DOG
EAT
DOG

DOG
EAT
DOG

MICHAEL BROWNING

A STORY OF SURVIVAL, STRUGGLE AND TRIUMPH BY THE MAN WHO PUT AC/DC ON THE WORLD STAGE

ALLEN&UNWIN

First published in 2014

Allen & Unwin
83 Alexander Street
Crows Nest NSW 2065
Australia
Phone: (61 2) 8425 0100

Email: info@allenandunwin.com
Web: www.allenandunwin.com

Cataloguing-in-Publication details are available
from the National Library of Australia
www.trove.nla.gov.au

ISBN 978 1 76011 191 5

Internal design by Christabella Designs

Set in 12/21 pt Cambria by Post Pre-press Group, Australia

Printed and bound in Australia by Griffin Press

10 9 8 7 6 5 4 3 2 1

MIX
Paper from
responsible sources
FSC® C009448
www.fsc.org

The paper in this book is FSC® certified.
FSC® promotes environmentally responsible,
socially beneficial and economically viable
management of the world's forests.

I DEDICATE THIS BOOK TO MY WIFE,
ELIZABETH, DAUGHTERS BILLIE AND ROSIE,
AND SONS JAMES AND BERT

CONTENTS

INTRODUCTION

Over the past thirty or so years, my friends and business associates have been urging me to write a book based on my experiences managing AC/DC. Our shared journey began during the band's early Australian days and culminated in their emergence as an internationally acclaimed band, perhaps the finest rock band of their era—certainly the biggest band to emerge from Australia, at least until the rise of INXS, who I also worked with.

I've done a number of interviews about AC/DC for various books and documentaries, usually along with many others who at some stage came into contact with the band. But I was actually there—and that's the key point of difference between my story and the many books that have been written about AC/DC, with the exception of *Dirty Deeds*, bassist Mark Evans's delightful and vivid account of his experience with the band. Like Mark, I lived it. Mine isn't a book based on interviews; it's as close as you can get to the source, unless one of the guys in the band decides to write a memoir one day, which I think is unlikely. There are books that go into great detail about the band and their lives; among them Clinton Walker's great *Highway to Hell: The Life and Death of AC/DC Legend Bon Scott*.

The old saying that goes, 'If you can remember the '60s, you weren't there' rings true for me, and that's where my story really begins. But I'm lucky—while my story is drawn from memory, my memory remains pretty strong. My story is about the early days of the band, told from a manager's perspective. It's not your typical sex, drugs and rock'n'roll story. (Okay, there's a bit of that.)

I set out in this task not to be distracted by the constraints and preoccupation of getting things like timelines totally accurate. Rather, I've hopefully conveyed a feeling of what it was like to be in the position I found myself in, managing a band that came from nothing but had obvious international star power.

My AC/DC story is interwoven with my earlier work as manager for Billy Thorpe and the Aztecs, who began with their rise through the Melbourne pub rock world, the same 'beer barn' phenomenon that would have an undeniable influence on the development of AC/DC. I was heavily involved with the Melbourne club scene, an incredible breeding ground of great music. The story therefore broadens into an autobiographical account of my Melbourne days, being part of a highly energised and unique time in our musical history, a time that featured an amazing cast of young bands, entrepreneurs and characters whose stories have for the most part been ignored by history.

Melbourne is where it all started for AC/DC. Their relationship with Melbourne is a lot like the Star Club in Hamburg and the role it played in the evolution of The Beatles. Post-Melbourne, my journey continued with the band as their international career unfolded, and they became a true force to be reckoned with. Then there was the drama that unfolded which ended my five-year management relationship with AC/DC. Afterwards, back in Oz, I set up Deluxe Records, the first home of INXS, before managing another great Australian band, Noiseworks.

It's been a wild ride. Better buckle up.

PROLOGUE

NORTH AMERICA, MAY 1979

AC/DC had just flown in from London, where they'd recorded their latest album with their new producer, Robert 'Mutt' Lange. There'd been a treacherous lead-up to the recording, including the heartbreak created by the band being forced to move on from their long and close-knit relationship with Harry Vanda and George Young, AC/DC's record producers, mentors and, in George's case, family.

Their new record label, American powerhouse Atlantic Records, said it had to be done and I somewhat reluctantly agreed, making me complicit in the decision. So far, this big change had claimed four scalps. It was a difficult and emotionally charged transition for all of us. I'd been managing the band since 1974, during which time constant touring and good old-fashioned word of mouth had established AC/DC as an international force to be reckoned with. But mass radio airplay had eluded them and it had become essential to make an album that would change this. This was our shot at the big time. It wasn't going to be easy.

The band and I met in my New York office and we listened to the *Highway to Hell* album. Not only did it completely blow me away, but it contained that one track, the title song, that I knew was the missing link, the song that would establish the band internationally, break them wide open. So why was I picking up a strange and uneasy feeling?

The next day I met with Bob Defrin, Atlantic Records' art director, with whom we'd developed the now famous AC/DC logo. We arranged a photo session for the new album's cover, another important piece of the puzzle.

After a few days' rehearsal at SIR Studios in New York, the band started their two-month tour of the US. This tour, along with their new album, would propel the band to a whole new level; we all sensed it. On 22 May, I flew to Nashville to join the tour. The band was playing the Tennessee Theater; we'd come a long way since I'd first sighted them at the Hard Rock Cafe, my club in Melbourne, and set out on this shared journey of world domination.

After the gig the band came off stage and into the dressing room, and straight away I knew something was amiss. The atmosphere was very chilly. I can't remember what started it, but an almighty argument erupted between the guys and myself. Malcolm and Angus Young were like a pair of rampant pitbulls, tearing into me. A number of issues were tossed around, including the sacking of Harry and George. Mutt Lange had helped them achieve something incredible, but the band had had a gutful of the drama. I'd taken on a partner they didn't approve of, and had come to dislike spending so much time on the road—these were other volatile issues that bounced around the Nashville dressing room. Singer Bon Scott and drummer Phil Rudd also threw a few choice words into the donnybrook, while bassist Cliff Williams, who by rights should have erected a statue of me in his backyard, remained absolutely silent.

Quickly, the gut-wrenching realisation set in. Here I was, in Nashville, the middle of nowhere, getting sacked by the same ungrateful little fuckers that I'd grown to love over the past five years. Until now, *I* was the one who did the sacking. But AC/DC's dog-eat-dog mentality had claimed a new victim. Me. And I was devastated. Life as I had come to know it was about to change in a huge way.

TAKING CARE OF BUSINESS—
ON MOUNT MACEDON GOLF COURSE

Collingwood, the inner suburb of Melbourne where I was born in 1947, was a place that lived and breathed AFL. You either loved or loathed Collingwood. My entire family loved the team; our veins flowed black and white.

But my father, Bert, who was still recovering from his stint in New Guinea and the Middle East as a soldier in World War II, became disenchanted with the inner city, where he ran a plastic manufacturing business. He and my mother Nina (Nin) decided to move me, my elder sister Coral, younger sister Jan and my grandmother to the country town of Mount Macedon, about 100 kilometres northwest of Melbourne in the Macedon Ranges.

The north side of the mountain was all rugged terrain stretching to the legendary Hanging Rock—made famous in the 1970s movie—and beyond. The south side of the mountain was a gentrified, manicured weekend escape for Melbourne's elite and still has some of the grandest properties and gardens in Australia. It was also the home of Victoria's first Government House. It felt a lot like the more genteel parts of England. Early settlers planted deciduous oaks and elms and all manner of cold-climate plants, trees and flowers that would thrive in the cool climate. It was a world away from working-class Collingwood.

Nin was of English heritage, while Bert was of Scottish descent. Having sold the place in Collingwood, he'd purchased a long-term leasehold of the Mount Macedon Golf Course from the Catholic Church, who operated a convent from an old mansion adjoining the property.

My father, who I've been told was a pretty entertaining square-dance caller, ran things on the golf course; my mother looked after the restaurant in the clubhouse. Every Sunday afternoon, out-of-town golfers and their families would dig into my mother's roast lunch. It was a regular Sunday roast, but shared with a couple of hundred people. Along with Coral and Jan, I attended Mount Macedon Primary School and eventually Kyneton High School.

My entrepreneurial interests kicked in early on, purely out of necessity. My father was of the belief that any work you did for the family business was your contribution to its survival—and therefore unpaid. So if I was to have any cash for pushbikes or whatever I craved, I was going to have to raise it myself. In hindsight, not a bad lesson. Being the only kid allowed onto the golf course, I cornered the market in finding lost balls and then selling them back to the golfers. There was a creek running through what was a picturesque golf course, so there was no shortage of lost balls, hit into the drink. I'd watch the golfers' balls sink, then offer them my help—for two shillings a pop—to fish them out. Easy.

I also controlled the thriving business of collecting beer bottles from the picnic area and then selling them to the nearby bottler, for the prized sum of a halfpenny apiece. I ruled my turf with an iron fist; the other local kids understood and stayed away.

Each morning before school I mowed the fairways on an old Massey Ferguson tractor, then I'd be on the bus for the one-hour trip to Kyneton High, a typical rundown rural high school. It felt like I was taking some monumental journey to hell and back. The headmaster resembled some overweight southern US cop, straight out of *Smokey and the Bandit*. A loner, he lived in a room at the old Kyneton Hotel, which is now regarded as one of Australia's trendiest foodie destinations. But it sure wasn't fashionable in the late 1950s.

One teacher was a particularly nasty piece of work who'd slink around in brothel-creeper shoes trying to catch kids who he imagined were up to no good. And when he did make a score, he'd dish out, much to his delight, 'six of his best'—six strokes of the cane. They don't make them like him anymore, thank Christ.

The only subject that I showed any interest in—and in which I excelled—was music theory, thanks in no small part to a wonderful and caring music teacher, one Mrs Wilson. She must have known something that I didn't at the time, given where I ended up, and singled me out for special attention.

After school there would be more chores, dinner and then, finally, my favourite time of the day. I'd go to bed early and listen to the radio serials on my old AWA valve radiogram, which were broadcast nightly from 6 pm. *Dad and Dave*, *Bluey and Curly*, *Tarzan* and *Life with Dexter*—I loved them all. Television was a long way off yet—and when I did first hear about it, I figured it would be the same programs as the radio, only with pictures. What did I know?

Between serials, they'd sometimes play this strange new music that was coming out of America, something called 'rock'n'roll'. That's where I first heard Elvis Presley, Buddy Holly, Bill Haley & His Comets and The Everly Brothers. The music hit me like a thunderbolt. Before I knew it, I was starting to build my own collection of records, which I played to death on my new (and hard-earned) portable transistor phonograph, paid for with the money I raised fetching golf balls and recycling bottles.

Being way out in the boonies, I could only ever dream of seeing any of these new stars in the flesh, which added to my fascination and growing addiction. And then it happened: I finally got to go to my first concert in the late 1950s. My mother, who'd worked at the Tivoli theatre during the war years and loved show business—especially swing music—was now also getting into rock'n'roll. She took me to a matinee performance by 'the Wild One' himself, Johnny O'Keefe, Australia's first true rocker, at Melbourne's Her Majesty's Theatre on Exhibition Street. I'd like to think that this experience had a profound impact on me—and subconsciously it probably did—but my strongest memory is of being a bit overwhelmed by the whole experience, the screams of the crowd, the noise, the madness.

In 1960, when I was 13, my family was hit with a financial calamity. The Australian Defence Force had purchased the convent and adjoining golf course from the Catholic Church, turning the convent into the Australian Civil Defence School. Their commodore, a pompous (and, as it turned out, corrupt) character, used a loophole in defence laws to take back the golf course and terminate my father's lease for 'civil defence purposes'. What he really wanted, of course, was a private golf course for him and his fellow officers, because that's what it eventually became. It was a pretty shoddy way to treat a returned serviceman like my father—or anyone, for that matter. It ruined his dream of a life in the country for his family.

I learned a very big lesson. It was a defining moment in my life. Through this encounter, I developed a distrust of public officials, the people who had just stolen from us. This would stay with me forever. My father was forced to start again from scratch, commuting to Melbourne each day to a new job with an electrical retail chain. Fortunately, it was the start of the age of television; he sold sets by the hundreds.

I'd been having my own troubles. I'd just been expelled from Kyneton High School. The school's 2IC was convinced that my 'kissing room' under the school hall—which I'd set up as part of the school fete, as a fundraiser—was some kind of a brothel. To his credit, he read my mind—while it mightn't have been a bordello, it was a way to get closer to girls. I was really starting to dislike authority, the establishment. I wasn't sure exactly how it would manifest itself, but I had the feeling that one day I would be doing something that kicked against people like the commodore.

Out of financial necessity, we moved a bit closer to Melbourne, to Sunbury, a working-class enclave about 50 kilometres northwest of the city. I spent a long and immensely tedious year at Sunbury High. The headmaster had been tipped off by my previous school that I was trouble.

'So, you're Browning,' he murmured at me in the hallway.

And that was it. For the remainder of the year, I got the blame for just about everything that went on, anything the staff didn't like. Okay, some of it was warranted. Along with my red-headed larrikin mate, Larry Shepard, we certainly made those uptight, so-called teachers earn their money.

The only thing keeping me sane was my ever-expanding music collection. Larry, who I'd spend every possible moment with after school listening to my singles, shared my rock'n'roll passion. Between us, we had a great collection, which was growing a bit more radical with time. Our heroes, dudes high on our collective playlist, were Eddie Cochran, Duane Eddy, Gene Vincent and Carl Perkins. All had a bit of the outlaw about them, something we were drawn to.

My father came to realise I was wasting my time in school and managed to find me a job in the chinaware department at Myer's in the city, where he'd once worked. Understanding that I'd totally screwed up my education, I made a conscious decision to pull my head in, to try to make something out of the mess. I became extremely ambitious, diligently working my way up from trolley boy to second-in-command of the entire department. Myer's had big plans for me; they wanted to put me through a manager's course and eventually take charge of the department. But fate—and rock'n'roll—had other plans.

WELCOME TO SEBASTIAN'S PENTHOUSE

My mate Larry was working at an insurance office around the corner from Myer's; we'd get together during our lunch breaks. We'd clumsily chomp away at our national gourmet delight, Four'N Twenty meat pies, piping hot and hard to eat due to their tendency to drip gristly chunks of fatty meat onto our trendy suede shoes. One day we stumbled upon an old building in the centre of Melbourne, from which we heard the muffled sound of music wafting in the air. *What was that?*

Purely by chance we'd discovered a daily lunchtime live music club called the Bowl. It was described as a 'sound lounge'. My life was about to be turned upside down.

The Bowl was housed in the basement of an old Art Deco

building, typically Melbourne. The sounds that we heard were rising up through the entrance door below street level; we were drawn downstairs like pilgrims on a journey to the dungeon below.

The place was like a sauna, hot and very sweaty, the music loud and distorted. The room had been painted black and there were ultraviolet lights everywhere; they made everything that wasn't black look bright white, including the many girls in the room, who were mostly dressed in miniskirts and looked extremely seductive. The aroma was thick, a dizzying mixture of cigarette smoke, sweat and cheap perfume. From that moment on, for me there was something magical about basement gigs.

We went there every day. It was at the Bowl that I first heard The Beatles' 'Love Me Do', 'I Saw Her Standing There' and 'Please, Please Me', as well as Booker T & the MGs' 'Green Onions' and the Rolling Stones' 'Little Red Rooster'.

All thoughts of our old heroes, guys like Duane Eddy, Elvis and Eddie Cochran, rockers that we'd loved so much, were shelved, at least for the time being. This new beat music from England and this thing called 'rhythm and blues' coming out of the US were officially where it was at.

I didn't do things by halves and desperately wanted to immerse myself in this new scene. So I quickly transformed myself into a mod. I had no more need for those old pie-stained blue suede shoes, exchanging them for desert boots, a mohair cardigan and a Beatles haircut. Larry, however, took a bit of convincing; he wasn't going to lose his magnificent red rocker pompadour in a hurry. He just couldn't bring himself to make the change.

The Bowl really was the place. A new breed of Australian bands played there every lunchtime, including my local heroes from TV's *Go Show*, people like Normie Rowe, The Flys, Bobby and Laurie, and Steve and The Board. There was also a DJ playing the latest records from all over the world.

I found out later that Ivan Dayman was the owner and operator of the Bowl. Ivan was a colourful promoter out of Queensland, cut a little from the same mould as Colonel Tom Parker, Elvis Presley's manager. He operated similar venues in Brisbane, Adelaide and Sydney. He also had a huge dance venue in Brisbane, the Cloudland Ballroom. Ivan's company, Sunshine Management, represented a string of early Australian pop stars and bands, such as Normie Rowe— his biggest discovery—and Mike Furber, Peter Doyle, Bobby and Laurie, Tony Worsley and The Purple Hearts. He was a real player.

Ivan also owned Sunshine Records, one of Australia's first independent record labels, along with the legendary American-born producer Nat Kipner, whose son was the Steve in Steve and The Board. Over time Steve would become a go-to hit songwriter for some of pop's biggest names; he would even write 'Physical' for Olivia Newton-John. Dayman was a true pioneer; his business model, basically owning the whole shooting match, was a no-brainer concept.

My mate Larry ended up having to change his pompadour after all: he was called up for national service—I failed the medical—and sent off to war with a crew cut. A number one. What an insult. He was shipped off to Vietnam, to save us all from the dreaded 'yellow peril' that our fearless leaders had conned us into believing was a noble cause. Tragically, Larry came home in a body bag. I had no doubt that if I'd gone I would have been with Larry when he stepped on a landmine. From that day onwards, whenever I ran into someone who served in that war, I got feelings of guilt, as if they did their job for the country and I didn't. It complicated my feelings about the military and my dad, which had left such a bad taste in my mouth.

I'd made a new friend from Sunbury, a guy called Phillip Knight, and we decided to take our social life up a notch or two by making the big trek from Sunbury to the posh Melbourne suburb Toorak. We'd heard about a music club called Pinocchio's and were keen to check it out.

It was a tiny place, about the size of a modern-day Starbucks, run by a guy called Garry Spry. He was a pretty impressive character to us eighteen-year-old country hicks. Spry was the guy you needed to know to ensure you could get inside the club—and coming from Sunbury that was crucial.

Spry had spent some time in the US before opening Pinocchio's, which had quickly developed a rep as one of Melbourne's best clubs. What it lacked in size it made up for in atmosphere—it felt very sophisticated and upmarket. To a couple of blokes from Sunbury, the girls, who all seemed to be blonde, were untouchable; they were mostly snooty, wealthy Toorak princesses. Even though Phillip and I rolled up in his brother's Mark 4 Jag, they still looked down their noses at the two of us. We were a couple of rubes way out of our depth. We didn't belong. But that didn't stop us.

Pinocchio's was the venue of choice for the cast of *Kommotion*, a nightly TV show that featured Melbourne's hippest stars. A young Ian 'Molly' Meldrum was among the in-crowd who'd hang out there nightly. *Kommotion* was a bizarre show, with its so-called stars miming current hits. Somehow they'd become more popular than the original artists.

So suddenly I was socialising with these cool young TV stars. *Okay, I'm in the same building as them*, but I was eighteen and it felt great. The experience was starting to trigger thoughts of some kind of future that I might have in this exciting new world. But what exactly could I do? I hadn't figured that out yet.

I paid a lot of attention to Garry, the kingpin. It was he who would decide who'd get into his club, what bands would play there and when. He had the power. This resonated with me, although I was just as excited by some of the bands that were filling Pinocchio's. The highlight for me was seeing The Twilights play. They were as close as I'd get to experiencing The Beatles live; in fact they'd mimic The Beatles perfectly. If you closed your eyes you swore you were in the Cavern in Liverpool.

The guys in The Twilights had all migrated with their families to Elizabeth, 20 kilometres north of Adelaide, from various parts of the UK in the early 1960s, bringing with them their early influences of The Beatles and The Hollies. The Twilights' secret weapon was their powerful vocal harmonies, made easier by having two lead singers, Clem 'Paddy' McCartney and Glenn Shorrock, who went on to front the highly successful Little River Band.

Garry Spry also ran a management company and soon became the Twilights' manager, grooming them for international success. It wasn't to be—the Hollies, for starters, had a hit with a song supposedly reserved for the Twilights—but they were one of the first local bands to at least try to go global. It was a huge step.

■

Melbourne's largest employer was Myer Emporium, where I worked. It was Australia's biggest department store, having grown from a country store in Bendigo to what was now a huge city sprawl, spanning two blocks and joined by overhead walkways. Everyone in Melbourne shopped at Myer's.

Myer's was famous for its creative shop window displays and they always employed the city's most talented and creative young designers. Two of them—Ken Moat and Ron Eden—would also design and create the city's latest music club, the Thumpin' Tum, which opened in 1966. It was located in an old bluestone factory at 50 Little La Trobe Street; in a former life it had been one of the city's first pubs, in a relatively rundown, post-semi-industrial side of town. Moat and Eden even had a slogan for the club: 'Go-go to be seen at this swinging frugging scene' became their catchcry. The cover charge to see some great bands was ten shillings.

The guys based their fit-out around an Art Nouveau theme. There were umbrellas, snapped up from a railway lost property auction, hanging upside down from the high, dark, wooden cross-beamed ceiling above the dance floor, replicating, when lit, classic Art Nouveau fabric. They hung old Tiffany stained-glass lampshades everywhere.

The Tum, as it came to be known, was very bohemian, Melbourne's first real underground club. Unlike Pinocchio's, the bands that co-owners Philip and Jan Flint booked were darker and more rhythm and blues based. These included The Groop, The Missing Links, The Wild Cherries, Carson, The Purple Hearts and Chain, some of whom would break out of the underground. The clientele was a mix of very cool and edgy art students, serious music lovers, pill heads and hipsters. Even pop star of the moment Billy Thorpe was impressed. He admitted the place was 'much hipper than anything in Sydney', a big statement from a guy who'd been based in the harbour city since his teens. I'd get to know Thorpey well over time.

My new best mate Phillip Knight lived around the back of my parents' house in Sunbury, in a very large and elegant house called Kismet. We'd spend most of our spare time there, messing around with old cars, and making jewellery out of copper and enamel to sell what we dubbed 'The Phillmike Range', although I don't recall ever actually selling anything. We'd also arrange gigs at the local church hall, booking whatever local line-ups we could put together. It was my first foray into the world of music.

Phillip's father, Owen, owned an investment property, a typical cream-brick, Austin Powers–style three-storey block of flats opposite the beach in St Kilda, an inner bayside Melbourne suburb. It was once a gracious and opulent seaside playground for Melbourne's elite, but when we arrived it was a seedy and drug-fucked skeleton of its former self. St Kilda's trendy 21st century reinvention was then a figment of someone's imagination. The place was a dump.

Sitting atop the flats was a penthouse apartment of gigantic proportions with outdoor decks, games rooms and bars. Despite the size of the joint, St Kilda's dodgy reputation made it difficult to lease, so Phillip's father allowed us to stay there between tenants. It became a pretty handy and impressive hangout for a couple of teenagers fresh out of sleepy Sunbury.

Phillip and I decided to show off our amazing penthouse by throwing a party. I spread the word around Myer's, at the time full of hip and creative young types, and before we knew it, 300 people were spilling out the doors. The party was a triumph. We hadn't even cleaned the place when the two of us were already making plans for our next bash—but this time we'd charge 10 shillings admission. Why not?

It also inspired me to make a big decision. Goodbye, Myer's and a career in retail; hello, music business.

We christened the place Sebastian's Penthouse, and by 1964 it became a fully operational club in spitting distance of St Kilda Beach. Word got out and I was soon approached by the brothers Wayne and Rodney de Gruchy, two of Melbourne's earliest band managers. They were a couple of likely types whose father, Len, had decided, after wasting his money at Ballarat Grammar, to send them to Taylors Business College in the city.

The Bowl just so happened to be located in the basement of the Taylors building. The rest, as they say, is history—poor buggers, they didn't stand a chance; the lure of rock'n'roll was just too strong. Len quickly pulled the plug. But Wayne and Rodney had learned that you could make money from these new bands—they also found out that managing bands meant not having to get out of bed early in the morning and sit in a traffic jam.

The de Gruchys booked their young Beat bands into our club, who played in what was the original bar-cum-games room, on the floor in the corner. We didn't even have a stage, but it didn't seem to matter.

Word of mouth spread fast and it wasn't long before we had a queue of patrons winding way up the external staircase, past the doors of the many tenants whose palms we'd sufficiently greased, providing us with their silence and a hassle-free operation. The ten shillings admission also entitled you to complimentary crumpets—with butter and honey. No booze was provided; our place was strictly BYO. We hired young bands on the rise, especially The Boys, featuring David Pepperell, who'd later make his mark as a journalist writing under the name Dr Pepper. They performed the latest Stones, Animals, Beatles and Kinks songs. Their fee was £50 a night, which left our take at around £100, after deductions for crumpets and neighbourly-palm-greasing. Not bad considering I had made £10 a week selling crockery at Myer's.

Just when I thought things couldn't get any better, and with the help of my new friend Johnny Walker, I was seduced by an older woman, the wife of a prominent pop star. We adjourned to my adjoining bedroom and I lost my virginity to the sound of The Boys belting out The Troggs' 'Wild Thing' and The Kinks' 'You Really Got Me'.

My new career was starting to look very good. With my slice of the profits from Sebastian's, I purchased a classic MG TC, which I posed in around town like a spoilt young mod brat. No wonder the rockers hated us. I was doing pretty well until an extremely jealous copper decided that he could no longer bear the sight of me in my trendy sports car parked in Fitzroy Street with a good-looking girl in the passenger seat. The bastard slapped an un-roadworthy certificate on my motor, putting me and my pride and joy (and my ego) off the road.

The high life didn't last very long. It hadn't occurred to Phillip and me that we'd need planning permission from people like the St Kilda City Council, the health department and the liquor licensing authorities—each body was amazed at our level of stupidity and nerve when they chanced upon Sebastian's Penthouse. We lasted about three months and were then shut down. It hardly came as a shock.

Still, we'd made an impression. The brief success resonated with Phillip's family. His brother Anthony Knight was another talented interior designer—also a former member of the Myer's window display team—and one of Melbourne's original dandies. He dressed in immaculately tailored suits with all the trimmings. He also happened to be incredibly charming, good-looking and had a passion for fine antiques. Phillip's other brother, Richard, was just as charming but in a more down-to-earth way. His passion was restoring Mark 4 Jags. They could see the potential of launching a new Sebastian's in a more sensible—preferably legal—location.

The Knights were an interesting family, who had very graciously taken me in, almost as an adopted son. For a while they became my second family. Their house, the Kismet homestead, was originally a sprawling sheep station in Sunbury. It was full of glorious colonial cedar furniture and housed arguably Australia's finest antique clock collection, which Owen had lovingly restored. They also collected vintage Jaguars. I learned a lot about the value of the 'aesthetic' from them, which I've been able to apply throughout my life and career. They would learn a thing or two from me, too, mostly about the music that we were about to surround ourselves with.

We found new premises at 335 Exhibition Street in the city, in an abandoned millinery, three storeys high. It was just around the corner from the Thumpin' Tum. We set about establishing the second Sebastian's, but this time, at Anthony's insistence, it was named Prince Albert George Sebastian's II. It was the '60s, after all.

Anthony created a replica of an antique-filled Edwardian mansion. There was a ballroom on the ground floor, featuring a spectacular oversized chandelier above the dance floor. The entire concept was perfectly in tune with the whole swinging London/Carnaby Street/Edwardian fashion thing that was happening in the UK. It was different, creative and every bit as interesting as the Thumpin' Tum.

The customers, who'd come from all over Australia, were equally cool. This was all about music and fashion, something Melbourne always understood and did well. There was nowhere else in Australia that was as classy or hip as the Tum and Sebastian's II. They were at the vanguard of the counterculture and Melbourne bohemia. The Sydney clubs were vastly different, bland by comparison, mostly operated by the underworld.

Sebastian's II quickly became a hangout for all the coolest characters. Pop stars the Bee Gees would come on their nights off in Melbourne. John and Merivale Hemmes, from the House of Merivale, the biggest and best fashion boutique in Sydney, would fly down to Melbourne every second weekend to check out the club. (I'd like to think they may have picked up a thing or two regarding style, which they later applied to their hospitality empire.) The club was also frequented by roadies such as Wayne 'Swampy' Jarvis, Norm and John Sweeney, Mick Cocks and Lee Dillow, all ex-Sydney guys now working in Melbourne, some of whom were better known than the bands that employed them.

The next club to open was the Catcher, owned and operated by Graham Geddes, an eccentric renegade school headmaster and antiques expert. It was located in another old warehouse in the city, at the wrong end of Flinders Lane. The Catcher may have been Melbourne's largest club, but it was at the bottom end of the market. It had an industrial feel about it, hip by today's standards, but not so in the mid-1960s. It catered mainly for Melbourne's misfits, kids on speed with spiky dyed-red hair, who'd get off on manic bands like Running Jumping Standing Still. Unlike the Tum or Sebastian's, the Catcher let everyone through its doors, including the local sharpies.

Melbourne kids were fashion savvy, mostly influenced by the British Beat bands and mods, but the sharpies were something else altogether. These kids were mainly from the poorer, rougher northwestern suburbs; their uniform was black bell-bottoms, black chiselled-toe shoes and maroon knitted Conte cardigans. They looked sharp, hung out in packs and created havoc wherever they went. Greg 'Angry' Anderson was a sharpie before he joined Rose Tattoo; he'd later write the Aussie classic 'The Butcher and Fast Eddy' about two of his more notorious sharpie mates.

We agreed that sharpies were strictly off limits at Sebastian's, but the more we tried to keep them out, the harder they tried to get in. We were forced to hire some heavyweight security. We found Bob Jones, a former street kid who'd discovered karate and reinvented himself as a fighting machine from hell. He remains the toughest guy I've ever met, hands down. Bob also had good business sense; he parlayed his passion for karate into a national martial arts school. Eventually he became both minder and head of security for most international artists touring Australia. Bob combined brains and brawn.

Things could get really ugly. One night, at least 200 sharpies descended on Sebastian's; way outnumbered, we had no option but to lock everyone inside and pour boiling water on the invaders from the upstairs windows. Melbourne's police HQ was just around the corner in Russell Street, but they were never any help. When it came to dealing with the sharpies they stayed right out of it; they left that work to the club's bouncers.

Typically, the sharpies would lick their wounds and drive down to the Catcher, where they were more welcome. But there were some serious battles inside and outside the Catcher, involving not only sharpies but also sailors and army personnel on leave. One unlucky guy had his ear bitten off in a scuffle, resulting in a full military inquiry. The bouncer involved left the country very quickly.

The Catcher eventually closed in the early 1970s when a patron, after being chased by the bouncers, drowned in the Yarra River. Geddes ended up becoming Australia's most celebrated antique dealer, quite an about-turn after running a place like the Catcher.

FAST TIMES IN THE MELBOURNE MUSIC SCENE

My role at Sebastian's was to book the bands, the best of all possible jobs. Melbourne was becoming Australia's musical Mecca; bands would come from all over the country to base themselves there. A lot of the Adelaide groups were the kids of 'ten-pound Poms', the result of an immigration policy introduced after World War II. The Twilights led the exodus, followed by the Hollies' influenced Y4, plus Move, and Levi Smith's Clefs, whose singer was the cuddly and husky-voiced Barrie 'The Bear' McAskill.

Then the Masters Apprentices rolled into town, led by a charismatic and glamorous bloke named Jim Keays. With them came a stack of attitude, dirty rock'n'roll swagger—and loads of young female fans. It was the first time I'd witnessed real fan hysteria. The Masters' hits 'Undecided', 'Living in a Child's Dream' and 'Turn Up Your Radio' would all stand the test of time.

The Masters played occasionally at Sebastian's, but as good as they were, their following mostly comprised pimply-faced teenage girls—not our audience at all. The few times they played it became a problem for our security, whose job it was to screen the patrons. We had a No Bozos policy, and it applied equally to teenyboppers as it did to sharpies.

Then bands started coming from Perth. The first of these was The Valentines, who had two vocalists, Vince Lovegrove and a very young Bon Scott. They arrived in Melbourne looking like a teenage cabaret band: they wore puffy pirate shirts (just like that famous *Seinfeld* episode) and matching satin pants. Apart from a few dodgy songs, which they'd obviously recorded hoping for a bit of chart action, they were actually a very good band, especially when they got into the soul stuff.

But The Valentines, too, were in danger of falling into the Masters' category, although I booked them because I was a sucker for the fatal charm of Bon Scott and Vince Lovegrove, both very good schmoozers. Chain and The Beaten Tracks, featuring Warren 'Pig' Morgan on piano, soon also followed from the west.

Brisbane bands soon started heading south too; first off the rank was The Purple Hearts, named after a type of speed favoured by mods. The band drove to Melbourne in a beaten-up Kombi. They were led by the blond-haired, tall and charismatic Mick Hadley, one of Australia's all-time best frontmen. Barry Lyde—aka Lobby Loyde—was their guitarist; it was rumoured he was a distant relative of Oscar Wilde. Who knows if it was true, but Lobby certainly had a creative and philosophical streak.

Lobby quickly made a big reputation for himself, not only as a guitar player but also as one of music's biggest thinkers; he had an opinion on just about everything and could hold court on any subject for hours. Lobby would drop acid and ruminate on the future, how this thing called 'video' would emerge and change everything. I should have paid more attention; Lobby was really onto something. He quickly became Australia's first guitar hero, arguably the godfather of heavy rock in this country.

Bands even crossed the ditch from New Zealand. Among them was Max Merritt & the Meteors. With his gravelly, powerful voice, Max was the boss. Everyone in the Melbourne scene loved the blue-eyed soul of Max and his band, with their Motown influences and an obsession with the music of Otis Redding. They were amazing, with Dave 'Bruno' Lawrence (who became a highly regarded actor) on drums, Billy Kristian on bass—he'd reappear in the UK band Knight—and Peter Williams on rhythm guitar and co-vocals. Their road manager John Highlands also played a key role.

They had a hit, a cover of a song called 'Fanny Mae', which most people were convinced was a song Max had written about a local transvestite with a well-known obsession for him. The original had been recorded by Buster Brown, an African-American R&B singer. Funnily enough, a band also called Buster Brown, which featured Angry Anderson on vocals and the talented Phil Rudd on drums, operated in Melbourne at the time.

As for the Meteors, they changed into a more jazz-influenced band and should have been huge. Sadly they had a terrible accident on the way to a gig in Morwell, Victoria, about 150 kilometres southeast of Melbourne. Their new drummer Stewie Speer had both his legs crushed, both arms broken and lost the tops off several fingers. Max lost his right eye and his face was badly scarred. Bob Bertles, their sax player, suffered a broken leg. Somehow their new bassist Yuk Harrison, who was in the back with the equipment, escaped uninjured. It took them about a year to regroup. Max eventually moved to America, taking up residence in Los Angeles.

Another NZ band we booked into the club was the highly talented La De Das, with Phil Key on vocals and Kevin Borich, now a fully-fledged Australian guitar hero, on guitar. Bruno Lawrence turned up again in a band called Electric Heap. In the group was legendary Hammond organ player Claude Papesch. Claude was totally blind, but it didn't stop him from helping to lug this huge instrument in and out of venues. Claude would sometimes load it in the van and freak everyone out by jumping in the driver's seat and taking off.

Leo De Castro was this fabulous little roly-poly Maori guy, probably the most electrifying vocalist I've ever heard. But he was also big trouble. For reasons I think I've blocked out, Leo moved into my house and created total havoc. It got so bad that finally I had to get him professional help, but somehow Leo escaped. I got home and found him sitting there, wearing my clothes, as if nothing had happened. But it was hard to stay angry at a guy who could do Little Richard almost better than the guy himself.

I was a Jimi Hendrix obsessive, to the extent that I made enquiries about bringing him to play in Australia, which would have been quite the coup. But he had a resistance to flying long distances, apparently, and so it didn't happen. But Phil Key from the La De Das told me about a guy named Fred, a Maori guitarist.

'He's got all the Hendrix chops down,' Phil told me. 'He even looks like Hendrix.'

I was sold and flew to Auckland to meet with this Fred. However, he wasn't interested in coming to Australia. But he had a tip for me.

'There's this guy called Reno, in Wellington,' he said, 'and he does Hendrix even better than me.'

That was all I needed to hear and so I flew to Wellington; Reno happened to be playing that night in a big band. Reno and I spoke and he was keen on the idea, so the next day he arranged for me to see him play in a rehearsal studio with his drummer Paddy and bass player Ben. Reno was an incredible player, and given his physical resemblance to Jimi, it was like being in the same room with the guy.

I took charge and found them a place to live in South Yarra that I later found out was owned by Olivia Newton-John's sister Rhona. I covered all their expenses and booked them into Sebastian's at least once a week. I named them Compulsion. I truly believed in the band. They soon built up a strong following; I even got them a gig at the Royal Melbourne Show, the most bizarre job imaginable. Between sets, the band would be paraded on this narrow scaffold balcony high above the tent.

It wasn't the real thing, I knew that, but it was as close as anyone in Australia would get to Hendrix. Reno had the whole act down: the burning guitar, the upside-down Fender Stratocaster, the set-closing attack on his Marshall amplifier stack. The violence and destruction was thrilling. I thought it was fantastic, great theatre.

But Compulsion, the first band that I managed, wasn't built to last. Reno got heavily into drugs and one day, in a drug-hazed moment of madness, tried to hold up his local bank, a pair of sunglasses his only disguise. He ended up in jail, not surprisingly. I later learned that Reno and the guys burned every stick of furniture in the South Yarra apartment as firewood. As my management debut went, it wasn't anything to brag about.

At the same time, more and more bands were taking the drive down the Hume Highway; many of them had started out in Sydney venues like Whisky A Go Go and Chequers—where AC/DC would make their debut—playing to US troops on R&R from Vietnam. But these Sydney acts started heading south for more work, especially the soul bands that had earlier cut their teeth entertaining the US troops.

Bands like Billy Thorpe and the Aztecs, as well as Doug Parkinson In Focus, Python Lee Jackson, and Jeff St John and the Id, all eventually migrated south. Jeff was another powerful soul singer, confined to a wheelchair due to childhood polio, but it didn't stop him from working the stage. He was just like James Brown, but instead of dancing he did wheelies in his chair.

There was also an influx of acid-inspired bands from Sydney's Northern Beaches, groups like Taman Shud and Kahvas Jute. Their music became the soundtrack to the emerging surf subculture, a scene captured by young filmmakers and journalists David Elfick, Alby Falzon and John Witzig in their monthly magazine *Tracks*.

My favourite Melbourne band was The Loved Ones, who'd formed from the Red Onions Jazz Band and The Wild Cherries, jazz bands with a strong bohemian streak. They ditched the jazz and started playing bluesy rock with a strong Stones and Animals influence. Among their hits was 'The Loved One', which one day I'd have INXS record. Many years later, Dave Faulkner of the Hoodoo Gurus was a great champion of The Loved Ones.

There was a great rumour about The Loved Ones, that their lead singer, Gerry Humphreys, was the brother of great Australian comic Barry Humphries—apparently no one thought to check the spelling of their surnames. The band's bass player, Kim Lynch, was absolutely convinced that Gerry had mischievously spread the rumour himself. But although they shared great talent, a Carlton address and a thing for living on the edge, Dame Edna and Gerry didn't share parents. As to who was the maddest, well, who knows?

Even at their peak, with 'The Loved One' high in the charts, the band was starved for a strong story that would make them a household name. The best they could do was get pinched for nicking pillows from a prominent hotel, although the story did rate a mention on the front page of every Aussie daily, weirdly enough.

There's no doubt The Loved Ones had what was needed to make it internationally: the sound, look, uniqueness, an amazing frontman and, most importantly, the songs. Perhaps they just didn't have the appetite for the struggle. Maybe they just weren't hungry enough.

The Groop, who'd played at the opening of the Thumpin' Tum, were the darlings of the early Melbourne in-crowd/party set. A very young Molly Meldrum was so impressed that he became their roadie. Over time The Groop evolved, with the addition of Ronnie Charles and future Oz music legend Brian Cadd.

One band I booked into Sebastian's several times was named Somebody's Image. A fair-haired kid named Russell Morris was their vocalist. The guys from The Groop spoke with Molly, who'd moved on from roadie to record producer, suggesting that he should work on a solo project with Russell. Molly was so taken by the sweetness and quality of Russell's voice that he offered to produce a song for him written by Johnny Young. It was called 'The Real Thing'. And, surprise, surprise, Molly went over budget! Way over budget. Molly and engineer John Sayers made an all-time great 'psychedelic' record, which to everyone's horror went for six minutes. But 'The Real Thing' was so good that radio couldn't resist it and in June 1969 it went to number one, kickstarting both Molly's and Russell's careers.

Another act I booked regularly at Sebastian's was Mike Rudd's progressive rock group Spectrum, a favourite of mine. Their hit 'I'll Be Gone' would become an Australian classic, which very much defined this great period in Oz music.

Then there was the fabulously gifted blues singer Wendy Saddington, a tiny young woman with this huge head of hair and an amazingly soulful voice. One night in the late 1960s, a disillusioned Billy Thorpe, whose days as a pop star were fast running out, walked into the Tum and caught Wendy playing with her band The Beaten Tracks. As soon as he heard Wendy sing 'Looking Thru a Window', Billy was creatively reborn. If this was the standard of music to be found in Melbourne, it was definitely the place for him.

The Wild Cherries, an experimental rock group featuring former Purple Heart Lobby Loyde, were Sebastian's regulars. This was before Lobby joined forces with Thorpey in the Aztecs and set about inventing a beast that would be called Oz rock.

There was no band room at Sebastian's, which meant that between sets groups would hang out with the patrons, adding to the feeling that we were all one big happy family. Bands and punters usually arrived stoned, so once inside the atmosphere was very laid back, very cool. Mellow.

All of this music made Melbourne an incredible place to be in the 1960s—let alone in my situation, running a music club.

THE MYSTERIOUS WORLD OF ROCK'N'ROLL MANAGEMENT

Sebastian's was constantly alive with music. I booked two bands a night at the club; one would play the early shift, from 8 pm until midnight, then another would play the late shift, which ran from 12.30 until 3 am. On a Saturday, most bands in Melbourne would work four gigs: an afternoon pub, an early town hall dance, an early club shift then a late club shift—sometimes with a morning TV spot thrown in for good measure. Somehow they'd usually manage all this with one roadie and a dodgy panel van. And all the bands would help their roadie with their gear, something I haven't seen since.

In the mid- to late 1960s clubs started opening all over the city. There was the Biting Eye and the Surf Rider, the Mad

Hatter and Tenth Avenue. Then up popped the Garrison, which, unlike the other clubs, had a licence to sell booze. The others, Sebastian's included, only offered coffee and café food—usually a toasted ham and cheese sandwich. Drinking just wasn't a big part of the culture. There was a lot of speed about and pot, of course, was everywhere. Who needed booze?

My involvement with Sebastian's started to wind down. There were no big discussions about the future; I'd just lost interest in being at the club all the time, although I continued to book the bands. My partners, the Knight family, decided to open a second club.

They found the perfect building, the old Public Schoolboys Club, on the corner of Spring and Flinders streets. This once exclusive spot for the well-heeled had long been abandoned. It was an elegant and commanding five-storey building with a tower overlooking the Fitzroy Gardens. This time Anthony transformed the site into a replica of a Victorian mansion. He truly was a remarkable creative talent.

Anthony named the club Bertie's, after Queen Victoria's husband Albert. The doors opened in 1966. I wasn't involved with the partnership, but as compensation the Knights appointed me 'house booker' for life, a role that I relished. They hired my old friend Wayne de Gruchy as general manager.

I was all of twenty and I'd become the most powerful buyer of rock'n'roll talent in Melbourne, the liveliest music city in the country. If you didn't play my clubs you weren't playing in Melbourne. I set up my own agency, Michael Browning Enterprises, and picked up most of Melbourne's cool young bands that the established, 'straighter' agencies didn't want or understand. My criterion was simple: I needed to love the music. Despite coming from the boondocks I'd developed a very keen ear for this, and was able to spot things that others didn't. What's more, I was in love with the whole deal.

I ran the agency out of a terrace at 40 Park Street, South Yarra, Melbourne's trendiest inner suburb. With my share of profits from Sebastian's, I decorated the terrace with colonial antiques, a passion I'd acquired from the Knights. I lived downstairs and ran the agency from an upstairs office. It soon became a hangout for every manager, agent, roadie and club owner in town. It also held a certain attraction for every runaway and upwardly mobile groupie in Melbourne, something I had no problem with.

There was a great feeling of community among the bands, their girlfriends, agents, managers, roadies, bouncers, club operators and friends. We'd all hang out at the International Club after the venues closed at 3 am. It was a sly-grog steak restaurant on La Trobe Street, run by a couple of Greek guys. They had a limited understanding of English, and asked few questions about what we were up to. It suited everyone just fine.

They couldn't have spent $500 fitting out the joint. But it didn't matter; it was a great place, with loads of atmosphere.

Everyone would gather at about 3.30 am, drink Scotch and cokes, eat big juicy steaks at about two dollars a serve, and talk music and more music until daybreak.

I'd met a girl called Fran, a good-looking blonde who worked as a waitress at Sebastian's. Things got fairly serious between us—the word 'marriage' was even mentioned. At least that was the case until my 21st birthday, held at Park Street. Fran's mother, whom I'd just met, overheard my uncle Milton commenting on the size of her daughter's tits. Surprise, surprise—she went totally berserk, prompting him to offer up some friendly advice to his favourite nephew.

'Michael,' my uncle told me with a grin, 'take a good look at the mother—because that's what you're going to end up with.' I took one look at the mum and that was it. I was single again.

The Woodstock/Age of Aquarius generation was now in full swing and the Melbourne scene was all about live music, sex and getting stoned. Most of the bands in Melbourne weren't making records for the charts; it didn't seem to matter that much. The bands built their following from playing live. Older people, who either didn't care or didn't want to know about the scene, ran the record companies. They were irrelevant to what was happening in the underground scene.

Go-Set was a weekly music magazine based in Melbourne and established by Phillip Frazer, Tony Schauble, Peter Raphael and the ever-present Molly Meldrum. Lily Brett interviewed the bands and reported on the music news, while Colin Beard took the photographs. For the most part it was a labour of love for this formidable bunch, who all went on to greater things. Their loveable advertising manager Terry Cleary doubled as a crystal-ball-gazing psychic, writing the astrology column. Sadly, it didn't reveal Terry's future; he'd later be killed in a car crash.

Go-Set was very much the voice of the whole scene, created by young music lovers and directed at an equally young, hip audience. It was eagerly read by Melbourne's music fans and bands; it was the music industry's most important voice, its bible. For the clubs it was equally important to place ads that would capture people's attention. The Catcher's Graham Geddes—with Terry's encouragement—was the master of crazy advertising campaigns. One of the best parts of my week was visiting Terry Cleary to put our advertising program together. Lily Brett's chic café in East Melbourne became another industry hangout, where music was the only subject discussed over gallons of the city's best Italian espresso.

Go-Set eventually went national and was finally swallowed up by a big publishing company, but during its peak it was a highly valued Melbourne institution.

In 1967, the Sydney band Python Lee Jackson approached me about becoming their manager. I'd never been to Sydney, even though I'd been booking Sydney bands for a few years. My first trip up there was an interesting, eye-opening experience.

I stayed in the Paris, a two-star joint in Kings Cross, located in an alley above a French restaurant. The place had an early Italian espresso coffee shop and was the hotel of choice for touring interstate bands—with all the decadence that went along with it. I definitely felt like I had arrived in a big city for the first time; the Cross really lived up to its lively reputation as Australia's red-light capital.

There were illegal casinos, sly-grog joints, brothels and strip clubs everywhere, with spruikers doing their level best to tempt you with their deliciously seedy offerings. The paid-off cops turned a blind eye to everything that was happening in their front yard.

On the main strip, Darlinghurst Road, were the Pink Pussycat and Les Girls, the Cross's famous drag queen joint, home to the legendary Carlotta. There were soul food restaurants, something I'd not seen in Melbourne, catering for the many African-American servicemen on R&R from Vietnam, who'd end their long nights at the Bourbon and Beefsteak, a 24-hour place that had just opened. The B&B's owner, American Bernie Houghton, used to run covert ops for the CIA in Vietnam.

Around the corner from the walls of flashing neon lights that reminded everyone to drink Coke was the legendary Whisky

A Go Go nightclub, another favoured hangout of the American troops, a place I couldn't wait to check out. (And a place that would play its role in AC/DC's rise.) Levi Smith's Clefs, a band I'd got to know well in Melbourne, were appearing that night. But it was different seeing them in Sydney at the Whisky. There was a mellower vibe. To me, everyone in this city seemed to be stoned. The club life was soulful and sleazy, nothing like Melbourne's more bohemian scene, although it was still a lot of fun. And I was about to sign up one of its classic fixtures.

Python Lee Jackson was the epitome of cool, a Kings Cross-based band with an air of danger about them, a sort of menacing intellect. Not only were they all well read and intelligent, but you just knew they were the kind of guys familiar with everything listed on the 'dangerous and banned substances' act. They were one of Australia's first truly underground/counterculture bands.

Vocalist Malcolm McGee, whose brooding charisma reminded me of Jim Morrison, fronted Python Lee. The guy embodied sex, drugs and rock'n'roll. The rest of the band comprised keyboardist Dave Bentley, drummer Dave Montgomery, bassist Dave MacTaggart—who had a habit of joining in whenever a fight broke out in the crowd—and Mick Liber, a surly Brit guitarist who'd later join Thunderclap Newman, a band that had a number-one hit worldwide with 'Something in the Air'. Parents would have been terrified at the thought of their daughters hanging around with this lot, although that didn't seem to stop anyone—girls loved the band.

They'd recorded a version of the old Sam & Dave hit 'Hold On, I'm Coming', which achieved moderate success. But Malcolm left to join Lily Brett's brainchild, The Virgil Brothers, a vocal trio in the Walker Brothers/blue-eyed-soul mould, with matching peroxided blond hair and white suits. Lily must have been very persuasive, because it was a very different and, as it turned out, short-lived gig.

Malcolm was physically strong, a fine specimen of a man. When in Melbourne he was drawn into Bob Jones' martial arts world, along with John de Blanc, another security guy at the club. Malcolm quickly became very capable at karate, but his musical career went into decline. There were whispers that he was involved with distributing drugs, which came to a head as he was getting off a plane in Sydney and found himself on the tarmac, surrounded by five drug enforcement officers. His reaction was to fight his way out of it—which he managed to do—but his musical career was over.

Later on, without Malcolm, the band relocated to London where they had an international hit on John Peel's Dandelion record label with the Dave Bentley–penned song 'In a Broken Dream'. The vocalist was a young mod named Rod Stewart, who in lieu of a session fee was paid with some car seat covers for his beaten-up VW Beetle.

We didn't exactly set the world on fire as manager and band; however, Malcolm McGee from Python Lee tipped me off to a Sydney band called The Questions.

'They have this incredible lead singer,' he said. 'His name's Doug Parkinson.'

Malcolm was no lightweight; he was a man of impeccable taste, so I was on a plane back to Sydney within days.

The Questions, as it turned out, comprised the cream of the city's young and coolest musicians. They were holding down a residency at the Manly Pacific Hotel, a grand Edwardian-era pile directly opposite Manly's famous surf beach. Not only was I about to hear Australia's best singer, but I was also looking at the surf for the first time in my life. I came from Melbourne, after all.

Malcolm was spot on. I don't think I'd ever heard a better singer than Doug; he had this huge, husky, soulful voice with charisma and stage presence to match. He was a big lad, bordering on beefy, but very charming. The girls in the crowd wanted to hug this bear-like character. I just wanted to sign him up.

Doug had this corny gimmick: an eye patch. In hindsight, it probably wasn't a bad thing, knowing that Ray Sawyer from the US band Dr Hook virtually built his entire career around the same thing. But Doug didn't need this distraction, so with a bit of gentle encouragement from all directions, he decided to lose it. I quickly arranged a management deal and the band agreed to relocate to Melbourne.

Before heading south, The Questions were chosen to support

English bands Small Faces and The Who on their Australian tour in January 1968. It didn't last long: a drunken onboard party during a flight from Adelaide to Sydney, involving members of all three bands, led to their flight being diverted to Essendon, where they were met on the ground by the Federal coppers. Booze wasn't served on board; someone had smuggled bottles onto the flight, which were passed around. The British bands were escorted onto their flight to New Zealand, while Prime Minister John Gorton sent a telegram to The Who demanding they never return. As if this wasn't enough—ha!—they were banned from flying again with Ansett. That must have hurt.

The Questions moved to Melbourne in mid-1968 and got a new drummer, Johnny Dick, who'd previously played with Max Merritt and Billy Thorpe. Johnny was renowned in muso circles for both his exceptional drumming skills and for his ridiculously elongated, custom-made kick drum. I have no idea about the acoustic merit of the thing, but it sure looked impressive. Doug, Johnny, guitarist Billy Green and bass player Duncan McGuire—arguably one of Australia's best—changed their name to Doug Parkinson In Focus.

They'd arrived in Melbourne with an extended family of friends and relatives; there was Doug's wife, Suzi, her sister Louise (good-looking girls, those Clark sisters), and the band's roadie Peter, a Northern Beaches surfie on a permanent high, who could somehow load the band's gear, including a PA, into the back of his Ford Sandman. They set up house and I got them working. Our customers at Sebastian's and Bertie's couldn't get enough of them.

To this day, I don't think I've ever heard a better band. They were a soul–rock hybrid in a similar vein to English greats Traffic; when they were in the groove, they could hypnotise an audience, almost put them in a transcendental state. It wasn't long before EMI records came sniffing around.

I took a look at the contract and didn't have the foggiest idea what it all meant. I had no one to ask about it, either—lawyers with knowledge of music and copyright law were still unheard of. The record companies had what they called 'standard contracts'; essentially, the deal was sign up or move on. All I knew was they were paying for recording costs and the band was going to receive royalties. The way we figured, it would make things happen fast. The band would become famous and we'd all be better off. So that was it. A record deal.

Their debut single was a cover of The Beatles' 'Dear Prudence', which became a massive hit in June 1969. Along with Joe Cocker's 'A Little Help from My Friends', it's one of only two Beatles covers, in my opinion, that were better than the original. In Focus followed this up with Billy Green originals 'Baby Blue Eyes' and 'Without You', which were also hits. They were on their way. This record contract thing was good. I was right—the band became huge.

In the late 1960s, a confectionery company called Hoadley, responsible for Violet Crumble bars and Polly Waffles, ran an annual Battle of the Sounds competition. Everyone would enter. It was a prestigious event, the big prize a boat trip to London, the desired destination for any ambitious Australian band in the 1960s.

In 1969, the competition was intense. Bon Scott and The Valentines were convinced that it was their year. They were dressed to kill in their puffy pirate shirts and tight strides.

I was backstage at the Battle of the Sounds, staged at the sad and sorry Festival Hall, this rundown old boxing venue. I was at the urinal, taking a piss next to Vince Lovegrove from The Valentines, who looked over at me.

'So,' Vince asked me, 'what is Doug Parkinson In Focus going to be wearing?'

'I don't know,' I replied. 'Whatever they turn up to the gig in, I guess.'

It was a brief conversation—with limited hand gestures, as you could understand, given where we were and what we were doing.

Vince looked at me with the kind of smile that said, *I know we look stupid, but we'll do anything to win this competition— and get the fuck out of this country.*

Vince and Bon might have thought that was the case, but it was Doug's night. In Focus, the original stoners, probably the most free-spirited Australian band to ever make it big, one of the coolest bands I'd ever encountered, won the event, beating out The Valentines, much to Bon's distress. Bon had already imagined himself standing at the dock, waving goodbye, on his way to London. A week later he turned up at an In Focus gig at Bertie's, wanting to punch Doug's lights out. He was one pissed-off Valentine.

Soon after, I arranged for the collection of the prize, only to be told that the band had to literally sing for their supper (okay, their tickets). They'd have to play aboard the ship every night for the duration of their four-week trip to London.

'This isn't a prize,' I thought to myself. 'Any band could have made this deal.'

We agreed to tell Hoadley's where they could stick their so-called prize. London would have to wait. To their credit, Hoadley's arranged for a box of Polly Waffles to be delivered to In Focus whenever they played a new town, for which the band was eternally grateful. A 'rider', a backstage spread of food and booze that's now a rock'n'roll ritual, was unheard of in 1969.

My management and agency business was doing so well I decided to hire a guy named Peter Andrews, who'd come over from Perth as the manager of Beaten Tracks. Peter also happened to be part owner of Perth's only underground music venue, the Hole in the Wall Club.

Peter was a private school boy, well spoken, cultured, a bit of an old-school colonial-type complete with handlebar moustache. But once he discovered the counterculture he never looked back. He moved into the Park Street house, which by now resembled a boomtown den of iniquity. Peter's love of pot smoking had reached an all-time high. Visitors and friends soaked it up.

'Without You', which came out in October 1969, had become another big hit for Doug and In Focus and they were starting to shape up like genuine counterculture rock stars, the kind of band that authorities would fear. Things were really changing.

I was 21 and life was great. It was a far cry from life in Sunbury, where I'd break the Saturday night boredom by blowing up people's letterboxes with firecrackers. I'd just met a beautiful young girl called Bobbi, whom I'd spotted on the dance floor at Sebastian's wearing the shortest miniskirt I'd ever seen. No more stuck-up Toorak girls from Pinocchio's for me, thanks very much.

Everything was rolling along pretty smoothly—I was making great money, had a beautiful girlfriend, a great apartment, incredibly cool friends—until one night there was a loud knocking on the door at Park Street. It was the drug squad, who had a warrant to search my house and business.

I was on the phone to Peter when they entered. He'd just stepped off a plane from Adelaide.

'I've been busted,' Peter let me know.

The phone rang again. This time it was Johnny Dick from In Focus.

'I've been busted, too,' he told me.

It seemed the drug squad had been casing us for a while. Each of us was charged with possession of cannabis; it was all over the news and came as a big blow for me and the business. We were depicted as 'dangerous druggies', but the truth was something else altogether. The busts had been for a very small amount of cannabis, hardly enough for a couple of joints—that, incidentally, comprised the stash of a certain band member that was hidden behind the paintings in my office. The Stones had recently been busted in the UK and the Melbourne drug squad wanted their own rock'n'roll bust. All they got was Johnny Dick, who it has been alleged, may have done a quick plea bargain, Peter Andrews and me. I got dragged through the Prahran court, copping a possession conviction.

The Valentines, meanwhile, had been holding down a summer residency at the Jan Juc Surf Life Saving Club, near Bells Beach in Victoria. It seems they'd shared a fairly strong hash cookie with a young girl who had freaked out. Her father—an ex-cop from South Australia—made sure that his contacts in the Melbourne drug squad paid the band a visit and duly busted them.

Bon's drug conviction, and mine, would come back to bite us fair and square on the arse in the near future. All this hassle for a couple of joints.

As for In Focus, things gradually fell apart. Duncan the bass player felt he was incompatible with Johnny Dick, while their guitarist Billy Green wanted to live in Europe. But I never stopped believing in Doug's talent; I knew he was the best singer that Australia had ever produced.

Vince Maloney was the Australian-born guitarist for the Bee Gees and the first guitarist in Billy Thorpe's band the Aztecs. In 1970, Doug would spend some time in London with Vince, putting together a formidable band called Fanny Adams. Vince thought—and I agreed—that with a singer as good as Doug surely they'd be able to make inroads into the British rock scene.

But with no natural songwriting team and limited resources, Fanny Adams struggled. They did strike a deal with MCA Records and record an album, but they bit the dust in 1971, leaving only a cloud of discontent for all involved.

Doug had faced the same dilemma as so many great acts before him—The Easybeats, the Masters Apprentices and The Twilights, for starters—who'd had great success at home that they'd failed to reproduce overseas. When nothing happened internationally, they ended up spending the rest of their careers in Australia going over the same old ground.

Doug continued gigging with great players and scored some good theatrical roles in Oz, while we worked together on an album of American standards, in the days well before Rod Stewart and his Great American Songbook series. Yet despite such a great talent, the world outside Australia would be denied Doug's voice. It was a classic case study of a big local success not translating to the international market.

AC/DC, however, would change all this.

AUSTRALIA'S OWN WOODSTOCK

The 1969 Woodstock Festival shifted the entire direction of the music business—flower power was in full swing. I got a phone call from Peter 'Stripy' Langham, owner of Melbourne's most successful fashion boutique, the House of Stripes. Peter wanted to produce Australia's version of Woodstock and he wanted me to be a partner and produce the music program.

Sydney businessman Leon Fink provided the money, but I held the key to the music world. Well-known jazz impresario Horst Leopold, a friend of Leon's, came down from Sydney to watch out for his interests.

We were offered a site, located on a farm about 130 kilometres out of Melbourne in a town called Launching Place. The farm was the property and home of well-known Melbourne psychiatrist John Diamond, whom Stripy happened to know. We drove down and spent the day mapping out where the stage would be located, where people would camp and so on. It was a beautiful property with a natural amphitheatre—it was an ideal setting for the bands and the audience. Our own little Woodstock.

Stripy considered it much more than a coincidence that the festival would be held somewhere called Launching Place. It was meant to be. Accordingly, we decided to name the festival The Miracle. The reality was it'd take a miracle to pull the thing off and not lose Leon Fink's shirt.

This was an adventure steeped in total hippiedom, so we hired the very bohemian Adrian Rawlins to handle the PR. Adrian has been variously described as a beat poet, performer, promoter, raconteur, ratbag, stirrer, jazz aficionado and walking dictionary on everything Bob Dylan (whom he claimed as a friend). Above all he was a loveable lunatic. He moved into my Park Street house in order to help with PR for the event, along with four members of a cult group from Sydney, headed by a grey-bearded guy dressed in a kaftan. His name may have been ordinary—Fred Robertson—but this guy was from some other planet. He spent his time trying to convince everyone that the world was about to end.

We announced that the festival would take place on the 1969 Easter weekend. The mainstream reacted in typical fashion: Victorian Premier Henry Bolte, who was horrified that some hippie drugfest was about to take place in his state, did everything within his power to prevent it from happening. He instructed his chief secretary, Sir Arthur Rylah, to refuse our application, citing the theatres and Sunday entertainment acts, banging on that the possibility of pollution and drug trafficking concerned police.

Adrian wasn't exactly helping matters with his colourful press releases and press conferences where he and Stripy offered flowers and incense to the assembled media and government officials. But with the help of Solly Ellenberg, our attorney and resident sensible person, we got our permits and the festival was good to go. We expected a crowd of about 15,000, pretty ambitious numbers for 1969.

I had assembled a great line-up of bands, headed by cult Sydney underground prog rock act Tully, who'd started out as the house band for Harry M. Miller's local production of the musical *Hair*. Others on the bill were Billy Thorpe and the Aztecs, Spectrum, Healing Force, King Harvest and Wendy Saddington. We threw open the gates on a beautiful evening; people were streaming in, the vibe was perfect. Stripy and I went on a 'reconnaissance mission' and everything seemed off to a perfect start, apart from the shock of witnessing a car that came racing down the road, passed us at speed and flew over a fence into a nearby cow paddock.

Then at about 4 o'clock on the morning that the festival was to begin, the skies opened—it poured and poured. In fact, it was the highest rainfall ever recorded for that time of year. Great timing! A peaceful Good Friday turned into a quagmire, and a single note had yet to be played. The site was a disaster zone. The patrons who'd turned up were given a refund and the festival was cancelled.

We'd passed on rain insurance, because it simply cost too much, so we were staring down the barrel of a financial disaster. Stripy disappeared up a mountain somewhere to pray, leaving me, a 22-year-old who'd never run a festival before, with the mess of sorting out the bands. Leon Fink wore most of the financial loss, but both Stripy and I suffered big losses too. As if that wasn't bad enough, a few days later my so-called friend and partner Peter Andrews made a hasty exit and set up a rival agency with a guy named John Pinder, taking half of my roster of bands with them. It was a move I didn't see coming, and wouldn't be the last instance in my life of a rat jumping a sinking ship. John, a journalist by trade with leftist leanings, might have been a circus ringmaster in another life. He was that kind of character.

They called their business Let It Be; aside from the bands they'd taken from me, they also managed Daddy Cool and Spectrum, both big groups. Their greatest achievement, in partnership with Carlton-based advertising guru Bani McSpedden, was establishing the T. F. Much Ballroom (as in 'Too Fucking Much', a much-used expression), at the Cathedral Hall in Fitzroy. When their landlords, who happened to be the

Catholic Church, found out about the name, they weren't greatly pleased. Andrews and Co. quickly modified the venue's name to the Much More Ballroom. Perfectly acceptable.

It was an occasional live music venue that became the epicentre for all things cool and hippie. There was macrobiotic food, stalls offering up counterculture opinions and wares, and Gerry Humphreys performing his comedy routine, as well as being the in-house MC. Daddy Cool and the Captain Matchbox Whoopee Band provided the soundtrack, along with performances from magician Jeff Crozier. Much More also featured Australia's first psychedelic light show, which entailed placing paint and organic objects on a horizontal hot glass slide; when projected, the images were colourful, constantly changing and mind-fucking, a sort of large-scale lava lamp. (John Pinder became a major player of the fledgling comedy scene, establishing legendary Melbourne venue The Last Laugh.)

Peter eventually dropped off the scene and became a born-again Christian. He'd pen scathing letters to his 'heathen' acquaintances from his recent past, advising them of the evil of their ways. Fortunately, my name wasn't on his hit list. I had other problems to deal with, anyway. The failure of The Miracle, and the drug-hazed madness that went along with it, really did my head in. And this new alternative-based/hippie culture on show at Much More dramatically changed the taste of club-goers—the days were numbered for Sebastian's and Bertie's. As for me, I needed to escape for a while, lick my wounds.

I auctioned off the contents of my Park Street house, and after attending a screening of Dennis Hopper's trailblazing *Easy Rider* with Doug Parkinson, I took off for an extended stay on the Gold Coast with my girlfriend, Bobbi. I needed to take stock, think about my future.

I spent about three months in exile, a tough time for me. There I was, broke, in a beachside holiday town with no soul. I picked up a few dollars working in real estate—enough to get me a ticket back home—but I was in a very dark place. By the time I did return to Melbourne, Bobbi, who'd returned before me, was long gone. She'd become as disenchanted with me as I was with my life. The very talented jingle writer and singer/songwriter Terry Hannagan, the bastard, quickly moved in on her. (A few years later, I saw him perform on the ABC TV's *GTK*, a live music program produced by Bernie Cannon. Terry was wailing a very solemn tune called 'Blues for Bobbi'. It needed no further explanation.)

It was great to be back with my friends in the city that I loved. The Knights put me straight back to work on their club bookings; despite the emergence of the new hippie world and counterculture happening just up the road in Fitzroy, the Knights were still holding their own. Peter Raphael from the Australian Entertainment Exchange—a former rival—asked me to join his agency. Peter was a highly regarded music agent, but had decided to manage Max Merritt & the Meteors, who were in the process of relocating to London.

I teamed up with Peter's partner Ray Evans, an ex-drummer from Melbourne big band Bay City Union, to book the bands. While I felt a great deal of gratitude towards Peter for the opportunity, I just didn't want to be there. I wanted something that was mine, my own creation—and I just didn't love some of the bands I was booking. It was difficult.

One day I happened to be having a conversation with Michael Gudinski. We had a little history: he'd booked my bands for gigs at the Caulfield Town Hall. Michael would come into my Park Street HQ with a few of his Jewish mates, mostly during their lunch break from Melbourne Grammar. No older than seventeen, they'd just hang around, often for the entire day, eating their adoringly prepared sandwiches from their lunch boxes, driving me crazy until I gave them the bands they were after for the Caulfield gigs.

I liked them all, but it was obvious that Michael was the smartest of the bunch. He was direct and focused and had a dry sense of humour. Even though his family was hoping he'd follow his father into the building industry, to his mother's absolute horror Michael was hell-bent on making it in the music business.

We decided to form a new agency and represent the bands we liked, setting up a temporary office in the foyer of Sebastian's. Then we entered into a short-term lease for a place on Punt Road in St Kilda, a terrace listed for demolition. That didn't last long—when it came down, a few clients, who'd never let the truth get in the way of a good story, joked that we'd gone so far to avoid our debts that we'd had the entire street demolished. We eventually moved to new permanent premises in South Yarra.

We called the company Consolidated Rock, a tag dreamed up by Bob Dames, bass player from The Purple Hearts, who was himself something of an advertising genius—he'd come up with The Purple Hearts, as well as naming The Coloured Balls. The Consolidated Rock name had its advantages; we once hosted a fully catered conference at Melbourne's Park Royal Hotel and never received the substantial bill. We found out later the hotel's management assumed we were some big-time mining conglomerate, which they couldn't track down.

Consolidated Rock quickly became the biggest music agency in Melbourne, controlling almost the entire traffic of bands throughout the city in 1970. The only acts we were missing out on were some Sydney bands controlled by Peter Cunningham, who either dealt directly with Melbourne venues or dealt through another agency. It was time to sort this out.

Michael and I had a meeting about the Sydney bands.

'How can we solve this problem?' I asked. It only took a few minutes before we came up with a plan.

'Let's open an agency in Sydney,' we agreed. It was time to expand Consolidated Rock.

THE REBIRTH OF BILLY THORPE, HIGH PRIEST OF AUSSIE PUB ROCK

In order to expand Consolidated Rock we needed more staff—ideally people as driven as Michael and me. I'd recently met Michael Chugg, a young bloke from Tasmania with a colourful vocabulary. He'd arrived in Melbourne and had been hanging around the office trying to get dates for his Tasmanian band, Ida May Mack. He offered to work for us at Consolidated Rock and was prepared to start at the bottom.

To check out his bona fides, we decided to put him through a test. For a day job, Michael had been selling manchester, so we commissioned him to install curtains for the office windows. He passed the test with flying colours—and Gudinski christened him Chuggie, a name that would stick.

Chuggie told us how he'd been sacked from his last job as a race-caller in Tassie because he'd dropped the word 'fuck' on air. (He'd bet on the wrong horse, as it turned out.) Their loss, our gain. Chuggie's talent for booking bands quickly became apparent, so we sent him up north to establish the Sydney branch of Consolidated Rock, assigned with the task of wiping out Peter Cunningham.

Chuggie was joined by a young guy named Roger Davies, who'd also been hanging around, hassling us about dates for his band Company Caine. They eliminated the Sydney opposition in virtually no time at all. It's incredible, looking back at the careers we helped set in motion: Chuggie as one of the world's biggest promoters, and Roger, who has managed Sherbet, Cher, Olivia Newton-John, Tina Turner, Janet Jackson and P!nk.

Consolidated Rock was going great, so we decided it was time to treat ourselves. Gudinski fulfilled one of his dreams and bought a sparkling canary-yellow E Type Jaguar convertible, which he totalled a few weeks later. I bought myself a vintage Triumph TR2, which I drove maybe twice before it broke down and was relegated to life in a garage. We had better luck with Consolidated Rock, though, which was now a fully operating monopoly. If your band wasn't with us, they didn't work in Melbourne or Sydney.

But some very unhappy music industry people were out to get us. Among our critics was Molly Meldrum, who wrote for music weekly *Go-Set*. He'd rip into us in his column, complaining that some poor young band was unable to get a gig because of our 'unfair' monopoly. It was really starting to piss us off. Gudinski and I decided that the best way to shut him up was to put *Go-Set* out of business. What idiots we were.

So for all the wrong reasons, we started *The Daily Planet*, a rival music weekly that we were convinced would blitz them right out of the market. The slogan on our inaugural issue read: 'The People Shall Have an Honest Paper'. (All bullshit, of course.) We did at least succeed in pissing Molly off, which we did royally. He continued to abuse us, both privately and publicly.

In our naiveté, we hired just about every dope-smoking, out-of-work roadie in town. We made Jiver, Chain's roadie, the editor-in-chief, mainly because he was the only one we could find with a university education—and he seemed to know what he was doing. We also employed Lee Dillow, another Sydney roadie; god knows what editorial skills he had, although he could tell a really good joke. Lobby Loyde was a contributor; in typical Lobby fashion he was extremely radical on social issues, which soon overtook the music content. *The Daily Planet* quickly became more like an early version of *Rolling Stone* magazine.

The record companies, our financial lifeline, hated the paper. In one particularly damaging story, the purchase of product from CBS Records was discouraged, mainly because our intrepid reporter had been told that their affiliates supplied component parts used in weapons wielded by American troops in Vietnam.

Despite the paper's popularity with musicians and certain segments of the public, it lacked substantial advertising and was destined to become a financial disaster. We struggled into 1971, but were eventually wiped out.

By now the relationship between Gudinski and me had become strained. I'd lost all interest in being an agent. The thought of sending out bands to perform on the same old circuit, merely spinning their wheels, just didn't interest me. I had a new goal: I wanted to find a band and break them internationally. No one in Australia had achieved that before. Gudinski and I sat down and amicably resolved our relationship, a very unusual thing, at least according to the local music industry standard. Gudinski and Chuggie, who was still on board as an employee, continued with the agency business. They joined up with Ray Evans, who left the Australian Entertainment Exchange, along with the majority of its artists, and merged with the remains of Consolidated Rock.

In 1972, inspired by David Geffen's work in America with Asylum Records, the home to Jackson Browne and the Eagles and Neil Young, Gudinski created Mushroom Records, which grew into Australia's most successful independent record and publishing company. Soon after, he'd launch his equally successful Frontier Tours, making him the most powerful figure in the Australian music business. It was a rapid rise; it seemed like only yesterday that he'd been hanging around the office in Park Street, hoping I'd sling him a band or two for his dances.

As for me, both Sebastian's and Bertie's had finally run their course, with the Knights deciding to close them down in the early 1970s and focus on their wedding reception venue, on the site of Kismet, once their sprawling home in Sunbury.

We'd drifted apart. The Knights decided to return to a relatively sane existence, while I opted to continue with this madness called the music business. I chose to return to band management. All I needed was that one prize act I could break overseas.

In my teens I'd been a big Billy Thorpe fan, and he, along with his band, the Aztecs, became my first new signing. So here I was, post-agency, suddenly managing a guy who, in reality, had more life experience and time at the pointy end of the music business than anyone else. The way Billy read the situation, and the reason he agreed to work with me, was that I was from the left, I understood the counterculture and I could make things happen. Billy was craving a resurrection, on his own terms, and I was striving to make a name for myself internationally. We just seemed to click. And it was a thrill to be involved with someone who I respected and admired so much.

Billy had some miles on the clock by the time we got together in the early 1970s. He was born in Manchester, England, in 1946 and migrated to Melbourne with his parents, William and

Mabel, in 1955. While still in England, on holiday in Blackpool, Billy had been given his first acoustic guitar. His father, a keen tinkler of the ivories, soon had him strumming along to some of the early country music standards.

By the time Billy and his family relocated to Brisbane, he'd discovered his singing voice—he had a hefty set of lungs, which he set to work belting out Eddie Cochran and Hank Williams tunes. Gwen Iliffe, a Brisbane talent scout, gave him the pseudonym 'Little Rock Allen', and Billy made his public debut at the Cloudland Ballroom, aged eleven, accompanying himself on his new Gretsch electric guitar. A music star was born.

Even as a kid Billy threw himself into everything at full tilt; there was no such thing as half measures for Thorpey. He soon blossomed into the complete pop package, his good looks melting the hearts of teenage girls from one end of Oz to the other. Over time, these female fans would do their best to tear him to pieces.

In 1963, Billy heard about an audition for a Sydney-based band called the Aztecs. Billy's mind was set, so it was goodbye to a safe and protected life in sunny suburban Brisbane and welcome to sin city. A whole new world of rock'n'roll lunacy was about to consume him.

The audition, which he passed with flying colours, was held at Surf City, a Beat music venue in Kings Cross; this was the new centre of Sydney's bohemia, habituated by artists, poets and jazz musicians. Billy thrived in this lively new environment.

Billy and the Aztecs also scored a residency at Surf City, owned by Sydney bookie and 'colourful local identity' John Harrigan, along with the Wong family, who also ran Whisky A Go Go and Chequers. Harrigan became Billy's first manager— Billy soon became the adopted son of the Cross's gangsters, promoters, prostitutes and pimps.

In 1964 Billy and the Aztecs were signed by Ted Albert for his fledgling label, Albert Productions, who'd go on to play a pivotal role in the rise of AC/DC. Billy's second single, a cover of 'Poison Ivy', launched him and the band to national stardom, reaching number one in June 1964. By now Harrigan had them working all over Sydney; Billy and the Aztecs rocked the Bowl, one of Ivan Dayman's venues, and Beatle Village on Oxford Street, another of Harrigan's clubs.

More hits followed, including 'Mashed Potato' and 'Sick and Tired'; by the mid-1960s Billy was even more popular in Australia than The Beatles. He was the biggest homegrown star since Johnny O'Keefe, the Wild One, Australia's first rock legend. Billy had friends in places of influence, too, including media moguls the Packers; Clive and Kerry were both big fans and even hired Billy to play at a family party, where he won everyone over. Once Billy Thorpe charmed you, you were a friend and fan for life.

As my relationship with Billy developed, he told me about these wild times, how expat American promoter Lee Gordon had hosted decadent after-parties at his Sydney terrace, bathing (quite literally) in the many thousands of dollars in cash he'd just taken at the door of the Sydney Stadium. Strippers writhed with snakes, partygoers openly smoked pot, and Gordon offered guests the use of the coffin in the corner of his lounge room. Billy felt right at home among the madness. He was the toast of the town.

It was all happening so fast for him, in fact, that he had been poised to steal the crown from Johnny O'Keefe, the king of rock'n'roll himself, whose mentor had been none other than Lee Gordon. But Billy had taken a seemingly bizarre about-turn, releasing a string of syrupy ballads, including a version of his childhood favourite, 'Over the Rainbow'. He was no doubt pandering to the mothers who adored his clean-cut, choirboy-ish good looks. Many of the songs were hits, but Billy faced the possibility of becoming a cabaret act, a card-carrying member of the mainstream.

The guys in the Aztecs had become disenchanted and quit, forcing Billy to find a new group. His recruits included drummer Johnny Dick, later one of Max Merritt's Meteors. With his popularity still at an all-time high, Billy was offered his own national weekly TV show, *It's All Happening*, which screened on the Seven Network from March 1966. It was a live one-hour showcase for Billy and his band, along with the usual go-go dancers and guest artists.

Off screen, Billy dressed sharp and had a model girlfriend, Jackie Holmes, on his arm. Jackie was a gorgeous brunette, a refreshingly down to earth soul who just happened to love rock'n'roll. They raced around Sydney in a bright red Aston Martin. The reality was that Billy couldn't really afford the car, or the lifestyle, but he understood that appearances were everything; it was as though he based his image on Frank Sinatra. If you were the biggest pop star in the country, Billy figured, you had to behave like one. When he arrived anywhere by plane, Billy made sure that he was the first to alight; that way his screaming fans figured he'd been travelling in first class. The reality was quite different.

But Billy's recording career had started to wane—too many ballads—and his popularity faded. His TV show was axed with a year remaining on the contract. He was adrift and he couldn't afford to keep his band together. Billy was barely into his twenties and it seemed as though he was finished, washed up. Another fallen star.

Travelling in a cab from Sydney airport, Billy had read a newspaper headline, which screamed: POP STAR BANKRUPT. 'Wonder who the poor bastard is?' Billy asked himself. He didn't have to look too far for the truth.

By the time Billy first played at my club, Sebastian's, in August 1968, he was part of a blues/rock-based combo, a world away from the type of pop that had made him a star just a few years earlier. He'd let his hair grow long, and now sported a beard. The Aston Martin was gone, repossessed. Billy had reinvented himself. And he fell hard for Melbourne's counterculture—he'd had enough of the Sydney high life.

Despite his enormous success, the Melbourne rock fraternity frowned on Billy: to them he was a pop star with minimal originality and credibility, and if he thought he could waltz into the city's rock world and get respect, then he better damn well earn it. And that's exactly what he did. Billy was determined to change this perception and went to extremes to avoid anything that had links to his past. Max Merritt & the Meteors, Melbourne's band *du jour*, were in London, so the stage was clear for Billy's big comeback.

Billy wanted to start from scratch, turning his back on his old hits. This, too, divided his audience, some of whom would storm out, demanding a refund. But those who stayed were quickly in raptures with Billy's bold new style. Billy played his wildcard, recruiting guitarist Lobby Loyde, formerly of The Purple Hearts and The Wild Cherries. It was a smart move. It not only gained him credibility, but it gelled musically: the band was starting to kick some serious arse. They also played incredibly loud; Lobby revealed during an interview that a Melbourne doctor was supplying the band with laboratory-supplied Sandoz Laboratories LSD-25, which inspired The Aztecs' brutal, earth-quaking wall of noise.

Billy and the Aztecs now had the chops, and the sheer power, to win over the music community and blow away the opposition. They soon became Melbourne's most popular band—and Billy's second career was in motion. I was right in the thick of it.

Billy was convinced that the volume added extra dimension to his music, which in a live environment was hard to dispute. But trying to bottle that in a recording studio was a very different situation. Billy's seriously distorted guitar and wailing feedback sent VU meters—and recording engineers— into meltdown, and would create all sorts of tension in future recording sessions. It also derailed Thorpey's career in the UK, my first international foray.

The culmination of Thorpey's bold sonic assault was a legendary night at notorious Sydney venue the Bondi Lifesaver, which has gone down in Oz rock'n'roll folklore. In the upstairs area of the Lifesaver was an enormous fish tank, the owner's pride and joy, filled with a rich variety of stunning tropical fish. Billy and the Aztecs took the stage, plugged in, unleashed the beast and within half an hour every fish in the tank was floating upside down, killed by the sheer intensity and volume of their playing. Billy had killed the fish. It became one of those rock'n'roll events where, if everyone who claims to have been in the venue was actually there, all of Sydney somehow squeezed into the Lifesaver.

As his manager, watching Billy morph from faded pop idol to rock'n'roll guru, I felt as if I was watching a caterpillar turn into a colourful (and very noisy) butterfly. Acid, volume, Lobby, the counterculture—they all played their role in his transformation. Billy was truly reborn.

The money was starting to pour in but somehow Billy wanted to spend it just as quickly; he craved even bigger, even louder amps. Sound system rentals were creating a brand new industry, with companies like Strauss in Melbourne and Jands in Sydney licking their chops every time I called. Billy thrived in his new fuck-everyone environment. He not only attracted a huge new following, but acquired an entourage of devoted promoters, agents, road crew and worshippers. We became very closely linked. I stopped all other business to focus on Billy and set up a staffed office in St Kilda. It was really happening.

Billy had arrived in Melbourne with Jackie Holmes, but she found she couldn't compete with the obsession that was his new career, and they broke up, leaving a hefty gap in Billy's life.

Billy had checked in with me one day when I was still at Consolidated Rock, and he bumped into our new secretary, Lyn, a country girl from the Mornington Peninsula, who bore an uncanny physical resemblance to Billy. They were both diminutive, with very appealing personalities. They looked as though they belonged together. They'd met once before while she was working at the Australian Entertainment Exchange for Ray Evans. Billy was besotted with Lynn. She left the office at the end of the day on her scooter, with Billy in hot pursuit, craving a date. She finally agreed and so began an enduring relationship, which over time produced their two daughters,

Rusty and Lauren, and now a grandchild. Billy had found a keeper, a life-long soulmate.

As for me, I was very much the bachelor and loving the life, living in a great apartment in South Yarra. Managing Australia's biggest band certainly had its benefits. For one thing, all the guys in the band were in serious relationships, which left me with a clear run at some beautiful, nubile women. Life couldn't have been better.

THE UNSTOPPABLE RISE OF THE BEER BARNS

The inner-city club scene, with which I'd been so heavily involved while at Sebastian's, was starting to fade by 1970. But with the introduction of late-night liquor-licensing laws—long overdue, incidentally—a new phenomenon was developing in the recently built suburban beer barns. It would become known as pub rock. The smell of charred ham and cheese was fast being replaced with the stench of mouldy old carpet marinated in beer, sometimes piss.

Billy started to play a lot of the beer barns that began popping up all over the country. These were not your friendly little corner pubs, but purpose-built, binge-drinking-ready, brick-veneer monstrosities, all with inviting names like Springvale's

Waltzing Matilda, Ringwood's the Manhattan, the Sundowner in Geelong and the Matthew Flinders, among others. They were built to accommodate hordes of working-class drinkers keen to let off a bit of steam. I also made a point of sending Billy back to Sydney for some gigs, where beer barns were also sprouting like mushrooms. The audiences there, used to Billy Thorpe the pop star, were shocked by the change in the man. They looked on, their jaws hanging open, stunned.

Promoter Bill Joseph, the former king of the town hall dances, which the inner-city scene had killed off, was now well and truly back in business. Bill quickly became the lord of the Melbourne pub rock movement.

One of his rooms was the White Horse Hotel, located in the outer eastern suburb of Nunawading. I booked Billy into the White Horse every Thursday night; before long the word got out and the place was packed each week. The thousand-strong audience mainly comprised young working-class blokes who'd down vast amounts of beer, although some of it also spilled onto the sticky carpet. Perched on one another's shoulders, they'd chant 'Suck more piss! Suck more piss!' while Billy and the band blazed away.

Billy would play his version of the old standard 'Ooh Poo Pah Doo', a song he'd stolen from the Wild One, Johnny O'Keefe, which had first been popularised by New Orleans R&B legend Jessie Hill. The paralytic and vertically enhanced audience would chant the song's 'call and answer' passage at the top of their lungs. Billy would then take them even higher with a thundering version of the old Gene Vincent tune 'Be-Bop-A-Lula'. The crowd response was deafening, night after night.

Billy was by now the master rock'n'roll showman, comfortable enough to return to his act some of his old showbiz routines and material from his pop star days. Billy had been a keen observer of the great old-school soul revue performers, stars like James Brown, Little Richard and Bobby Womack, guys who knew how to work an audience. Billy's transformation was now complete. And the bucks kept rolling in.

In September 1970, Billy and the Aztecs recorded their breakthrough album, *The Hoax is Over*, consolidating their newfound rock'n'roll arrogance and screw-you attitude by including only four tracks, three of which were Billy originals. The album was dominated by the old Johnny 'Guitar' Watson song 'Gangster of Love', which ran the entire length of side one, and Billy's own 'Mississippi', which clocked in at 20 minutes. Billy told me that the band recorded on acid and jammed, while engineer Ernie Rose let the tapes run.

The album was released on Festival Records, a Sydney-based record company owned by Rupert Murdoch, a once powerful and fully independent record company with a wonderful roster of the best Australian and international artists. But at the time of *The Hoax*'s release, Festival was in decline. Without consultation with the band, or me, they decided to delete the band photos from the inner sleeve.

'Too expensive,' was the answer I was eventually given. This was how they treated the biggest band in the country? We needed a new label.

Lobby Loyde only lasted two years with the Aztecs, but his influence was enormous. Billy had clearly absorbed Lobby's influence; his playing had improved to the point where he became the Aztecs' lead guitarist when Lobby left in late 1970. Billy also continued dabbling with acid and grew his hair even longer. Rather than trying to replace Lobby, he enlisted electric piano player Bruce Howard from New Zealand's La De Das, which gave the Aztecs more of a boogie-shuffle feel. Billy also added a new member, Kevin 'The Beast' Murphy, the hardest-hitting drummer alive. Billy and the band blitzed audiences with their stacks of amplifiers and oversized PAs, not so much a wall of sound as a mountain of noise, the type of assault that shattered windows and left patrons' eardrums buzzing for days afterwards. Billy likened the experience to rocking out while standing astride a pair of Boeing Jumbo engines.

As for Lobby, he felt the need to be in a band where his LSD-inspired leanings would be better realised, so he left and formed The Coloured Balls, along with a motley bunch of young, energetic Melbourne musos who played everything full bore. They sported rat-tail/bogan-style haircuts and found their audience in the tail-end of the sharpie movement, which had now crossed over to more of a *Clockwork Orange*-inspired hybrid. The Coloured Balls' rock'n'roll opus was referred to as G.O.D.—Guitar Over Drive or, sometimes, Guitar Over Dose. Lobby cited Beethoven and Wagner as inspirations.

Lobby's contribution to creating a distinctly Australian guitar sound didn't go unnoticed; he would be hailed by musicians far and wide for years afterwards, including Nirvana's Kurt Cobain, Pavement's Stephen Malkmus and Henry Rollins.

As for Billy, his label problem was solved by Rodney de Gruchy, my old friend from the days of the original Sebastian's. Rodney was involved with a label called Havoc Records. It was a small, independently distributed outfit that put out the occasional international release. It was owned and operated by the highly regarded sax player Frank 'The Lion' Smith, in partnership with Eddie Floyde and Col Jones, owners of the 1960s venue Tenth Avenue and the Bunny Club in South Yarra.

Rodney had a vision: to make the Havoc label a home for Australian artists. Billy had grown a little weary of big record companies making creative decisions, and Rodney offered him a recording contract—with full creative control over his music, production and album art. Admittedly, this was a little bit like handing over the atomic bomb to Adolf Hitler. Billy's extravagant ways, after all, had previously sent him broke in Sydney—despite his transformation, Billy and money just didn't belong in the same room, so Rodney was in for a wild ride. I'd learned a bit more about record contracts, and the deal we struck up was very artist-friendly, way ahead of its time. But artists weren't usually given such free rein and Havoc Records would prove to be aptly named.

■

Michael Gudinski and I planned a series of Sunday night concerts at the Melbourne Town Hall, a concept we'd stolen from promoter Harry M. Miller, who'd made this work at the Sydney Town Hall. The first concert was to be Billy and the Aztecs, featuring Warren 'Pig' Morgan playing the Town Hall pipe organ, reputedly the biggest in the southern hemisphere. The concert was to be filmed and recorded by Havoc Records. The gig was set down for 13 June 1971.

Slightly out of character, I'd been to the ballet a few months earlier, enticed by a beautiful young woman I hoped to know better. I was hugely impressed by a stage prop, a sculpture of a starfish with tentacles about 30 feet tall, made from clear plastic. A compressor blew air into the starfish, making it move, all synched to the music. When lit, the effect was breathtaking. The artist/designer was a brilliant but somewhat out-there Melbourne guy named Rodney Currie. Although he'd never touched a drug in his life, Rodney was just on a continual high with his work.

I explained his work and concept to Billy, who loved the idea, but in typical Billy Thorpe fashion he had an additional idea.

'Can he make the tentacles about 70 feet high? And can I have ten of them?'

When I asked why, he explained that 70 feet was about the distance between the top of the stage and the ceiling at the Melbourne Town Hall. Sounded good to me.

The concert was a sell-out and the Aztecs got off to a great start; Pig was perched high up in the air, pumping away on the pipe organ. The only problem was there was a substantial 'delay' between the organ and the rest of the band, so while the live effect was amazing, on later playback of the recording, the sound was abysmal.

There was another problem. The starfish sculpture was hitting the ceiling; Rodney Currie was having enormous difficulty controlling it. Before long it fell down, narrowly avoiding the audience before knocking over all the band's amps and equipment. (And this was pre *Spinal Tap*!) It didn't help that the band was on acid. Rodney eventually managed to get his creation under control and the Aztecs completed their performance, which was released as *Aztecs Live at the Town Hall*, organ problems, wild starfish and all.

The next Sunday night show we staged was equally impressive—the first major concert performance by a rising phenomenon named Daddy Cool, a group of rock'n'roll revivalists about to give the Aztecs a run for their money.

Soon after the Town Hall show, I received a call from Jim McKay, a producer at Channel Nine. He was interested in staging a music festival at Sunbury, my old hometown, on a farm that he'd located. It would run over the 1972 Australia Day long weekend. After my Launching Place disaster, I was a bit gun shy when it came to festivals—but this time neither my money nor my reputation was on the line.

'If you can get me Billy and the Aztecs to headline,' Jim told me, 'I can make it work.'

Billy was packing out the Melbourne pubs, including the wildly popular 'suck more piss' night at the White Horse; McKay felt he could parlay all this into surefire success at the Sunbury Festival. He offered us the pretty impressive figure of five grand, a hefty fee.

We took a trip out there so Jim could show us around. Unlike the picturesque Launching Place, the Sunbury site was no idyllic rural farm. Rather, it was barren, dry and rocky, with a dried-up creek its one natural 'feature'. It wasn't what you'd call pretty. But there was an upside: if it rained, unlike Launching Place, it wasn't going to turn into a disaster zone.

We struck up a deal where Havoc Records would have rights to the proposed recording and documentary.

Billy and the band, along with friends and partners, immersed themselves in the whole festival experience. They arrived the morning of the gig and set up in tents behind the stage near the creek. It was going to be a big night (and day). Come nightfall, huddled around their campfire, Billy and the guys were determined to indulge in substances of one kind or another, to ensure that when it was their time to play, band and audience would be all on the same level. They envisaged a giant version of the White Horse, with thousands of blokes on each other's shoulders, chanting 'suck more piss, suck more piss' deep into the night.

Sunbury was no Woodstock. It was certainly no 'peace and love' tribal gathering, but the 35,000-strong audience revelled in it. Billy was their hero and the festival, which could only be described as 'quintessentially Australian', was a huge success. Sunbury would continue on an annual basis for a while, but the glory of this first event would never be surpassed. Also on the bill for Sunbury '72 were the La De Das, Max Merritt & the Meteors, Spectrum and Madder Lake. Gerry Humphreys was the MC. In the spirit of the times, clothes weren't mandatory at Sunbury. Molly Meldrum, who was covering the event for *Go-Set*, was a bit surprised by all the nudity. 'What sort of made you . . . just get up and shed your clothes like this?' he asked one naked female punter. She just smiled and kept on dancing.

I figured that sidestage was the best place to take in Billy's performance, although I suddenly wasn't so sure when a can or two of Fosters flew past my head, hurled by yobbos in the crowd. The perpetrators were usually dealt with by other members of the audience, a very Aussie twist on the hippie ritual of brotherhood. Undeterred, Billy and the band kept on playing; 'Ooh Poo Pah Do' becoming a sprawling jam that extended for more than 15 minutes.

Billy had another of his great ideas for the proposed double live album. He insisted on a pop-up cardboard album cover, replicating a scene from the Sunbury campsite. I engaged graphic artist Ian McCausland to create this masterpiece, but it nearly sent Havoc Records broke and left Rodney and myself with a lot less hair. Still, *Aztecs Live! At Sunbury* reached number three in the charts when it appeared in August 1972 and remains an essential document of that wild first festival.

Nothing, however, could surpass Billy and the Aztecs' next big gig, in early 1973, this time staged at the Sidney Myer Music Bowl, a man-made amphitheatre close to the centre of Melbourne. It could well be the biggest Australian gig ever staged, about 200,000 people in all, sardined into a space designed to comfortably accommodate about 30,000. The trees at the back of the park, loaded with people trying to get a glimpse of the stage, swayed in time to the music. It was an incredible sight. Police closed off all the nearby roads to traffic; there was just no way to move.

The gig was put together by one of Australia's staunchest rock supporters, Trevor Smith, from radio station 3KY. The day after the gig, the headline of the *Melbourne Sun* declared: AZTEC ENERGY DRAWS 200,000 PEOPLE. 'Aztec Energy' was a phrase I coined after reading about the ancient South American nation of sun worshippers.

Clearly inspired, Trevor organised a second memorable gig in an outdoor amphitheatre, this time at Rosebud, a coastal holiday town southeast of Melbourne. The crowd that descended on the town created an impenetrable traffic jam, backing up about 30 kilometres from the site of the gig. Billy, the band and I got stuck—on the way to Billy's own gig. A bikie gang was winding their way around the traffic jam and happened to notice us.

'Need a ride?' they asked, pulling over.

Our chopper-led journey to Rosebud took us through the back streets and across a golf course, directly to the backstage area, minutes before the gig was due to begin. I've never seen a man as relieved as Trevor. It also taught me—and everyone else—a lesson in the value of making a memorable entrance, something I'd later draw on with AC/DC.

Billy was now the undisputed king of Oz rock, the biggest star in the country for a second time. His ego, however, was starting to get a little bit out of control. He was repeatedly arrested for swearing on stage, and it was left to me to get him out of trouble. During a show in Tasmania, he opened the set with a rave about how a cop told him 'you can't go around saying fuck on stage'— and was duly arrested yet again. On one occasion, after a gig in Perth, we got stuck in the lift at the Sheraton Hotel. There was a telephone in the lift, so via the hotel operator I put in a call to Patti Mostyn in Sydney. Patti was Australia's best publicity agent, perhaps the best in the world. And we had history.

Patti and I had a very short-lived romantic fling, volatile and dramatic (and well before she got hitched to Eric Robertson, owner of Jands Audio). Patti had sprung me in the middle of a threesome at the Cosmopolitan hotel in Double Bay with two very attractive room service girls. One had earlier planted a joint on my lunch tray order, which begged the question: 'What time do you finish your shift?' She turned up later in the day, along with her colleague. Patti, who was expecting to have dinner with me that evening, was singularly unimpressed— and that was the end of that. Fortunately, we somehow stayed friends and I immediately thought of her when Billy got stuck in the lift.

'Patti,' I told her. 'I've got a great story for you, one you won't believe.'

I told her that Australia's biggest rock star was trapped in a hotel lift. She immediately called the Perth media, who all descended on the hotel, attracting the attention of the police. Two hours later, when they finally got the lift working, Billy was fuming. The doors opened on the ground floor and he burst out, telling everyone within earshot to get fucked. Unfortunately, this also included the local cops, who threw Billy in their paddy wagon and carted him off to the watch house for an overnighter. I had to post bail and Billy eventually went back to Perth for court, where he received a hefty fine.

Billy was pretty much a law unto himself, but there were times when it would have been really helpful if he had known— in the words of the old song—when to hold them and when to fold them. But that just wasn't his style.

THE AZTECS ARE COMING!

Billy, Lynn, and Pig and his wife, Nina (the subject of their song 'Momma'), had all moved into a house in Hawksburn Road, Toorak. There was a nightly ritual of sitting around a huge central dining table, eating fine food—a favourite past-time of Pig's, hence his nickname—and drinking, followed by a dessert of hash cookies, a house specialty of Momma's. Once all that was digested, a jam would break-out, with Billy and Pig swapping licks and exploring ideas for a future recording project that they planned to make as a duo.

In 1973, Billy and Pig wrote and recorded their album, which they named *Thump'n Pig & Puff'n Billy*. The concept, from what I can recall through the haze, was both a creative outlet for the vast amount of material they'd written during their jams, and a chance to consume as many of Momma's hash cookies as humanly possible—and then capture the outpouring on tape.

The album came out in July 1973 and, while not a commercial hit, it had a lot of character and remains an enduring reminder of Pig's unique boogie-style piano playing. It really captured the essence of their special friendship and musical connection, which had begun in Perth several years earlier, at the Hole in the Wall Club run by my ex-partner Peter Andrews. The album's memorable tracks included 'Captain Straightman' and 'Early Morning'.

The next stop was the Mulwala Festival, in country New South Wales. Havoc Records had chartered two planes and had the words 'Aztecs Are Coming' painted under the wings. It ensured maximum hype, especially when we made a low sweep over the festival site before landing at a nearby dirt airstrip. It was a far cry from the band's organic, grassroots connection with the Sunbury Festival. We'd learned about the impact of a big entrance from our arrival via Harleys at the Rosebud Festival. Now we took that to a whole new level. Anticipation for the gig was at fever pitch.

Americans Canned Heat and Stephen Stills were the festival headliners; the Aztecs followed Stills and were to go on immediately before Canned Heat. As good as both acts were— and anyone who's seen the *Woodstock* film knows how great

Canned Heat could be—they didn't stand a chance at Mulwala, following on from the Aztecs, now at the absolute peak of their popularity, with a huge crowd bellowing, 'Suck more piss!'

Some time later I bumped into Skip Taylor, Canned Heat's manager, while in LA. Skip told me that as soon as they returned to the States, he'd put in a call to Lillian Roxon, a hugely influential Australian reporter based in New York.

'Billy Thorpe and the Aztecs are the best thing happening in Australia,' Taylor informed her.

My challenge was how to transform this praise into something tangible. I craved success on a global level.

Rodney de Gruchy and I, via our connection with Havoc Records, had become close friends and I moved into his house on the corner of Darling Street and Alexander Avenue in South Yarra, a busy throughway. Rodney was the manager of The Coloured Balls, Lobby Loyde's band, and given that Lobby had once been a member of the Aztecs and they were now playing the same beer barn circuit, there was a bit of good-natured rivalry between the two bands, mostly drummed up by the press.

I was driving a huge old 1964 Pontiac—everyone called it the Whale—which just happened to catch on fire one night (from a cigarette, I think) out the front of the old Waiters Club in a laneway off Little Collins. I came out of the club to find the interior totally engulfed in flames and smoke. I raced to a nearby parking station, grabbed a fire extinguisher and put out the fire, leaving a mess of white foam, totally burned-out upholstery and a spike of a steering wheel. I managed to start the car and drove it home, where I parked it out front. Then I went to bed.

The next morning I walked to a nearby deli and looked down at the newspaper stand. There was a photo of my burned-out car on the front page of *The Truth*, one of Rupert Murdoch's racier tabloids. The headline read: THORPE'S MANAGER'S CAR BOMBED. The story 'revealed' that it was a 'revenge bombing', arranged by The Coloured Balls. It was written by a local journalist and mate, Dave Dawson, who loved to play around with colourful stories. Ironic that it ran in a daily called *The Truth*. Rodney and the guys in The Coloured Balls couldn't believe the story made it into print. We thought it was hilarious.

Before Billy and Pig's *Puff'n Billy* collaboration, the band had recorded what would become Billy's signature song, 'Most People I Know (Think That I'm Crazy)', which was released in March 1972 and packaged in a psychedelic painting of Billy, courtesy of Ian McCausland. It became a huge Australian hit, peaking at number two and spending almost six months on the charts, and is widely regarded as one of the classics of Oz rock.

'Most People I Know' was highly autobiographical, Billy having a strong spiritual belief in the powers of the universe. Billy and I were both big fans of Dr Norman Vincent Peale, world-renowned author of *The Power of Positive Thinking*. We went to the Melbourne Town Hall to hear Peale speak, which was a powerful experience, and one I believe had been a big influence on the song. You don't go through what Billy had gone through—and me, to a lesser degree—and come out on top without a bit of help from a higher source.

I received a call from Alan Keen, head of the British-based Radio Luxembourg, one of the UK's infamous 'pirate' radio stations. Alan was in Sydney and heard 'Most People I Know' on the radio.

'That song,' he told me, 'should be a hit in Britain. And the guy to release it is Mickie Most.'

I couldn't argue with Alan. Most, a record producer and label boss, had huge hits with Herman's Hermits, Eric Burdon and The Animals and Donovan, and was a massively influential man in UK music circles. True to his word, when Keen returned to London he played the song to Most, who loved it.

Next thing I know, a telex from Keen hit my desk, strongly suggesting that I get straight over there and do a deal. It was an opportunity too good to refuse. A few days later I jumped on a Pan Am 747, on my first big international trip, to sort out a deal with Mickie to release Billy's single on his highly successful Rak Records. Mickie was currently producing his latest signing, leather-clad rocker Suzi Quatro, a humble and likeable kid Mickie had plucked from obscurity in Detroit. She just about lived at the Rak office, plotting her launch to stardom.

Soon after arriving in the UK, I teamed up with my old friend Wayne de Gruchy who was living in London. It was time to get down to business. The deal with Rak was very quickly consummated, and Wayne and I set ourselves up in a phone booth in Curzon Street, just down the road from Rak's office in Mayfair. After making the daily trek from Surrey on the train, we'd spend most of the day in the phone booth trying to drum up support for 'Most People I Know'. Mickie found out about our humble HQ and gave us an office, where we worked closely with him and his brother Dave, who was head of promotion at Rak.

Billy had found a new career and home in Melbourne; he'd become re-energised. International success was high on his agenda, although he'd never admit to it and would occasionally dismiss the prospect. But I knew this was just an escape clause, in case it didn't come off. Billy was well and truly on board and knew that 'Most People I Know' was the vehicle to get things going. Making it a hit in the UK was a huge priority for both of us.

Before leaving Australia I'd seen an audiovisual contraption, made by a company called Fairchild, housed inside a briefcase, on display in a Myer's window. When you opened the case, a screen popped up and it would play film footage that had been transferred on to a cassette. I thought that it would be a great way of showing people what Billy was all about, so with the help of Fairchild, I had the film clip of 'Most People' transferred onto cassette. I took the machine with me to London. As far as I could see, no one else carried such a device.

Dave Most loved it and thought the Fairchild would be a good way of introducing the song to BBC Radio 1. He made an appointment with the Head of Programming and off we went. As my machine had been made in Australia, in order to screen Billy's video to the producer, we jimmied up something using matchsticks and exposed electrical wires. The next thing we knew, we'd short-circuited the entire BBC Studios. Fortunately, they loved the record—when we did get everything working— and put 'Most People' into high rotation. We couldn't have dreamed up a better result.

But despite receiving heavy airplay on the most listened-to radio station in the world, the British public just didn't get the record, which failed to chart. In an attempt to rescue it, it was agreed that Billy and the band come to London and perform at London's Speakeasy Club, which had a history of launching many outstanding careers, including The Jimi Hendrix Experience and Deep Purple. 'The Speak' was *the* hangout for the British music industry.

I'd been in London for six months now and had become a regular at the club. Wayne de Gruchy had been working there, so we'd hang out there most evenings. I developed a good relationship with Nino, the club's manager. Nino did me a huge favour by giving my unknown band—whose single had failed to chart in the UK—a gig in his famous club. I arranged for a number of influential and well-connected people to come down and check out Billy and the Aztecs. This was our last shot.

The band had been used to playing festivals and huge beer barns in Australia, so the Speakeasy was a huge downwards adjustment. It was a tiny basement club with a front bar, a dining room frequented by music industry insiders, and an area where the bands played. The place could hold maybe 150 people at a squeeze. Come the night of Billy's gig in December 1972, I'd invited the Most brothers, plus agents from Chrysalis whom I had been desperately trying to convince to represent the band, and a big contingent of musicians, including visiting Australians. It turned out a bit like the Bondi Lifesaver gig when Billy killed the fish—if everyone who admitted to being there was in the room, the place would have been shut down before the gig even began.

Unfortunately, in typical Billy Thorpe fashion, he insisted on turning up the volume to ridiculous levels for such a small place. Barely a few songs in and the club owner did what some Australian club owners would have liked to have done to the Aztecs: he pulled the plug. Afterwards, Billy went to some lengths to smooth over what had been a total disaster, writing it off as a publicity stunt and so on. It simply wasn't true. He'd just tried on his 'fuck you' attitude at the wrong place and the wrong time.

It was a complete train wreck. I couldn't even get the Most brothers on the phone afterwards; the deal was dead. It was time to go home, but not before Billy and I found ourselves heading up to Oxford in a vintage Rolls Royce with a young

Richard Branson at the wheel. We were on our way to check out his Manor Studio, where we were considering recording an album before returning to Australia. It didn't happen but we were lucky enough to hear Mike Oldfield's massive *Tubular Bells* LP through the same speakers on which it was recorded and mixed. At least we ended the disastrous journey in style.

Things in London were now hopelessly in tatters, so we all headed back to Australia to headline the 1973 Sunbury Festival, which was scheduled to begin on 27 January, only a few days after our return. There would be no camping in tents this time; we arrived at the festival only an hour or so before showtime.

When we reached the site I happened to notice this 'ocker' bloke on stage, telling jokes and doing something silly with a rubbish bin. I hadn't contractually okay'd any of this prior to the Aztecs' performance time, even though this guy seemed to have a good rapport with the audience and was going down well. It was going to be hard for Billy to follow. I demanded that the organisers get the comic off stage, which contractually they were compelled to do.

In all the time I'd been living in London, I'd missed the beginning of Paul 'Hoges' Hogan's career—I had no idea who the guy was. By now, of course, he was a big star. I wish somebody had filled me in.

The Aztecs eventually went on and got a great response, though perhaps not as fanatical as the previous year, when it was all new and exciting. By now, Billy was running the risk of becoming overexposed; I could sense the public was starting to grow tired of hearing about him. It was a big problem, especially now that any chance of international success was gone.

Johnny O'Keefe was also on the Sunbury bill that day, one of his last major appearances before passing away a few years later. Johnny played such a huge part in the development of the Australian music industry. It was partly because of his early efforts that Australian artists were finally given the opportunities they deserved via such vehicles as the TV show *Six O'Clock Rock*, which JOK hosted. Johnny had also been a big influence on a young Billy Thorpe back in the early Surf City days. It was great to see the new generation of rock fans at Sunbury give this legend such great respect and love. Watching him up there on stage, at this drug-, mind- and alcohol-fucked outdoor rock festival, dressed up in his stylish suit and white shoes, looking dapper, was a rare and wonderful sight.

Billy loved JOK, despite a few run-ins. Johnny had referred to Billy and his band as a bunch of 'long-haired poofters' when they were due to appear on his TV show *Sing, Sing, Sing*. But Billy was right there with Johnny at Sunbury that day, showing his respect and affection from the side of the stage. Johnny was having a red-hot go at being a tough act for Billy to follow, even to the point of reclaiming his old song 'Ooh Poo Pah Doo', which

Billy now played, and nearly pulling it off. It was like waving a red rag to a bull—and Billy thrived on a challenge.

Around this time, there were personnel changes in the Aztecs. Kevin Murphy, who had been playing drums since the departure of Jimmy Thompson, was replaced with Gil 'Ratso' Mathews. We now had a 'Ratso' and a 'Pig' in the band. The sequence of these events remains hazy to me—nothing, of course, to do with Momma's cookies! Sketchy as I am about specifics, I can tell you one thing for sure: every line-up rocked its arse off—and the world's best roadie, Norm Sweeney, was always there to keep everyone in line, which was never easy. Billy, especially, was a fucking handful.

The American producer Lou Risner reached out to me; he wanted Billy to perform as the Pinball Wizard in his proposed Australian production of The Who's rock opera *Tommy*. Billy loved the idea and the deal was soon done; the show was slated for March 1973. Rehearsals were to take place in Melbourne. Billy really embraced the role made famous by Elton John, putting his heart and soul into it. The coupling of Billy and The Who's Keith Moon, who was playing the role of Uncle Ernie in Australia, promised interesting times ahead. Two madmen, from opposite hemispheres, with a shared love of Courvoisier cognac and a genetic need to create chaos; well, anything could happen. But to everyone's surprise, it all went off smoothly and the tour was a success, despite some poor reviews. Billy would never admit it, but I know these reviews affected him.

He sometimes felt like he was another victim of the tall poppy syndrome.

Many years later, I walked into a café in the New South Wales seaside town of Port Macquarie. I noticed some gold records on the wall. Turned out it was run by Keith Moon's sister, who'd migrated to Australia.

'I once got pissed with Keith,' I mentioned as I left.

'You and a thousand others,' she laughed.

Having now done hard yards with Havoc, a small independent record company, the time seemed right for Billy to sign to a label with bigger resources and connections to the American market. The obvious choice was the Australian branch of the American-based Atlantic Records, owned by the powerful Warner Brothers (WEA Records), the label of choice for Led Zeppelin and, later on, AC/DC.

The Aztecs' first album for Atlantic, recorded at Armstrong Studios in Melbourne and aptly called *More Arse Than Class*, came out in May 1974. The album cover featured a photo of the band standing in a row bending over and flashing their arses—a classic Aussie browneye. While very Billy, it wasn't exactly a pretty sight or an 'I must own this' piece of album art. This was followed in early 1975 by the live album *Steaming at the Opera House*; the Aztecs had been the first rock band to play at this newly opened Sydney icon.

Despite both being essentially good albums, neither lived up to sales expectations. The audience, having been served up a load of Thorpey, had simply moved on. The time was approaching for Billy to undergo yet another reinvention.

Following the Hunter S. Thompson–inspired 'Fear and Loathing' tour of Northern Queensland, decadence and over-indulgence was really starting to take its toll on all of us. Too much equipment, too many drugs, too much booze—and not enough paying customers. The tour lost so much money it put the touring company into voluntary liquidation; we simply had no money to bail it out. It was a sobering time and we all became a little disenchanted. Working with such a great talent had been a privilege, but Billy and I both needed to move on.

We met in May 1974 and while we agreed to split, we still had great respect for each other. International success, which I craved, just wasn't going to happen with Billy. But the London experience would prove to be a valuable one—for me, that is, not Billy.

I hooked up again with my friend Rodney, while Billy eventually signed a management deal with Robert Raymond, a well-known Australian promoter of international artists. Robert had toured Frank Sinatra, who, as the story goes, chose Robert to be his Australian promoter after watching him go through his pitch routine—directly through a one-way mirror at his agent's Los Angeles office. It was quite a statement. A film, *The Night We Called It a Day*, was made of the disastrous Sinatra tour.

Robert, Billy and their respective families packed up and moved to Los Angeles in the mid-1970s, where Billy began the third instalment of his amazing career. He signed to Pasha Records, a small independent production company with its own recording studio, located on Melrose Avenue near the Paramount Studios—and opposite my favourite Mexican restaurant, Lucy's. Pasha was run by well-known American producer Spencer Proffer, who'd produce Billy's American albums.

Just as I expected, Billy reinvented himself, this time as a classic progressive rock artist. His first US album, 1979's *Children of the Sun*, was released through Capricorn Records. The label's legendary owner, Phil Walden, gave it the big push and it would have a reasonable amount of success, particularly in the southern states.

As for me, I was about to meet the band that would achieve everything I'd hoped to achieve with Billy.

LAUNCHING THE HARD ROCK AND MEETING A
SCHOOLKID NAMED ANGUS

Just around the corner from the Rak office in London was a recently established restaurant called the Hard Rock Cafe. I noticed that every day there was a huge queue of people from all over the world waiting for a seat. Sometimes I joined them. Not only did I like the cheeseburgers, but the whole concept appealed to me.

Back in Australia, post-Billy, I was having a chat to Rodney, my confidant and best friend, and mentioned how popular the place was.

'Well, why don't we set one up in Melbourne?' he asked me.

Fair enough, I figured, and before I knew it we were drawing up plans.

We made calls to the owners in London and soon realised they weren't into doing a franchise deal. So we figured, what's stopping us doing it anyway? We researched the name rights and discovered that a greasy spoon in the inner suburb of Brunswick had registered the Hard Rock name. But they had recently shut down and were no longer using it. So we simply purchased it off them; the name became ours. We decided to set the Hard Rock up in the old Bertie's building, which had been sitting vacant for several years and still had all of the amenities in place—including the all-important kitchen.

My old friend Bill Joseph from the White Horse days agreed to finance the operation and join the partnership. We designed what we felt was an Australian version of the original Hard Rock, with an FJ Holden, courtesy of 'Ross the Wrecker', a colourful Melbourne character who'd fly Billy and the Aztecs to country gigs in his private plane. The FJ was parked above the entrance of the imposing five-storey Victorian building.

The basement was the live room, while the ground floor had a record shop called House of Wax, set up by Gil Mathews, the Aztecs' drummer, as well as various reception rooms and the office. The first floor was a coffee shop-cum-soda bar with about 50 pinball machines. The second floor was the main hamburger joint with classic 1950s/*Happy Days* booths. Diners could bring in booze; we had a licence for BYO. On the rooftop was a high stage, built into what was the original squash court viewing balcony. We opened up the remainder of the rooftop and imported tons of beach sand, for that all-important Aussie beach party feel. The whole building was accessible via a huge winding staircase left over from the Bertie's days. It was a great fit-out.

We had a huge opening night celebration; despite the winter chill, 1000 people turned out, the who's who of the Melbourne music and social scene, including politicians and rock stars. The night was a triumph.

About five o'clock the next morning I was woken up—I'd barely gone to sleep, to tell the truth—with a phone call from Claudia Wright, going live to air on her ABC radio program. Claudia had been at the Hard Rock the night before. Next thing I know I'm in a heated discussion with the owners of the Hard Rock in London, who were abusing the shit out of me for stealing their name, threatening me with an injunction. As I slowly woke up, I let them know I was the owner of the name, at least in Melbourne.

It didn't matter to us—we'd created a sensational club, a very Australian slant on the whole 1950s diner theme—and we'd covered all the potential legal loopholes, too. In hindsight, we could have chosen a totally original name, but using the Hard Rock tag sure didn't hurt. We were packed from day one, and it quickly became the place to be seen and a great venue for the cream of Australia's bands to play. It became the venue of choice for bands wanting to showcase themselves to the music media and industry as well. It was also where I ran into AC/DC.

The Hard Rock was open every night except Tuesday, which we set aside for Melbourne's more out-there gay community. Six nights a week, two bands would appear in the basement with the occasional showcase for a music business audience, staged in either the second floor restaurant or the rooftop garden.

The current prescription drug of choice was a muscle relaxant called Mandrax, known to its many users as 'Mandies'. It was a well-known 'leg opener'. When mixed with alcohol it made everyone fall over—especially the girls, who loved the stuff. But it created a nightmare for our security staff, who had a full-time job saving these horny, spiky-heel-wearing young girls from tumbling down the stairs.

The price of admission to the Hard Rock was $2.10. Why the odd figure? Mark Evans from AC/DC once asked me this question. The 90 cents change was earmarked for our 50 pinball machines. As for me, I was back to my old job as the band booker. I'd be there with my partner and friend Rodney most nights, enjoying myself in the ground floor office, socialising with the bands and their agents and managers.

It wasn't exactly how I saw my future, but I felt it was a great place to continue the wound-licking process, while having some fun and keeping my eyes open for a band with whom I could fulfill my dreams. Meanwhile, I'd met a girl called Julie who told me that her family owned a winery in McLaren Vale, South Australia, called 'Pirramimma'. She sure as hell got my attention; I mean, really, a beautiful girl with access to a winery? Julie had spent most of her youth in a posh Adelaide private boarding school, so her understanding of my rock'n'roll world was minimal, but somehow I liked that. I'd been the bachelor for a while, living large with Rodney on a nightly basis, and was becoming tired of it. Suddenly I was falling for this girl—within months we were married.

In early 1974 I was talking with my old mate Michael Chugg, now a Sydney-based promoter. I asked him casually if he had heard of any new bands from Sydney that I should be booking into the Hard Rock.

'Well,' he said, 'the younger brothers of George Young from The Easybeats have started a band. It's called AC/DC. Maybe you should check them out.'

Immediately bells started going off in my head: The Easybeats were Aussie music royalty, a band that I loved. Of course I'd check out the younger Youngs.

I put in a call to booking agent Frank Stivala at Premier Artists. As well as providing many of the bands for the Hard Rock, Frank had been my agent for Billy Thorpe and the Aztecs and was also a good friend.

'Chuggie has tipped me off to this band from Sydney,' I said to Frank. 'Do you know anything about AC/DC?'

It so happened that Frank did—and he'd been considering bringing them down to Melbourne for some dates. He explained there'd been a buzz developing around them in Sydney's industry circles; they'd been playing gigs at Chequers nightclub, a run-down relic of a once classy venue, in a sleazy part of downtown Sydney. This had somehow slipped under my radar; AC/DC had not only held down this residency, but also landed the national support for the upcoming August tour of American rocker Lou Reed. I booked them into the Hard Rock on their night off in Melbourne.

I was keen to see them, considering these recommendations and their brother's impressive credentials. On the night of their gig, I walked downstairs to the Hard Rock's live room, in the basement, full of anticipation. To my surprise, I saw this scrawny little schoolkid walking around the room, with a bit of a cocky swagger; apparently he was part of the entertainment. The kid was dressed in long shorts, a private boys school uniform, complete with a leather satchel on his back. He wore a school cap with the letter 'A' embroidered on it. A cigarette was hanging out the corner of his surly mouth. He looked like he'd walked off the pages of *Mad* magazine.

Then I noticed this other little guy whose name I learned was Malcolm. He was dressed a bit like a jockey, in shiny clothes and high boots.

'This can't be the band,' I thought to myself. 'This is a venue for grown-ups. What's Chuggie on about?'

I tried to put their strange appearance out of my head when they started playing. Within about 20 seconds of their first song I was beginning to get excited; it was a song ignited by one of Malcolm's beautifully crafted guitar intros, which would become his signature.

'This,' I started thinking to myself, 'is pretty good.'

Then the schoolkid kicked in with some blistering lead guitar. His head was bobbing up and down in perfect groove. The little fucker was going off, doing this Chuck Berry duck-walking routine, the whole deal. But that wasn't all. Then he fell to the ground and, with his legs kicking the air, he wriggled around on his back, continuing to play without missing a single note. I thought he was having a seizure.

As for the rest of the band, their vocalist Dave Evans seemed okay, although I thought his glam-rock image was out of step with Malcolm and Angus, despite Malcolm's seriously dodgy Melbourne Cup-winner's outfit. Their songs were melodic, potentially commercial. But I just couldn't take my eyes—or my ears—off Angus and Malcolm.

By the end of their set, the assembled crowd, which wasn't huge, were dumbfounded. Me included. What had we just seen?

I soon learned their backstory. The Youngs, including older brother George, the creator and guitarist of The Easybeats, were all originally from Scotland. They immigrated to Australia post-war on what was known as the 'ten-pound scheme'. Only eldest brother Alex stayed behind in the UK; he became involved with Apple, the Beatles label, who signed his band Grapefruit.

After arriving by ship in the middle of an abnormally wet and cold winter, the Youngs were accommodated at the Villawood migrant hostel, southwest of Sydney, a strange, spooky, spider-infested dump with a leaky roof. Welcome to Australia.

At the hostel, George met Harry Vanda and Dick Diamond, a couple of Dutch immigrants, along with Stevie Wright, another recent arrival from the UK, and Gordon 'Snowy' Fleet. They began jamming together and decided to form a band.

They'd rehearse in a hall at the hostel; sometimes they'd play for the new arrivals. They called themselves The Easybeats. It wasn't long before they were spotted by a hotshot real estate agent-cum-talent scout, a guy called Mike Vaughan. He introduced them to Ted Albert, an immigrant himself, with Swiss and Russian roots. Ted was the boss of J. Albert & Son, Australia's premier music publishing and record production company.

A stream of local hit singles poured out of the band: 'She's So Fine', 'Wedding Ring', 'Woman', 'I'll Make You Happy', 'Sorry'. It was the mid-1960s and Australia now had its own version of The Beatles. Hysteria and chaos erupted wherever they went. Hordes of girls would camp out in front of the Youngs' new home in the Sydney suburb of Burwood. Eventually it would fall apart, but it was a crazy few years.

George's brothers Malcolm and Angus, barely in their teens, looked on with no small amount of interest. Clearly, they could see the benefits of a career in music. The evidence was all over their front lawn. They began to practise furiously, pumping out some of the early Australian hits by The Delltones and the guitar instrumental hit 'Bombora' by local surf band The Atlantics. Once they had that down, they moved onto the more challenging blues-rock of Mike Bloomfield, Chuck Berry and Eric Clapton.

The brothers both left school at fifteen, much to the concern of their father, William, who'd just seen George's band The Easybeats come undone. Malcolm began working in a nearby bra factory, but Angus never really had what you would call a proper job. He would just sit on the edge of his bed all day playing his guitar.

Malcolm joined a blues band called Beelzebub and another band that, for some inexplicable reason, called themselves The Velvet Underground, later known as Pony. They were into the bluesy rock of British band Free. Angus's first band was called Kantuckee (later Tantrum); they'd cover songs from Deep Purple, Jimi Hendrix, The Rolling Stones and Jeff Beck. Big brother George, however, suggested they join forces.

They put their obligatory sibling rivalry aside and agreed. Dave Evans joined on vocals, Larry Van Kriedt on bass and Colin Burgess, formally of the Masters Apprentices, was their drummer. They decided that Angus would play lead guitar and

Malcolm rhythm. All they needed now was a gimmick or two, which was how Angus came to wear a school uniform. The rest of the band put in a half-hearted attempt to dress glam rock style, with satin shirts and matching satin pants, tucked into their high-heeled boots. That was the tragic outfit Malcolm had been sporting the first night I spotted him at the Hard Rock in August '74.

Angus's guitar hero moves had come about by accident, when he tripped over on stage and to save embarrassment, continued to play guitar while lying on his back. Simple. This, along with a few Chuck Berry duck walks, was enough to give the band a semblance of a stage show. Their first official gig as AC/DC had been on New Year's Eve 1973 at Chequers.

The Youngs' older sister Margaret, who had been a big supporter of The Easybeats, had come up with the school uniform idea, which allowed Angus to really emerge from his shell as a performer. They swiped the name AC/DC from the power rating sign on a sewing machine, owned by George's wife Sandra. It had to be better than Kantuckee—or even The Velvet Underground, the name of Lou Reed's earlier band. Angus claims to have been totally oblivious to any sexual connotation in the tag AC/DC. Malcolm, who was savvy to the glam rock bands coming out of the UK, probably would have been a bit wiser.

That night at the Hard Rock, I knew straight away that I'd found something special, something that I had to be involved with. My ambition to manage a band to an international level may have taken a hit with Billy Thorpe in London, but I knew this was different. AC/DC was going to be the one.

After packing up their equipment, Malcolm and Angus came into the office to collect their $200 fee. The Hard Rock office was a bit like Ivan Dayman's office at the Cloudland Ballroom in Brisbane, which the Purple Hearts singer Mick Hadley had colourfully described as 'the place where cheques and wisdom were dispensed'. It was the social hub of the venue, a former drawing room in this wonderful old Victorian building, where wine flowed freely and joints could be smoked without any concerns about security.

The Youngs and I had a good chat and I mentioned how much I'd enjoyed their band. They told me that they were off to Adelaide and Perth and that they might come back through Melbourne on their way home to Sydney. I immediately booked some return dates. I couldn't help but notice how polite and endearing they were; they were not at all like your typical rockers.

A few weeks later the phone rang.

'It's Malcolm,' said the voice down the line.

He was calling from Adelaide, with some bad news. Their manager, their third within a few months, a guy named Dennis Laughlin, had apparently abandoned them.

'We're stuck,' reported Malcolm.

Laughlin had been the singer for Sherbet in the days before Daryl Braithwaite, and could best be described as more a friend of the band than their manager. His focus was on keeping them happy, mostly with promises of better things to come: dope, booze, endless fish and chips, Kit Kat chocolate bars and packets of Benson & Hedges. (The latter two, I was to learn, were Angus Young staples.)

Malcolm explained to me what had brought about the breakdown. They'd taken a three-day trip across the desert in the back of a van, sitting on amplifiers and drum cases, in 40-degree heat, with no air conditioning, only to arrive in Perth, baked in red dust, to learn they were supporting a drag act. Laughlin had neglected to tell the Western Australian promoter that AC/DC wasn't some gay cabaret outfit. They managed to get back to Adelaide, but that's where it all fell apart. They had no manager, no money, and seemingly no way to get back to Sydney and start again.

Malcolm had a question for me.

'Can you lend us some money? Enough to get us to Melbourne and play some gigs—yours included?'

I didn't have to think too hard before replying.

'Are you kidding? Of course I can.'

I couldn't wait to hear them again and, frankly, I could see that this was going to help my thus far silent ambition of signing them up to a management agreement.

I wired Malcolm the funds they needed and they arrived in Melbourne the next day, looking the worse for wear. After their return appearance at the Hard Rock—another impressive performance despite the dodgy outfits and suspect lead singer—Malcolm and Angus again came back into the office. They thanked me for sending them the money. We chatted about their future plans.

They were unaware of my management background; as far as they knew, I was the part owner of the club and the guy who booked the bands. But we got on well and I mentioned that I'd be interested in managing them. I told them about my past experiences, including my recent odyssey with Billy and the Aztecs. Given Billy's enormous success and stature, his 'fuck you' attitude and rock style, I sensed that they realised I knew a thing or two about managing bands. I could be the right guy for them.

I had decided to stop managing bands for a while and open the Hard Rock, but I still held onto the thought of being the first Australian to break a local band internationally. AC/DC was the only band I'd seen who I considered genuinely capable of pulling this off.

The band—specifically the Youngs—already knew where they were headed. They would tell potential band members and anyone else who would listen that one day they'd be a huge international act, like the Stones and The Who. Australia just wasn't big enough for AC/DC. So we were definitely singing from the same book. While most people would reply, 'Yeah, sure you are,' I knew instinctively that they knew what they were talking about. Until now, Billy Thorpe had been the only artist that I'd seen who'd give his absolute all on stage; I was witnessing it again in Angus. I realised that nothing was going to stop Angus and the band from achieving their goal.

We were driven by the same ambition: to conquer the world.

But first I had to convince big brother George Young that I was the right guy. George, along with Harry Vanda and The Easybeats, had nearly pulled it off with their big global hit 'Friday on My Mind', one of the best songs to have ever come out of Australia. They'd toured internationally with The Rolling Stones but eventually fell short of really establishing themselves as a major international band.

Apart from the usual drug problems, it seems that The Easybeats had also experienced some so-called management issues along the way. Their manager, Mike Vaughan, had been their original connection with Ted Albert, from J. Albert & Son, a relationship that had obviously been an enormous boon to the rise of The Easybeats.

But The Easybeats' recordings had been assigned by Mike, territory by territory, to a multitude of different companies throughout the world, which wasn't ideal. It wasn't easy to get deals back in the mid-1960s; bands from Australia were considered by most multinationals as too expensive to deal with, given their distance from America and the UK. No one wanted to know about them.

This territory-by-territory set-up would have made it very difficult for any one of the companies to think about the band in a global, long-term sense. There were also rumours that Mike may have licensed the same recordings to two different companies in the same territory. If this was correct, it would go a long way to explaining the feeling of paranoia George had towards the music business in general and managers in particular.

Mike became the whipping boy for the band's failure to reach the top, yet Alberts, being the owner of the recordings, would have been aware of these deals. Ted Albert, the company's chief executive, would have signed off on them. So why wasn't he copping a bad rap? This was all pretty intriguing to me.

The Easybeats had also been frustrated following up on the success of 'Friday on My Mind', which hit the UK Top 10 in late 1966. To find that next elusive hit, they strayed off the rock'n'roll path. George knew this, too; when he was interviewed for *Rolling Stone* magazine he admitted: 'We were a rock'n'roll band—and what was a rock'n'roll band doing with this cornball schmaltzy shit?' George said he'd walked away from the wreckage of The Easybeats with nine shillings to his name.

So George was quite rightly concerned that his younger brothers didn't make the same mistakes. I fully understood this and endeavoured to make all my dealings with AC/DC as transparent as possible. I respected George's relationship with the band, his role as their adviser and guru. George and Harry were also the production team behind AC/DC and were involved on a partnership level with Albert Productions. That was an interesting arrangement, in a continual state of negotiation, never fully laid out in writing. Allegedly, George and Harry felt they'd signed enough paperwork to last a lifetime, so the set-up with Alberts remained a 'gentlemen's agreement', although the company had snapped up the band's recording and songwriting/publishing rights. All this and the band had recorded just one single, 'Can I Sit Next to You, Girl', a modest hit at best.

George was not only looking after his younger brothers' best interests—he and Harry had a lot at stake career-wise. They flew down to Melbourne and we agreed to meet at the Sheraton Hotel, next door to the Hard Rock.

Meeting George and Harry for the first time was a big thrill for me. I'd always been a huge Easybeats fan; without doubt they were nothing less than Australia's most talented and important band. Their singer, Stevie Wright, was the best frontman I'd ever seen. He pulled out all the stops, from backflips over the top of the drum kit, to singing ballads that would leave the audience in tears. He had this cheeky smile when he sang, too, something I'd later see in Bon Scott.

As I discovered, whatever went down between them and Mike Vaughan—and I never got a clear picture of what that was—sure as hell put the fear of hell into George's head. To him, managers were a necessary evil; they were all rogues and thieves.

My experience so far was to break bands through playing live and then go after a record deal when I had a much better bargaining position. The major record companies and music publishers were generally run by a bunch of overpaid old fogies, who never made their presence felt in the live music world.

It was usually left up to independent entrepreneurs like Ted Albert to set up labels and make third party deals with the majors, which generally meant that the big label would be responsible for marketing costs and promotion. The independent labels would take care of the record production— including recording costs—which were sometimes paid for by way of an overall advance from the majors. This was the arrangement that Alberts had with EMI Records.

I was impressed with George and Harry's general understanding of the music business—and I loved their vision. It was clear that AC/DC were the chosen ones, who'd achieve on a global scale what The Easybeats had been unable to do. However, what was missing was the master plan. They were somewhat guarded about everything until it became clear we were all on the same page.

Harry and George appeared to have made a smooth transition from pop stars to businessmen and, most importantly, record producers. I'm sure their mentor Ted Albert helped them, too. Oddly, I noticed that Malcolm, whom I hadn't known for that long and was at the meeting, suddenly lost his broad Aussie accent in the presence of his older brother. He broke into this heavy Scottish brogue.

'Where does this come from?' I thought to myself, though I didn't say it out loud.

We all put our stereotypes and preconceptions aside and struck up a deal. But George insisted that I put my money where my mouth was in order to stabilise the band's financial situation, which was dire. I soon learned that I hadn't signed a band; I'd signed a clan.

A few weeks later I flew up to Sydney for more meetings with the band. By now they'd grown apart from their glam rock–styled lead singer Dave Evans. As Malcolm would later explain, Evans's thing for Gary Glitter meant that the beer-swilling yobs in most crowds targeted the singer. Sometimes the band would tell him to take a break and they'd play a rockin' boogie for half an hour and win back the unruly mob. Clearly, Evans wasn't right for AC/DC, who wanted to tap into the middle ground between the Stones and the blues. Malcolm later summed it all up when he admitted: 'The day we got fuckin' rid of him, that's the day the band started.'

I never actually met Dave. However, it'd be fair to say it was a case of him being in the wrong band at the wrong time. But not in a million years could I have guessed the guy they'd choose to replace him.

ALL HAIL AC/DC

Bon Scott had met the band in Adelaide, after their gay cabaret disaster in Perth. Bon spent some time in the back of the same non-air-conditioned van in which AC/DC had crossed the desert.

In May 1974, Bon had been playing in Adelaide in a band called the Mount Lofty Rangers, The Valentines having split a few years earlier. After a rehearsal, Bon jumped on his Suzuki 550 motorcycle and crashed into a car. He ended up in a coma, perilously close to death. He'd broken his collarbone, lost most of his teeth, cracked some ribs, busted his jaw. Bon was a mess.

In Adelaide, on crutches, Bon had been hired by his friend and former bandmate Vince Lovegrove as a general dogsbody, hobbling about the office, putting up posters and chauffeuring around the bands—including a very young Cold Chisel—that Lovegrove was importing into Adelaide for Jovan, his newly established agency business.

Lovegrove's latest import happened to be AC/DC—knowing the band's financial circumstances, Bon wouldn't have been a highly paid chauffeur. While acting as the band's driver, Bon talked to the guys. He tried and failed to convince them he'd be a good drummer for AC/DC, but then talked them into a boozy jam session at the home of Bruce Howe, his former mentor and bandmate in a group named Fraternity, a progressive rock band from Adelaide. Bon was certain that he could show the young upstarts from Sydney a thing or two about how to rock.

Apparently Bon turned up with two bottles of bourbon, some dope and some speed. When Angus saw this stash, he spoke to Malcolm. 'If this guy can walk, let alone sing, it's going to be something.' Prophetic words, as it turned out.

At 28 Bon was already a hardened rock'n'roller. Of course I'd known him from the days of The Valentines, when he went head to head with Doug Parkinson In Focus during the Battle of the Sounds. We'd also crossed paths when he was the singer for Fraternity.

Although born in Kirriemuir, Scotland, Bon had grown up with his family in Melbourne and then Fremantle, Western Australia. At North Fremantle Primary, Ronnie, as he was then known, was taunted about his Scottish accent and was nicknamed Bonny by his classmates, which he hated. It was eventually shortened to Bon, which stuck. At John Curtin High School, Bon, like most kids, developed an interest in rock'n'roll, which grew into a passion: he loved Elvis and Little Richard and then all the bands from the British Beat invasion.

Bon left school as soon as legally possible, and took on any job that came his way. He became a crayboat fisherman, then an apprentice washing machine mechanic. But he lived for something else: the adrenaline rush and attention he'd get from singing the occasional song or two with the band at the Saturday night Port Beach Dance.

Bon was no choirboy. He discovered booze and, soon after, pot. He was constantly in trouble with the police for stealing cars. During one altercation, he beat up a cop but escaped the charge due to lack of evidence. Following the theft of another car, which he used for drag racing, Bon met a young girl at the Port Beach Dance, with whom he was alleged to have had carnal knowledge—then Bon protected the young girl from a group of young blokes who he thought were about to pounce. Bon fought them off until the police arrived and carted him off to the watch house. Bon did eighteen months in a juvenile detention centre known as Riverbank, which housed the worst youth offenders; his only outlet was learning to play the drums and sing with some of the more musically inclined inmates.

After his release, Bon eventually found his niche as the second singer in The Valentines, alongside Vince Lovegrove. Fraternity, Bon's next band, was almost the antithesis of the poppy Valentines: they were hippies in their musical style and outlook. They based themselves in London for a few years and had a crack at the tough British music scene. But Bon was, to my mind, a high-voltage rock'n'roller, who'd been waiting for a band like AC/DC all his musical life.

Back in Oz in late 1973, after Fraternity folded, Bon took whatever work he could find: he boasted about being a 'shit shoveller' in a fertiliser plant; he also scraped the barnacles off fishing boats. Then he had his bike crash. He was in a coma for three days—the doctors asked his wife, Irene, if she'd like a priest to come and give the last rites. But Bon knew that he had unfinished business.

AC/DC would become his new surrogate family—and Scottish blood brothers. The Youngs were from the Gorbals on Glasgow's River Clyde, a heavy industrial area; Bon's roots were in the slightly posher Kirriemuir, birthplace of J.M. Barrie, the creator of Peter Pan—another mischievous boy who never aged.

Bon returned to Sydney with AC/DC in October 1974, itching to get things going. Without knowing the band's repertoire he winged a few gigs with more than a bit of ad-libbing and a few covers, until he had a chance to fully immerse himself. But with Bon now on board, the band had acquired a new sense of purpose as well as a sense of humour and uniqueness. Seriously, Bon was one of the world's best street poets, as he'd prove with his funny, razor-sharp lyrics. First though, he had to lose his Quaker-style beard, long hair and hippie beliefs left over from his Fraternity days, which he did with a few encouraging words from Malcolm.

Along with the guitar skills of Malcolm and Angus, Bon would set AC/DC apart from every other band on the planet. Now all they needed was a rhythm section to match.

By late 1974, pre-production and the recording for the debut album had already commenced at Alberts Studios in Sydney, with Vanda and Young producing and the highly capable studio drummer Tony Currenti helping out. But the band needed a permanent drummer. After that recording session, I moved the band to Melbourne, which would be their base for the next year.

Enter Phil Rudd, whom I'd known from the tough Melbourne suburban band Buster Brown, a group that, because of their big sharpie following, I'd never booked at the Hard Rock. But I was fully aware that Phil was respected by his fellow musos. He was a great drummer, rock solid.

Buster Brown had recorded an album, which was produced by Lobby Loyde for Gudinski's Mushroom Records. Things were looking promising until Phil had a falling out with singer Angry Anderson over money. Phil was 21 and working in a car wash when Trevor Young, a friend from school days and a member of The Coloured Balls, told him that AC/DC was searching for a drummer.

Phil became integral to AC/DC's musical style and was over time admired worldwide by his peers for his wonderful timing and feel. He was influenced by Free's Simon Kirke and the great Ringo Starr. Phil was all about 'feel before flash', perfect for the engine room of a band with plenty of the latter.

AC/DC was also still looking for a permanent bass player. George Young had been filling in whenever he could, and despite it not being his first instrument, he was more than capable. But they needed someone full-time. They finally recruited another young street-smart kid from Melbourne, Mark Evans, in early 1975, a few months before Mark's nineteenth birthday. Evans had been a resident of the notorious Prahran Hilton, the not especially accurate name given to one of Melbourne's first Housing Commission high rises.

As the story goes, Mark fell down the stairs of the Hard Rock, having been thrown out by the bouncers—only to land at the feet of Malcolm and Angus, who were coming in the front door. The other version of Mark's story is that he was involved in an incident at Melbourne's Station Hotel; Mark had been banned due to some past trouble with the bouncers. He had to talk his way back into the venue to jam with AC/DC. Urban myths? Perhaps. I recall it more as part of dogma designed to complement the street image we were working on at the time.

In actual fact, Mark was tipped off to AC/DC by his old mate and occasional roadie Steve McGrath, who told Mark the band was auditioning bass players at a house in Lansdowne Road, East St Kilda. Mark was told to come back the next day for a 'blow', which he did. Despite no visual signs of excitement from Malcolm and Angus, and/or words of encouragement or congratulations, Mark had apparently passed, because a few days later he was playing a gig with them at the Station Hotel as their new bass player.

Mark had only just swapped over from playing guitar; by his own estimation he wasn't a world-beating bass player. But he had what they needed: a straight-ahead, no-bullshit style; he could lock into a groove with Phil and Malcolm without any flashy virtuoso leanings.

I now had the band's signatures on a very basic contract, which had been drawn up by my lawyer, whose specialty was real estate. I was scheduled to fly to Sydney to meet with the enigmatic Ted Albert, head of the organisation.

I'd heard all sorts of glowing reports about Ted from the band and George, who seemed to be almost overwhelmed by him and his background of wealth, culture and social position. It was all very alluring for both the working-class Youngs and myself.

So this didn't really feel like a meeting; it was more like an audience with royalty. Ted's office was on the sixth floor of a building named Boomerang House, one of many he owned. It was an older-style building on King Street in the heart of Sydney. It had an antique lift with metal concertina doors, like you'd see in old department stores, with a lift operator who'd apparently been working for the Alberts his entire life; he had become one of the family.

It really was like stepping back in time. Ted's office was straight out of a colonial gentlemen's club, with its walnut wall-to-ceiling panelling. I expected David Niven to stroll in any second wearing a dinner jacket and nursing a martini. Everyone in the building—with the exception of George, Harry and Chris Gilbey, the head of marketing—referred to him as Mr Albert. I just wasn't used to this type of formality.

I discovered that despite being a part of the Albert family, Ted was strait-laced, avoiding the indulgences that once made the family legendary among Sydney's eastern suburbs social set earlier in the century. The Alberts called home a lavish Spanish Revival–style mansion on the waterfront at Elizabeth Bay called Boomerang. There was a massive, elegant timber yacht, also named *Boomerang*, moored outside. The sight of *Boomerang* sailing through the Pittwater heads would herald the beginning of the 'social season' at Palm Beach, where the family had an impressive holiday house. The company also had a string of highly successful radio stations to their name.

The family had made their fortune in the early twentieth century, first importing violins and then publishing sheet music. They also manufactured the Boomerang mouth organs, along with other musical instruments. Like I said, it felt as though I was meeting royalty—at least Sydney royalty.

Yet Ted seemed very unaffected by the family's history and affluence. I met an immaculately dressed, charming and astute man with a passion for music and recording studios. He'd been a record producer himself, having worked on some of the early Easybeats records; he'd also recorded Billy Thorpe and the Aztecs, and on the fifth floor of the King Street building had built one of Australia's best recording studios, in which he took great pride. This was where all the Vanda and Young productions took place. With Ted at the helm, Albert Productions would become the nearest thing Australia had to a hit factory.

Englishman Chris Gilbey was in charge of the day-to-day running of Alberts. Chris was a former member of a band named Kate who followed The Beatles' footsteps in Hamburg before tragically imploding. To escape the fallout, he decided to migrate to Australia, and with the help of a written introduction from a prominent British publisher, landed a job at Alberts. Straight away, Chris impressed me with his intelligence. He was in charge of the marketing for all of their artists; the man was a dynamic PR machine. He was a bit like a kid in a candy shop, given free rein to organise photo shoots, film clips, album art and generally hype everything up.

Over time, Chris would be responsible for the early AC/DC album covers, including the *High Voltage* concept, which featured not-so-flattering letters from the band members' schoolteachers on the back cover. He was also the creator of the lightning flash that separated 'AC' from 'DC', amping up the electrical connotation, while giving the bisexual angle a bit of distance.

'Which one are you?' a dull journo once asked Bon, when talk turned to the band's logo.

'I'm the lightning flash in the middle,' Bon grinned.

Chris Gilbey's PA was the very astute and efficient Fifa Riccobono, an impressive woman of Sicilian decent. Fifa had joined the company straight out of school and had become a faithful and integral part of the organisation. Her role extended beyond the office; she took the utmost care of people's lives, not just their careers. Fifa was another member of the extended Albert clan, an insider.

Yet I always felt that Chris Gilbey was underrated and unappreciated by Alberts. His sometimes brash manner probably didn't win him many allies; an extremely conservative mode of operation prevailed inside Boomerang House. However, Chris could get the job done. He helped make Alberts the strongest independent player in the local music industry. Over time, their artist roster read like a who's who of Australian music: Rose Tattoo, The Angels, Stevie Wright, Ted Mulry Gang, John Paul Young, William Shakespeare—or, as Angus would ask, 'Will he shake?' They all had amazing chart success. But AC/DC were the leaders of the pack.

GROUPIES, ROCK DOCTORS AND 'THE JACK'

The band's finances were in an appalling condition when I became their manager in late 1974; it was the first thing that needed sorting out. Part of my deal with them was to shift their base to Melbourne. Then I put all the guys on a wage of $60 per week for the next six months. With these two objectives accomplished, things started to stabilise for the band.

Sixty dollars a week may sound laughable, but in 1975 it provided them with food, cigarettes and booze, their basic necessities. I covered all expenses, which included, but were not limited to, equipment, transport, accommodation and the road crew. It worked well, but if they ran short, there was always Angus. Being a non-drinker he would be cashed up;

in fact, Angus was like the band's very own banker, a regular Milburn Drysdale (of *Beverly Hillbillies* legend). He'd give out loans to support the other members' drinking habits. I found out that he had a long history of being a good saver, ever since he was a kid and craved his first guitar, which he bought with his own money.

I'd receive all the income from gigs, which would (hopefully) offset my costs and, with a bit of luck, perhaps generate a small profit. After a six-month 'trial', I'd be on a straight 20 per cent commission of the gross income from then onwards. Naturally, I was highly motivated to get things going fast.

Although there was good word of mouth spreading about the band, the early performances were to a very small group of dedicated fans, probably no more than 50 punters. The fees ranged from $200 to $500. But the number of patrons had no impact on the band's performance; they gave 100 per cent whether they were playing to 50 or 5000.

Fortunately, Bill Joseph, my business partner, was flush with funds. Bill was a veteran of the Melbourne scene and had been the original manager of Bon's old group The Valentines. Bill may even have had something to do with those puffy shirts they had worn, although I never dared ask him. Bill was also my partner in the Hard Rock. So we had a number of venues that we could slot AC/DC into, and, boy, did we make them work—expenses were mounting up. Between late January and mid-April 1975 they played the Hard Rock perhaps a dozen times, and then another seven times in May alone, along with regular gigs at the Station Hotel and elsewhere.

At Bon's suggestion, and with the help of Ralph—a faithful old friend and roadie of Bon's from the Fraternity days—we purchased a bus that we could convert into a touring van, for about eight grand. It was an old 1950s Ansett Pioneer Clipper Coach with a sloping back; it was similar to one that Fraternity had owned. It looked great. Bon's thinking was solid: the bus would accommodate the band and the crew, and house the equipment in a discrete compartment at the back.

This was great in theory but there was one problem: we'd purchased a lemon. It kept on breaking down. I was writing cheques every week to a garage called Queens Bridge Motors, which was draining away our profits. The bus had no air con or heating; on winter runs the guys would either freeze or huddle together with the female passengers I'd explicitly banned from transporting for insurance reasons. Sometimes they'd be forced to push the bus the final kilometres to their gigs. It wasn't quite like Thorpey and the Aztecs arriving by chartered plane.

On one occasion, in April 1975, the band was running late for a gig at Melbourne's Festival Hall, where 5000 screaming girls eagerly waited, hoping to drag them off stage. The bus had broken down and the band was forced to push the damn thing for the final few blocks. When they finally arrived it had been best to give everyone a wide berth for a while. The mood was not great.

TOP LEFT: Spending a day at the beach with my father Bert, my mother Nina and sisters Coral and Jan before we moved to the leafy splendour of Mount Macedon.

TOP RIGHT: The interior of the Thumpin' Tum, one of Melbourne's first truly 'bohemian' clubs. Their slogan? 'Go-go to be seen at this swinging frugging scene'.

ABOVE: I did my best to look dapper at Bertie's, where the Knight family appointed me 'house booker' for life. Half-mast trousers and daggy sandals were apparently chic back in 1967.

In order to deter sharpies from our club, Sebastian's, we were once forced to pour boiling
water from an upstairs window onto the gang gathered in the street below.

TOP: Wayne (left) and Rodney de Gruchy, both good friends and invaluable mentors to me as I immersed myself in the Melbourne club scene.

ABOVE: Phillip Knight, another great friend and business partner, inside Sebastian's, the club where I managed to book virtually all the great Australian bands of the late 1960s.

© Phillip Knight

THIS PAGE: Sebastian's exterior (left) and the foyer (below). Phillip Knight's brother Anthony created his own version of an Edwardian mansion. © Phillip Knight

OPPOSITE: Guitarist Phil Manning and singer Wendy Saddington, one of the great voices of Australian music, someone I booked as often as I could. © Philip Morris

Admit One

Prince Albert George Sebastian II
355 Exhibition Street, City.   34 3000

THE Chief Secretary, Sir Arthur Rylah, is trying to prevent the Easter "Launching Place Miracle" pop festival.

® REFUSED a permit to hold a pop festival — from left: Solicitor Solly Ellenberg and organisers Sue Rees, Peter Langham, Michael Browning and Adrian Rawlins.

PHILIP SHOCK —NO BEER

Pop fest —Rylah says no

BANKS
From P. 1

Last night police were still looking for the two men they say tried to get money at Lilydale.

The two men detained at Ivanhoe were driving a car registered in NSW.

Sgt. Mudge said that the operation was "almost certainly Sydney inspired."

He said certain teams appeared to have been assigned to certain areas.

Early today, three men were charged at the City Watchhouse with conspiracy and fraud.

WELLINGTON, Fri. AAP. — Prince Philip said as he left New Plymouth today: "I'll always remember it — it's the city with no beer."

At a civic luncheon for himself and the Queen, Prince Philip had asked for a glass of beer.

The embarrassed caterers admitted that they had every drink except beer.

But eventually they found a bottle of beer at the airport building and Prince Philip got his glass.

At Lake Taupo, North Island, today Prince Charles hooked a 5 lb. rainbow trout after two hours' fishing.

Prince Charles and Princess Anne are spending a two-day holiday in the lakes district.

● Students at the University of Papua-New Guinea, in Port Moresby, have decided not to acknowledge the Queen's Australian tour.

The organisers plan to go ahead and "do their thing" at the holiday weekend.

They expect more than 20,000 people to attend the festival, at Coonara farm, about 40 miles from Melbourne.

Sir Arthur said yesterday these people would be "wise to make other plans."

He refused applications by the festival promoters for permits under the Theatres and Sunday Entertainments Acts.

Without these, the promoters may not charge admission.

Sir Arthur said he had asked the Crown Law Department for "urgent advice" on whether the festival could go ahead.

Sir Arthur said the possibilities of pollution and drug trafficking worried police.

A director of the promoting company, Mr Stripes Pty. Ltd.,

Mr Peter Langham, 27, later said "the festival will go ahead as planned."

Mr Langham offered reporters bowls of fresh fruit while incense sticks burned in the background.

He said the organisers "complied in every way to abide by all regulations when planning the festival."

He said: "We will lose more than $15,000 if the festival does not go on."

The company's solicitor, Mr Solly Ellenberg, said Sir Arthur's attitude to pop music was "entirely wrong."

---

waterfront we "competition in Minister for Lab Service, Mr Sne night.

They were doing t positions and advar causes, he said.

Mr Snedden was commenting in a written statement on the national wharf strike of at least five days beginning at 7.30 a.m. today.

It will be the biggest for more than 15 years, involving 19,000 watersiders in 35 ports.

About 4000 would strike in Melbourne.

Mr Snedden said that, because of the Communist action, the general secretary of the Waterside Workers' Federation, Mr C. H. Fitzgibbon, and other officers were willing to promote the strike to retain their positions.

"It is no secret that much of the trouble in the two major ports of Sydney and Melbourne in recent

---

MAY 1975 PROGRAMME

Fri. 9th	Jets (early)
	Captain Matchbox
	Woopee Band (late)
Sat. 10th	Red House Roll Band (early)
	Billy Thorpe & The Aztecs (late)
	& Guest Support Group
Sun. 11th	Breeze
	Ayers Rock
Mon. 12th	"Holiday Hard Rock Cafe"
to Fri. 16th	1 p.m. till 3 p.m. daily Starring AC/DC, Jets, Finch, Buster Brown & Cloud 9
Fri. 16th	Mainstreet (early)
	Renee Gayor (late)
	& Sanctuary
Sat. 17th	Richard Clapton (early)
	AC/DC (late)
	& Guest Group
Sun. 18th	Benefit Concert Bangladesh (details to be advised)
Fri. 23rd	Rock Granite (late)
	Daddy Cool (late)
Sat. 24th	Jets (early)
	Madder Lake (late)
	& Guest Group
Sun. 25th	Ayers Rock
	& Guest Group
Fri. 30th	Coloured Balls (early)
	Dingoes (late)
Sat. 31st	Split Enz (early)
	Hot City Bump Band (late)
JUNE	
Sun. 1st	SPECIAL AC/DC & Guests

CNR SPRING & FLINDERS STS. CITY
PHONE: 63 7144 63 9089

PROGRAMME

Sat. 25th Jan.	Jets
	Ariel
Sun. 26th	La Do Das
Thurs. 30th	AC/DC
Fri. 31st	Exclusive to Hard Rock 3 nights only
	Black Feather
	Ayers Rock
Sat. 1st Feb.	Black Feather
	Shadowfax
Sun. 2nd	Black Feather
	AC/DC
Thurs. 6th	La Do Das
Fri. 7th	Madder Lake
	Direct from South Africa
	Black Magic
Sat. 8th	Pantha
	Skylight
Sun. 9th	Ayers Rock
Thurs. 13th	AC/DC
Fri. 14th	Shadowfax
	Ariel
Sat 15th	Jets
	Dingoes
Sun. 16th	Geoff St. John
Wed. 19th	SPECIAL
	AC/DC in Concert
	Performing new Album
	"Hi Voltage"
	Admission an AC/DC
	Eye shades on $1.00
Thurs. 20th	Hot City Bump Band
Fri. 21st	Geoff St. John
	Bootleg Family Band
Sat. 22nd	Hot City Bump Band
	Marcia Hynze and Arthur Funk
Sun. 23rd	Ariel

OPPOSITE: Doug Parkinson, Australia's best male vocalist, hands down. He and his band In Focus, one of the first acts I managed, were formidable.
© Tim Harrison

ABOVE: Me (second from right) with my fellow founders of the aborted Miracle festival, March 1970. How did we know it would rain? *The Sun*, 21 March 1970.

LEFT: Early bills for the Hard Rock Cafe, where I booked the bands in 1974. A few months earlier I'd met a broke but inspirational AC/DC for the first time.

Lobby Loyde (standing, left), Australia's first guitar hero, and his 'psychedelic skinheads', The Coloured Balls, the group he formed after blazing brightly in Billy Thorpe's Aztecs. © Philip Morris

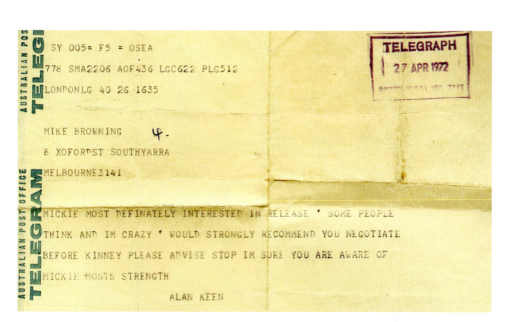

TOP: An April 1972 telegram from London, expressing interest in Billy's 'Some People Think and I'm Crazy'. They almost got it right.

ABOVE: A newspaper feature implying that the rivalry between Billy Thorpe and Lobby's bands was fierce enough to have my Pontiac fire-bombed. A good story, but not *The Truth*!

OPPOSITE TOP: The dynamic trio of The Who's Keith Moon, Doug Parkinson and Billy Thorpe on-stage during the Oz production of *Tommy*, March 1973. Not a bottle of Courvoisier in sight. © Philip Morris

OPPOSITE BELOW: Billy and his Aztecs raised the roof of the Melbourne Town Hall in June 1971. The band was dwarfed by a giant starfish sculpture, which almost ended the show.
© Philip Morris

ABOVE: Billy Thorpe (centre) and his wife Lynn, along with Molly Meldrum (back row, left) and me (back row, right), taking in an apparently underwhelming Elton John show at Kooyong Stadium, 1972. © David Porter

TOP: Billy Thorpe (centre) with fellow Aztecs, Bruce Howard and Paul Wheeler, and a disinterested onlooker, in Melbourne in the early 1970s. © Philip Morris

ABOVE: After a few lively years riding the Thorpey rollercoaster, Billy and I announced the end of our management arrangement in May 1974. We remained good friends. © Philip Morris

The Sunbury festival, which ran from 1972 to 1975 and was everything the Miracle was not.
Billy Thorpe featured prominently, the masses chanting 'Suck more piss!' as he played.

Bon Scott in his prime, charming the locals at the Moorabbin Town Hall, 1974. Bon was a great street poet, even though he dismissed his lyrics as 'toilet poetry'. © Rennie Ellis Photographic Archive.

OPPOSITE: Some pages from the early AC/DC account ledgers, 1975. Dr Goldberg (top), aka the Rock Doctor, did pretty well from a band nicknamed The Seedies.

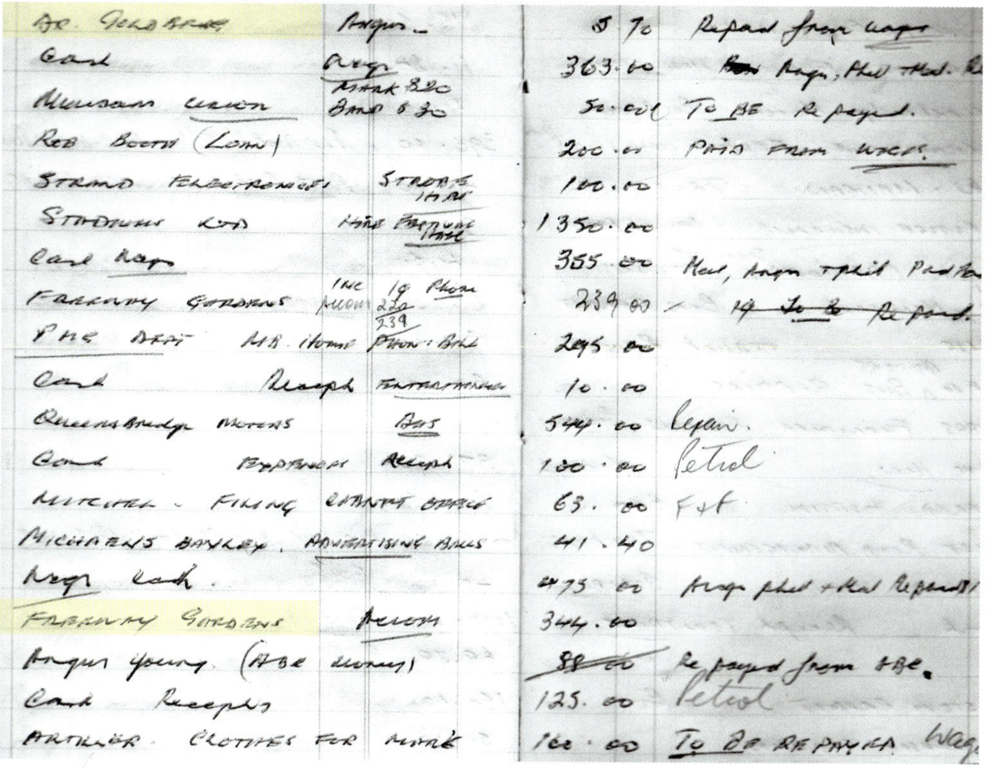

Top ledger page (left entries / amounts / notes):

Dr. Gold Bros	Angus	5.70	Repaid from wages
Cash	Angus	363.00	Angus, Phil, Mal...
Musicians Union	Angus & Mal	50.00	To BE repaid
Rob Booth (Loan)		200.00	Paid from wages
Strand Electronics	Strobe	100.00	
Stramer Ltd	Hire Telephone	1350.00	
Carl Hay		355.00	Mal, Angus + Phil Pocket...
Freeway Gardens	Phone	239.00	...14 To be repaid
The Flat	M.B. Home Phone Bill	295.00	
Cash	Receipt	10.00	
Queensbridge Motors	Bus	544.00	Repair
Cash	Typhoon Receipt	130.00	Petrol
Mitchell - Filing Cabinet Office		63.00	F+F
Michaels Bailey. Advertising Bills		41.40	
Angus Cash		475.00	Angus, Phil + Mal Repaid
Freeway Gardens	Accom	344.00	
Angus Young (SBE money)		88.00	Repaid from SBE
Cash Receipts		125.00	Petrol
Arthur. Clothes for Mark		100.00	To BE REPAID Wages

Bottom-left ledger page:

Date		Venue	Amount
4	. .	S.S.6.	150.00
31 Dec 74		Hard Rock Cafe	200.00
			$350.00
7 Jan 75		Station Hotel	130.00
8	. .	Sundowner	150.00
9	. .	Hard Rock Cafe	175.00
10	. .	Matthew Flinders	225.00
11	. .	Colosseum Hotel	120.00
11	. .	Hard Rock Cafe	160.00
12	. .	106 Lands	130.00
			$1150.00
14	. .	Croxton Park	130.00
16	. .	Sundowner	175.00
17	. .	International Hotel	100.00
17	. .	Hard Rock Cafe	175.00
19	. .	Frankston Rol.	250.00
			$950.00
		BANKED IN T/P A/C.	
23	. .	Hard Rock Cafe	175.00
24	. .	Matthew Flinders	225.00
25	. .	S.S.6.	150.00
26	. .	Sorrento	60.00

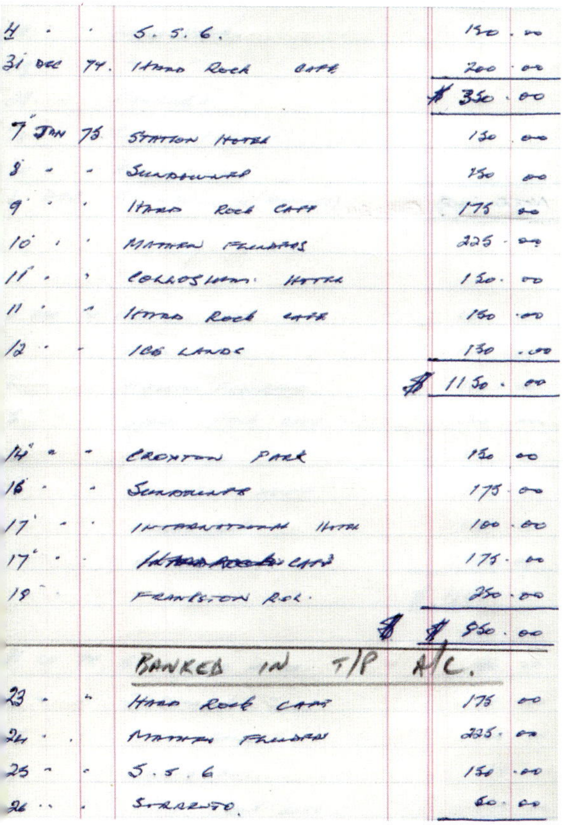

Poster:

AC
DC

WED 30   SAT 2   SUN 3

thu 31 HOT CITY BUMP BAND
fri 1 DINGOES & SKYLIGHT
sat 2 AC DC & BAKERY

CUP EVE

Hard Rock CAFE

STEVIE WRIGHT

GERRY & the PACEMAKERS

car finders - spring sts city

Angus in one of the great early *Countdown* segments, this time dressed as Zorro. The show was a huge supporter of the band early on. © Australian Broadcasting Corporation Library Sales

Bon kicked in the upstairs dressing room door, while John Wren, the owner of the venue, which had been in his family for years, watched on. (The Wrens had been immortalised by the novel and TV series *Power Without Glory*.) John was extremely unimpressed and placed an immediate ban on AC/DC.

'You'll never play here again,' John told the guys.

Then I pointed out how much money John stood to make, and he backed down. Five thousand screaming fans amounted to some serious change. The band played Festival Hall throughout 1975 and filled the place every time.

Their 1950 Clipper bus finally conked out, conveniently and very suspiciously, in the car park of Canberra Airport. The band, who'd had a gutful of the thing, waved farewell to the old lemon for the last time and caught a plane back to Melbourne—at my expense. Someone eventually tracked me down and made an offer to buy it for a miserly sum. I wasn't about to have it towed to Melbourne, so that was it, although it's since been traded for way more than it's worth on the basis of its place in AC/DC history.

One of the more interesting rumours to emerge from my early days with AC/DC was that I'd banned the guys from wearing watches. Apparently, I was working them so hard that I didn't want them to be aware of the time, which is laughable, absolute nonsense. It's true that I didn't like the guys wearing watches, but that was because of my beliefs about 'star quality'. Growing up as a fan, in awe of the rock star image, I wanted to believe that rock stars lived beyond the daily grind, with no dividing lines between art and life. I never saw Jimi Hendrix wearing a watch—if he did, it would have appeared as if he was bound by the constraints of time. No free spirit wore a watch in my book. As H.G. Wells once said, 'We must not allow the clock and the calendar to blind us to the fact that each moment of life is a miracle and a mystery.'

I also discouraged the guys from using public transport, for the same reason. After all, you didn't see Elvis Presley or Mick Jagger catching a bus home from the recording studio; that would have totally spoiled the rock star aura surrounding them. I was dismayed when I once spotted Melbourne pop duo Bobby and Laurie on a tram. That wasn't how pop stars should get around, surely. I wanted to install this principle in the band; it was as simple as that.

Yet these stories got twisted to the point where I was made out to be a slave driver, which of course was not true—although, looking back, the group may disagree! They did become the hardest-working band in the country by mid-1975 and it was starting to pay off for them. 'High Voltage' was their first Aussie Top 10, in July 1975.

Around this time I lost my Christian name. Everyone in the band simply referred to me as 'Browning'. It took a bit of getting used to—at first it sounded a little hostile—but the name stuck. Browning it was.

As part of my management agreement, I found the band a sprawling furnished house in the quiet and leafy neighbourhood of Lansdowne Road in East St Kilda. They shared the place with their road crew, Ralph the roadie (and also the bus driver) and Tana Douglas, an attractive young lady who could throw a Marshall amp over her shoulder with ease and mix it with the best of them. As far as I knew, Tana was the only female roadie in Australia.

The house turned out to be ideal for the band, a great place to write and rehearse new material. But as well as having a practical purpose, it fast became the 'do-drop-in' for every single wayward groupie, out-of-town muso and off-duty St Kilda hooker. They all joined in the action that was happening there on an almost daily basis.

Malcolm has been quoted as saying that these 'were some of the happiest days of my life', which is easy for him to say, as I was paying the damage bills and dealing with the concerns coming from their houseguests' parents, who were threatening all sorts of physical and legal action.

One distressed father turned up to the house and dragged Bon through the once glorious and now tragically neglected rose garden, in the process knocking out Bon's front teeth plate, which he'd acquired after his motorcycle accident. The guy literally wiped the smile off Bon's face. Afterwards, we had to find his plate. We preferred his new smile, for one thing, but there was also no provision in our contract for replacement teeth.

After our first six months together, the band was now required to stand on their own feet, financially speaking, and I reverted to a straight management commission. This meant that the house had to go. It was a good thing, in a way, because it wouldn't have been long before they were evicted. It had become an eyesore to the locals and a nightmare for the authorities.

Now, oddly enough, it's a place of reverence, where the same authorities are planning to erect a plaque in the band's honour. And don't get me started on Melbourne's AC/DC Lane; I can't recall them ever setting foot there. It's a serious stretch. Swanston Street, or Spring Street, where the Hard Rock was situated, would have been more fitting locations. I can assure you that when AC/DC first set up base in Melbourne, they were hardly the well-respected denizens of the city they are today.

I re-accommodated the band at a motel called the Freeway Gardens in North Melbourne, conveniently located right next to the on-ramp of the Melbourne airport freeway. It soon became the accommodation of choice for every band visiting Melbourne; the owners were happy (at first) to have found a niche for their noisy, two-star cream-brick dump. The traffic noise far outweighed any racket the musos created, making it the perfect new HQ of depravity.

The word spread fast that this was where the action was, and it soon became party central, open 24/7. It was Lansdowne Road all over, but now more discreetly located. I can't imagine that there'll ever be a scene like this again. The girls would be lined up around the block, patiently waiting their turn, and the bands wouldn't disappoint. The only social diseases to be feared could be treated with a dose of penicillin and a quick trip to the 'Jack Clinic', which all the bands could have driven to blindfolded. I eventually worked out an arrangement with Dr John, a medico friend of mine, who'd do house calls, keeping an eye out for any other ailments that may have been bothering them. This is how the band became affectionately known as 'The Seedies'.

Although I was still very much involved with the Hard Rock, my focus and passion had shifted in the direction of the band. Things were building nicely and my thoughts of getting them to the UK grew stronger. There was never any thought of bypassing the UK and heading directly to America. London was the place every muso aspired to. The work permits were easy to get, coming from a Commonwealth country—even easier because we had band members born in the UK. The way we saw it, America always followed London's trends—if you made it there and gained word-of-mouth and print media exposure, the vibe would eventually find its way across the Atlantic, making the eventual push into the States an easier mission.

As 1975 rolled on, I'd started to develop a very good working relationship with Malcolm. I would run everything by him on a daily basis and he'd then convey things to the band. Apart from being a gifted rhythm guitarist and songwriter, Malcolm was also the business brain behind the band, very switched on as to what needed to be done. He always took care of business. We were a great team.

Bon had been working on some lyrics for a song called 'The Jack': 'She was 9-99 on the clinical list and I had to fall in love with that dirty little bitch.' George pulled Bon aside; he was worried about the blatant nature of the words and urged him to make a change. Bon came back the next day with revised lyrics that illustrated the genius of the guy, who, as well as getting his share of 'the jack', was also getting into what I have always thought were amphetamines.

Around this time I got a call from Bon's girlfriend, letting me know he'd been admitted to hospital, having nearly overdosed on a mixture of booze and amphetamines. By the time I reached the hospital Bon was sitting up in bed as if nothing had happened, flirting with the nurses, who were telling him that he'd been a 'very naughty boy'.

Bon bragged to me that the last time he'd been in that hospital was to visit two girls—total strangers to one another—who were in the maternity ward having his babies. It turns out that Bon might have been indulging in something stronger than amphetamines. His girlfriend and her friend had dared him—

even assisted him—to inject some of their heroin, promising the ultimate high.

Instead of getting 'higher than he had ever been', as the girls had promised, Bon plunged into unconsciousness and turned a frightening shade of blue. He was gone. To try to bring him back they injected him again, this time with speed. It didn't work so the girls dialled triple-O, keeping him upright until the ambulance arrived, when Bon was given mouth-to-mouth resuscitation.

After his recovery and discharge from hospital nothing much more was said. Bon knew only too well the horror the Youngs had experienced with Stevie Wright going down this path.

AC/DC were now permanent residents at the Freeway Gardens, while other bands would come and go. This meant that all good times revolved around the AC/DC quarters. They really held court, led by teetotaller Angus, who'd sit there like Little Lord Fauntleroy, a funny little fucker keeping everyone amused with his pearls of wisdom and humorous one-liners. Angus would be completely sober, chatting away with people who could barely walk, let alone talk. Angus, apart from his guitar wizardry, was a natural comedian, one of the best comedic minds I've ever come across.

Bon wrote the lyrics for 'Whole Lotta Rosie' after an encounter at the Freeway Gardens. Bon had been attracted to the real-life Rosie for a number of reasons—one of them being that because of her hefty size, she may not have been carrying the dreaded Jack, which he was doing his best to avoid. I thought she was a sweet girl—a sweet girl, that is, who became immortalised in song.

What made the Australian music industry unique during the 1970s was the rise of pub rock, with its HQ in outer suburban beer barns. In order to deal with the 'dead sound' of the carpeted rooms, where no thought or planning had been given to acoustics, there was more of an emphasis on a loud snare and kick drum, along with a driving bass and the repetitive guitar riffs. This provided the perfect soundtrack for the hundreds of young drinkers who'd gather at these brick houses. The live music program of these venues had been taken to new heights a few years earlier by the success of Billy Thorpe and the Aztecs and The Coloured Balls. AC/DC also fitted right in.

The punters wanted their rock 'hard and loud'; 'suck more piss' was still their chant, as it had been back when Thorpey was at his peak. These blokes—and they were mainly blokes— weren't actually listening to the music in the normal sense; they were feeling it, with the help of buckets of booze. They were really into the music, but in a different way to your typical punter.

This beer barn phenomenon wasn't a strictly Melbourne one. It was happening all over Australia, from the Largs Pier Hotel in working-class Port Adelaide, to Sydney's western suburbs and Northern Beaches, places like the Sundowner and the Royal Antler, where bands such as Rose Tattoo, The Angels and Cold Chisel would provide the soundtrack.

Not surprisingly, these beer barns could get really rough, sometimes totally out of control. The bouncers always seemed outnumbered by drunken yobs. The bands were often confronted with threats of personal violence from drunken idiots, in the shape of fists in the car park or flying full beer cans—and glasses—while on stage. Angus developed a way of dealing with the chaos; he just kept moving on stage. It was always harder to hit a moving target.

But there were times when it got really frustrating for him. Nothing could put off a blazing guitarist more than a full beer can to the side of the head. One night, after a particularly dangerous show, he pulled me aside.

'Browning,' he raged, 'I want you to put up safety nets in front of the stage from now on. I'm sick of dodging beer cans.'

Thankfully, once he calmed down, he forgot all about the idea, which would have been an interesting one to pitch to publicans.

But the beer barns and their rowdy audiences were absolutely crucial in the development of AC/DC's sound. The experience of winning over the audiences at these tough

Aussie venues was something they were able to draw on for their entire career. Making these unruly mobs actually take notice of you, let alone get them on your side, was a massive accomplishment.

AC/DC was about as far away as you could be from the gay scene, but the gay community was initially attracted to them because of their name, which had already caused the disaster in Perth that almost killed the band. When not packing the beer barns, they played the weekly gay nights on the Hard Rock's rooftop stage. Bon would have a ball camping it up, teasing the gay guys with a whip. Thankfully, this was before the days when Angus started mooning the audience. Who knows what kind of message that would have sent.

HIGH VOLTAGE AND TEENAGE RAMPAGE

In January 1975 AC/DC was scheduled to appear at the Sunbury Music Festival, where, as Billy Thorpe's manager, I'd learned the value of a good appearance. It can make or break an act's reputation. I had no fears about which way it would go for an unleashed AC/DC, on a big stage, before a large audience. It was also an opportunity for the band to play to a genuine rock audience, albeit a bunch of drunks, rather than screaming teens. To mark the occasion we made thousands of cardboard replica Angus schoolboy hats, which were distributed throughout the crowd, who loved them. The scene was set for a big night. The fee for the gig was a whopping $300.

British rockers Deep Purple were headlining, scheduled on stage from 9 pm until 10.30 pm, which meant AC/DC would be on stage at 11 pm. This was good timing: the pub-rock-loving yobs out there would be totally off their faces and raring to go. When Deep Purple finished playing, their production managers said they wanted to break down all of their equipment, including their lighting rigs, before AC/DC's crew could set up. An international band and crew behaving like big shots. It meant AC/DC would not be able to go on until after 2 am, maybe even later. This wasn't going to work.

The Aussie stage manager was nowhere to be found; he was obviously off somewhere avoiding the conflict that was unfolding. The foreign road crew thought they were running the show. I pulled Ralph the roadie aside.

'Take our gear up on stage,' I told him. 'Set it up—and ignore these bastards.'

Ralph and the crew did just that and, as expected, all hell broke loose while the crowd looked on. An all-in brawl erupted between Deep Purple's crew, their management and us. George Young, who was going to be playing bass for that gig, threw the first punch.

'Don't fuck with me,' Deep Purple's stage manager told him, 'I'm from the Bronx.'

'Are you now?' asked George, unimpressed. 'Well, I'm from Glasgow.'

Then he thumped him. It was on for young and old. Strangely, we all seemed to find our perfect sparring partner: I ended up trading blows with Purple's manager, Bruce Payne, who'd inform me a few years later during a meeting in New York that my ring opened a nasty gash on his chin. Fortunately, he didn't hold a grudge.

Local security and production personnel eventually intervened, and we were forced to back off. We were given a choice: wear an early morning slot the next day, or tell the promoter where he could shove his festival, and split. We chose the latter and it turned out to be a career-changing lesson.

I believed then and I still do now that it was a pivotal moment for us—and a big lesson for up-and-coming bands. This conflict and punch-up was the catalyst for getting the band out of Australia as soon as possible. Sunbury's promoters, producers and security were all subservient to the big-shot international artists—who were behaving badly—rather than doing the right thing and letting an Australian band carry out their performance in accordance with their contract. We all knew from that moment on that if you wanted respect in Australia, first you had to make it overseas. It was the end for Sunbury, too; 1975 was their last festival, due to higher ticket fees, lower attendances and money-related issues.

Ironically, Deep Purple—who pocketed $60,000 from the gig—spent the next night jamming at the Hard Rock, totally unaware that they were performing in my club. A few years later we were able to have a laugh about this with their guitarist Ritchie Blackmore over post-gig schnapps in a Hamburg bar. Ritchie needed a laugh; he'd just endured the stress of having his three ex-wives sitting in the front row of the show.

AC/DC's debut album *High Voltage* was released in March 1975 and a few months later was receiving massive airplay and sales. The pubs were constantly packed, but the audience was changing from hordes of male drunks, who'd take pleasure in throwing stuff at them, to hordes of teenage girls who wanted to tear them apart.

Myer's, the prominent Melbourne department store where I'd first worked, were promoting the opening of their new youth fashion department, the Miss Melbourne Shop. Foolishly, they booked the group for a lunchtime launch in August. Thousands of young girls jammed into the youth fashion department. Myer's wasn't familiar with the needs of rock'n'roll bands, and had built a very low stage, which the band accessed from an adjoining dressing room. There were no security barriers. It was simply the band, a very low stage, a few thousand screaming teens and a whole lot of hormones.

Even before the band struck a chord in anger, the girls rushed the stage. The guys dropped their instruments and scattered for whatever safety they could find. It was a mob scene. The newly fitted-out department was completely trashed, the next four planned Myer's gigs swiftly cancelled. Bon was last seen that day tearing through the ladies lingerie department with a fearsome pack of screaming young girls in pursuit, his best mate, Pat Pickett, at his side. The lanky, red-haired Pat was one of the early Catcher misfits, who'd befriended Bon and the band. Angus referred to him as the 'human Redhead matchstick'.

The mayhem at Myer's was just the beginning of the brief 'teenage mayhem' phase of the band. There was chaos wherever they appeared; hundreds of girls would faint and have to be rescued by security and then revived by the ever-present St John Ambulance personnel, who were now at every gig. And these were big crowds—at Melbourne's and Brisbane's Festival Halls and Sydney's Hordern Pavilion, the average audience was about 4000 strong, mostly screaming and hysterical young girls.

Despite the chaos, there was something special about the affection that the audience had for the band at these gigs. They'd put their wellbeing on the line just for the chance to jump up on the stage and touch the guys. But this would be short-lived. Soon after, the screaming girls would be replaced with hordes of air-guitar-wielding young blokes who wanted to be just like Angus and Malcolm. Guitar heroes.

Don't let anyone tell you that there is no competitive spirit in the world of music; competition in the local music business was fierce, especially in the mid-1970s. The bands would never admit to it, but there was a friendly but lively rivalry among them all, for the hearts and minds (and pocket money) of these young fans. AC/DC didn't go much for friendly, it should be said. Everyone was a rival.

Hush were a popular glam rock band from Sydney that had scored a number-one hit with a cover of 'Bony Moronie' in September 1975. The band featured two Asian guys, guitarist Les Gock and bass player Rick Lum. Angus affectionately renamed them Blue Suede Thongs.

Sherbet, led by the talented vocalist Daryl Braithwaite, were another hugely popular pop rock band, also from Sydney, who had enormous chart success and a loyal following, mostly comprising young girls. Angus had a name for Sherbet, too: they were tea-towel rock.

Then there was everyone's favourite glam rock band, Melbourne's Skyhooks. Everyone's favourite, that is, except for Malcolm and Angus; just the mention of the band's name got them seething. They had a strong hatred of Skyhooks; they were the enemy. Skyhooks were killing them in the charts and in the pubs with their catchy, accessible songs about Melbourne suburbs, especially on their iconic album *Living in the Seventies*, which had been produced by Daddy Cool's Ross Wilson. That record was unavoidable in 1974 and 1975, just as AC/DC started to find their audience.

While AC/DC played songs about getting 'the jack' and laying overweight women, Skyhooks sang about their friends getting married, women in uniform and horror movies, 'right there on my TV'. They were entertaining and very popular with the girls—another good reason for AC/DC to hate them—especially the loveable Shirley Strachan, their lead singer, with his curly blond locks. Despite having shades of KISS and the New York Dolls, they were somehow regarded as quintessentially Australian.

Their manager was my old partner Michael Gudinski, who managed to pull off what he described as a 'million-dollar deal' for them with Mercury Records in America. The Australian music media obviously hadn't been privy to the fine print in the contract, which, of course, Michael wasn't volunteering. The press was hyping it up, saying it was a groundbreaking deal for an Australian band. Had Mercury stuck with the band it may well have been, but that failed to materialise. Gudinski, however, was a good hype merchant, and within a short space of time Skyhooks became enormous, at least in Australia.

One of my favourite Skyhooks stories involved their volatile guitarist Bob 'Bongo' Starkie, who was upset about a gig that their (and AC/DC's) agent, the very unassuming Frank Stivala at Premier Artists, had booked. Bongo stormed into Frank's office and split his desk in two with an axe, while Frank was sitting there, engaged in a telephone conversation. I could only imagine the horrified look on Frank's face, watching this go down. Bongo was an intense, rebellious type; after Skyhooks split he flew to Rio on a mission to find God. Instead he found a new friend, Great Train Robber and exile Ronald Biggs, with whom he shared a house as well as a musical collaboration—the Sex Pistols were also involved.

On the strength of *High Voltage* and constant gigging, it wasn't long before AC/DC's popularity surpassed Skyhooks', rendering their enemy status obsolete. But hating other bands that people had the nerve to praise in their company was a favourite pastime of AC/DC's. They had nothing positive to say about anyone. Angus would occasionally sing the praises of Fats Domino, Mr 'Blueberry Hill', but even legends like Jimi Hendrix weren't above a caning. Angus once told a reporter that he wished Hendrix was still alive, so he 'could blow him off the stage'. American veteran Bo Diddley got a shit-canning one day when we shared a flight with him.

As for me, I thought, 'How could you not love a guy who has made a career out of one guitar riff?' But this rivalry was all part of AC/DC's bravado and band doctrine. As soon as a band was no longer a threat to their market share, they were soon forgotten.

The driving force behind this new teen movement was *Countdown*, a weekly national TV show that had begun screening on the ABC in November 1974. Former roadie, journo and record producer Molly Meldrum had reinvented himself as the show's chatty, nervous and hugely influential host. The program was loosely based on the successful formula of the UK's *Top of the Pops*, with one major difference: *TOTP* would only feature artists whose records were already charting. *Countdown*, however, would give a shot to young emerging Australian artists whom Molly liked. Fortunately, *Countdown* liked AC/DC.

The show's producer, Paul Drane, always liked to do something a bit different with AC/DC. When they played 'Baby, Please Don't Go' on *Countdown* in March 1975, Bon dressed up as a ciggie-smoking schoolgirl wielding a mallet, which caused a bit of a stir. In their 25 May 1975 appearance, rocking 'High Voltage', 'Baby, Please Don't Go' and 'Good Morning', Angus got dressed up as Superman and suddenly appeared with his guitar from inside a telephone booth. During another appearance Angus was Zorro, then he was an ape breaking out of a wooden cage. Mac, my in-house carpenter at the Hard Rock, was kept very busy building stage props.

Paul Drane, at the request of Alberts, made a video clip for the song 'Jailbreak', shot in the western suburbs of Melbourne. The site was an unused quarry with a makeshift jail cell, from which Bon made his dramatic escape, while homemade explosives blew up around him. Bon burst out, miming the lyrics about copping a bullet in his back, then fell on the ground dead. Part of the set blew up during the shoot, leaving a shaken Angus—in his convict pyjamas—stranded on a rock playing a very nervous guitar solo. Occupational health and safety wasn't a big concern in 1975. If you watch the clip, you can see Drane running for his life when the explosives start detonating.

Paul also produced the now-famous video for 'It's a Long Way to the Top (If You Wanna Rock 'n' Roll)', or, as Angus would re-name it—as he had a habit of doing for almost everything— 'Long Way to the Shop if You Wanna Sausage Roll'. The band was driven down Melbourne's Swanston Street on a flat-bed truck, miming to the track, accompanied by three members of the Rats of Tobruk pipe band, much to the bemusement of passers-by. They simply didn't have a clue what was happening.

This clip has become iconic, but in reality it was just another day in the life of AC/DC. The audience were just ordinary people going about their business—very few witnessing the event had any idea of what was going on, or how famous the clip would become. I was walking alongside the truck, wearing a white T-shirt and for some reason carrying a briefcase. I still can't recall why—I probably wanted to look important.

I had sent copies of the *High Voltage* and *TNT* albums to my sister Coral in London, along with the live film clip of 'High Voltage', showing the band at its best. Chris Gilbey had arranged with filmmaker Larry Larstead to shoot the video. Larstead was making a big-budget Coca-Cola TV ad in Melbourne during the same week the band was playing a gig at Festival Hall. We only had a modest budget; I guess you could say that Coke inadvertently sponsored our clip.

I did everything I could to best promote the band in the shoot. I organised a flashing AC/DC sign, similar to the one that became the backdrop for the American band KISS in their early days. With this in place, and a roaring crowd as the backdrop, the clip made AC/DC look like a big-time international outfit. I transferred the film onto a cassette suitable for my Fairfield AV machine, the same unit that I had used to show Billy Thorpe's film clip to the BBC.

Coral (and the Fairchild machine) had stayed in London after the Billy Thorpe crash and burn, working for such labels as Motown and A&M. At the time I sent her the AC/DC package she was working for Bob Marley and the Wailers' management, who also repped John 'Rabbit' Bundrick, an American songwriter and keyboard player. Phil Carson, the head of Atlantic Records' UK and European operation, was in the process of signing him. Bundrick was slated to replace Mike Montgomery in the new band Back Street Crawler, which featured Free's troubled guitarist Paul Kossoff. Back Street Crawler would come to play their own weird role in AC/DC's international odyssey.

Coral started shopping AC/DC around London's record companies, including A&M and Anchor Records, when she received a call from Phil Carson asking her to drop in and finalise the deal on Rabbit. Carson, a former muso, the bass player for Dusty Springfield, was now a dynamic record executive, a highly respected and powerful guy. He'd started out as the UK head of Polar Music, the Swedish record and management company owned by Stig Anderson, the manager of ABBA. When he joined Atlantic, Phil set up a deal between Atlantic America and ABBA. He'd also become the go-to guy at Atlantic for Led Zeppelin and their eccentric and difficult-to-deal-with manager, Peter Grant. Grant pretty much refused to have anything to do with anyone at Atlantic without Carson's direct involvement. Phil was a good guy to know.

When Coral met with Phil in early 1975, she had the Fairchild machine under her arm. She left quite the impression on Phil, who'd often talk about the meeting, describing my 29-year-old sister as a 'willowy brunette'. Once the deal was done for Rabbit, Coral moved on to other business.

'My brother in Australia is managing this group, AC/DC,' she told Carson. 'They've sold over 100,000 records.'

Carson's initial response could best be described as 'who the fuck cares?', but then Coral opened up the Fairchild and played him the 'High Voltage' clip. After about two minutes, Carson told her to turn it off. She thought she'd blown it, and feared that he hated the band. Instead, he looked at her and said, 'Get your brother on the phone now. Let's do a deal.'

Carson called me in Melbourne, waking me up at some ungodly hour.

'How quickly can you get to London?' he asked me excitedly. 'We need to talk about AC/DC right away.'

Even though I was still half asleep, I couldn't have been more thrilled. In hindsight, I choose not to consider whether Coral's 'willowy' good looks had any influence on his decision; it's probably safest not to. While I was planning on getting the band to the UK no matter what, Carson's enthusiasm accelerated everything. But without his call AC/DC might still be playing the White Horse in Nunawading, Angus dodging flying granny knickers rather than half-full VB cans. Really, who knows what might have happened? It wasn't easy to get Australian bands an offshore record deal; they were generally considered behind the times and too expensive to deal with. Carson changed all that with AC/DC.

I flew to London in March 1975 for several meetings with Phil and the key Atlantic staff. The label's general manager was Dave Dee, an original of the English pop group Dave Dee, Dozy, Beaky, Mick & Tich, who'd scored a big hit in 1966 with the song 'Bend It'. Within a week we had struck up a deal. I'd spend much of the next year bouncing between the UK and Australia, putting things in place for the band.

It may not have been the most lucrative record deal ever made; I'll admit that. The initial advance was $25,000, with an option graduating by $5000 for each option exercised, which was purely at the discretion of Atlantic and was dependent upon their ongoing faith in the band. It was more like a 'life sentence', should Atlantic exercise all their options (which they ended up doing). The band's royalty rate commenced at 12 per cent. This would go into the coffers of Alberts, who'd then pay the band half of the receipts after the recoupment of tour support. But it was still a deal.

For my part, Alberts paid for my airfare—and that was it. I did the deal because no one else was in a position to; I simply wanted to make things happen. It was a bargain for Atlantic, a lot less money than they'd normally spend signing a band and starting from scratch.

Typically, Jerry Greenberg, the President of Atlantic America and another ex-musician, would sanction all new deals, but he happened to be away on leave. So Carson went ahead with the signing, confident of his power within the organisation. From where the band and I stood, the deal was going to provide the opportunity to get out of Australia and on the road to achieving our objectives. I knew enough to know that deals can always be re-negotiated in the future; this was fine for now.

Everyone—the band, Harry Vanda, George Young and Ted Albert—were over the moon when I told them about the deal. We all shared a good feeling that this was going to work. With a live band as good as AC/DC, I knew it was all about getting them in front of audiences over a sustained period. Now we had our chance.

I believed that Atlantic was a good match for the band. Not only had they launched the careers of many of the legendary American soul and R&B artists, such as Ray Charles and Aretha Franklin, but Atlantic was also the worldwide home of Led Zeppelin, along with British rock bands like Cream and Yes, who, having established themselves in the UK and Europe, entered the American market through the back door.

The contract was actually between Atlantic and Alberts, AC/DC's production company. I proposed a deal to Ted Albert in which the advance paid to Alberts would be re-invested back into the band's overseas touring expenses and support them being based in London, which he agreed to. The band was back on salary, slightly more than the $60 a week they earned in Australia, enough to cover the basics in the UK. Now all they had to concern themselves with was getting on stage and blowing people away live—and schmoozing the crap out of the notoriously fickle UK media.

Just before Christmas 1975, the band started recording their third Australian album, *Dirty Deeds Done Dirt Cheap*, and performed their farewell gig at Sydney's notorious Bondi Lifesaver, the same club where Billy Thorpe had killed the fish. Shame I missed it; I was already in London. Thorpey was in the room and got up on stage with the band for their usual closer, 'Baby, Please Don't Go', a jam that probably went on forever, considering both Billy and the band loved a big finish.

Just before leaving for London I married my girlfriend Julie. The very traditional ceremony took place in an Adelaide church with only close personal friends and family in attendance—no rock'n'roll reprobates were invited, even though by now Julie had developed a keen interest in my progress with AC/DC. She accompanied me to London—off we went, with the band to follow once the album was done, ready to conquer the world, all within a year of my signing the band. It had been quite a ride already.

LIVING ON THE EDGE IN ENGLAND AND EUROPE

Soon after arriving in the UK, I appointed the London-based agent Richard Griffiths, from Headline Artists, to represent the band. Richard, who'd first been exposed to AC/DC via my Fairchild machine, was a true British gentleman, with an unmistakable private school accent. Despite his refined and cultured manner, Richard was an agent in the classic sense, as cunning as the proverbial shithouse rat, a natural and necessary characteristic of most talented agents.

Richard and Phil Carson quickly arranged for AC/DC to be the support on the forthcoming Back Street Crawler tour of the UK, which was scheduled to begin on 25 April 1976. It looked like we'd hit the ground running.

The band, along with their road crew Ralph and Herc, the lighting guy, landed in the UK on 2 April 1976, work on the *Dirty Deeds* album now completed. Spring was in the air and there was a feeling of optimism and excitement about what lay ahead. Their first UK single 'Long Way to the Top' had just been released and was already receiving some airplay on the pirate station Radio Luxembourg, who'd helped with Billy Thorpe's 'Most People I Know'.

Coral and I met the band at Heathrow in two huge black Daimler slope-back limos, provided by Atlantic. They were the first and last limos we'd see for a while. London and its history was wasted on the band; as we drove along, Coral and I would point out yet another famous landmark and the guys would shrug and bury their heads back in their comic books.

We arrived at their new home, a terrace house in London's Bayswater. There was a mad scramble for the best bedrooms. It was an exercise in futility, really; there was already a well-established pecking order within the band. Accordingly, there was a single room each for Malcolm, Angus and Bon, and a shared room for Mark and Phil and the crew. They were used to living together at Lansdowne Road, so they knew the deal, how tricky it could be for seven people living in a relatively small space. Thankfully, I wasn't part of it. As a newly married man, I managed to find nice little basement digs in Mayfair's Shepherd Market, which also served as my business HQ. It was a step up from the phone booth I commandeered while trying to get things happening for Billy Thorpe.

Atlantic and WEA threw a welcoming party for the band in April; it was the first chance for the staff to meet this strange and colourful band from Down Under, with a chain-smoking schoolkid and a singer with dodgy teeth and a cockatoo tattooed on his arm.

Hospitality was a specialty of the WEA group of companies; they were well known for their attention to artist relations. And the band's reputation for a good time had preceded them— most likely via Coral, who was now working as my assistant— and Atlantic arranged for more than the usual quota of booze. That night, the Atlantic and WEA staff learned a whole new language and received an insight into the Australian psyche. It was the beginning of a new and long-lasting relationship— and a great starting point for what was going to be their first British tour.

Among the invitees that night was Derek Taylor, the former press officer for The Beatles. Not that the AC/DC guys gave a shit. Derek came on like a pompous git, trading on his former glories. He dared to ask Bon, 'What do you do around the place?' Bon stuck it right up him. I, though, was slightly more impressed; The Beatles would always be royalty.

The following day, however, I got a call from Richard. He had some startling news.

'Paul Kossoff is dead,' he told me.

Shit.

Back Street Crawler's guitarist, a drug addict of some notoriety, had died suddenly from heart failure, on a plane en route from New York to London. He was 25. The tour was over before it even began.

This was a tragic piece of news for everyone: Kossoff's family, his band and adoring fans (including me), as well as AC/DC, who'd just travelled 12,000 miles to play with the guy. Bon summed up the situation in his typical fashion with a few well-chosen words when he spoke to *RAM* magazine.

'That cunt Paul Kossoff has fucked up our first tour.'

So what to do? The way we saw it, this misfortune presented us with an opportunity to do what we knew best: play the pubs and build a following from scratch. Australian bands were used to dealing with adversity and AC/DC was no exception.

But there was a potential problem starting to gather momentum down on King's Road, one that I hadn't anticipated. Designers and provocateurs Malcolm McLaren and Vivienne Westwood, who ran the SEX boutique, were plotting a musical and cultural revolution. It was designed to kill off the existing music establishment, which they considered boring and prehistoric. It would be known as punk rock; the movement's mouthpiece was a group of misfits called the Sex Pistols, led by a ball of rage named Johnny Rotten, whom McLaren would manage. Punk was something we'd soon have to deal with.

We also had another, more immediate problem. The album cover sleeve that Atlantic had come up with for the UK release of *High Voltage* in late April was a disaster. It was a very loud, pink-based cartoon image of Angus and Bon. Because of time constraints there was nothing we could do about it—but we all hated it. Short of putting a stop to the whole schedule, we just had to deal with it. It sucked, though.

I was forced to put a positive spin on it to the band. Years later, when I watched the movie *Spinal Tap* and their manager defended their ridiculous all-black LP cover, I absolutely related. Here I was praising this pink pile of junk and how it would stand out in record shops. Not surprisingly, the guys weren't buying it.

'It's crap,' they told me, repeatedly. I silently agreed.

But they eventually stopped moaning about it. Richard, in the meantime, had good news—he'd booked four London gigs, commencing on 23 April at the Red Cow, a tiny pub in Hammersmith. The band was booked to play two sets, for a fee of £35. London was about to have its first taste of real and raw Aussie pub rock.

We got our first shock even before we set up. The publican owned two huge Dobermans, trained to kill, who all but ripped us to shreds as we entered just before opening time. That little problem overcome, any concerns the guys may have had about their first gig in this new country soon disappeared. There were only about 40 punters in the room; they all looked like regulars who just happened to be drinking there when AC/DC played. But after the initial shock of seeing some schoolkid prancing around on the small stage, they really started to get into it.

During the break, between sets, I noticed a line of people waiting to use the pub's payphone. When the band started their second set, the place was suddenly full. It seemed that everyone in the room for the first set had called their friends, urging them to get down to the pub, and quickly. The now large audience went crazy. It was a great start.

The next gig that Richard booked was at the Nashville, a small pub in West Kensington, on 26 April. The night was billed in the music press—by the well-intentioned but misinformed venue manager—as an 'Antipodean punk extravaganza'. Jesus.

Angus introduced the unsuspecting crowd at the Nashville to his table-walking routine, where he'd bounce from tabletop to tabletop, with roadies following behind holding his guitar lead and collecting the upended beer glasses he left in his wake. Angus was a big consumer of chocolate bars and milk; one of the downsides was that while he played he would occasionally emit gallons of what Mark Evans described as 'a snot cyclone', which the front row would end up wearing. As he strutted from table to table, the punters down front at the Nashville wore the lot, much to the amusement of the other patrons, including me, Julie and Coral. It was a wild sight, Angus in overdrive.

Two gigs in and everything was looking rosy, but something—or someone—had popped up unexpectedly, threatening to bring everything undone. It was Silver, Bon's old girlfriend from Australia, with whom he'd had an affair while still married. They'd reluctantly broken up but it seemed the flame still lingered. She turned up unannounced at the Red Cow gig.

Silver was an exotic and attractive woman of the world, a seriously connected rock chick with a cold and calculating manner. She had been living in London for some time, and had established herself as a rock'n'roll insider; she was on a first-name basis with members of the Stones.

The band was singularly unimpressed with the couple's shallow, drug-fucked bullshit. They'd sarcastically refer to Bon and Silver as 'Rod and Britt', a nod to the superstar couple of the hour, Rod Stewart and Britt Ekland. They knew of Silver's potential to lure Bon into dark and dangerous places. And Silver did live recklessly; she just didn't fit into Bon's 'other life'—the band, who'd just put their collective balls on the line to set themselves up on the other side of the world. They could all sense her potential for destruction, her negative influence. Bon would eventually move in with Silver; they set up a love nest on the other side of town, which heightened the band's concerns. We'd see her from time to time; occasionally Silver would join the band and me for dinner, but she rarely came to gigs. While I was apprehensive about Silver, I kind of liked her, too. But AC/DC was just not cool enough for her.

Bon would sometimes accompany Silver on her adventures, which included one trip to Paris he'd often talk about. It was a lively soirée; the pair socialised with Keith Richards and Ronnie Wood for a few days of absinthe- (*la fée verte*), drug- and Gitanes-fuelled partying in the city's Latin quarter. It had taken Bon more than ten years to be hanging out in an environment as cool as this. The rest of the week he spent recording vocals with his new drinking buddy Bernard Bonvoisin, from the French band Trust, who just happened to be recording a punked-up version of AC/DC's 'Love at First Feel'.

Within days of Bon and Silver's reunion, Coral and I got a call from the hospital; Bon had been admitted in bad shape. When we sat down with him at his bedside, Bon started spinning more of the same old crap, saying he'd had one too many pills and that when mixed with some booze, it took him over the edge. I later learned that it was a cocktail of heroin and booze that caused him to OD, this time snorted rather than injected. I've never been able to determine whether Angus or Malcolm knew what went down. Bon certainly wasn't giving too much away.

Richard had another gig booked, this time at the Marquee on 11 May. Jack Barry ran this legendary venue, which had featured in the rise of so many important blues-based rock bands over the years, including The Yardbirds, The Rolling Stones and The Animals. Jack was so impressed by AC/DC that he gave them a weekly residency, along with a spot at the huge Reading Music Festival, which he also ran. Jack wrote a note to Atlantic, the kind of AC/DC artefact I wish I'd had framed. In it he said AC/DC was 'the best band to appear at the Marquee since Led Zeppelin'. High praise.

The punk rock revolution that I'd noticed brewing on King's Road was now in full ascendancy, led by the Sex Pistols and The Clash. A few music industry insiders somehow imagined that AC/DC was going to be a part of this movement, but nothing could have been further from the truth. AC/DC hated the whole punk scene; they found it shallow and pretentious, more about fashion than music or passion. Punk was, however, the hot topic of 1976; the focus of the music press had shifted to the 100 Club in Oxford Street.

The victims of this new movement were the bands who'd been around for a while, building a following, doing the hard yards. They were now viewed by the music media as dinosaurs, hopelessly out of touch. The two weeklies, the *New Musical Express* (the *NME*) and *Melody Maker*, were all over punk like a rash.

I have to admit, though, that I thought the Sex Pistols were amazing. They had good songs and a great image that had been well planned by Rotten, Vivienne Westwood and McLaren, who I considered a marketing genius. There was no doubt they were a relevant and provocative force to be reckoned with, at least until Sid Vicious was brought in; then the bullshit began and they became a parody of themselves.

I saw the Pistols and The Clash a few times at the 100 Club. The club's audience was right out there, having embraced the whole punk concept and taken it to an extreme new level. The Clash added an interesting twist, throwing paint on each other during their performance. As for the other British punk bands, well, they left me cold. But it wasn't possible to even hold a conversation with AC/DC about punk without them getting totally pissed off.

All this was making it very difficult to get AC/DC's records on radio, which meant they were not charting, leading to one very nervous record company. In spite of this, foundations were being laid through playing live and the band was having a ball—as long as no one mentioned punk rock or Silver. The guys knew that the music industry's obsession with punk would eventually fade. The band kept their heads down and worked.

As a substitute for the aborted Back Street Crawler dates, Atlantic arranged the 'Lock Up Your Daughters' tour throughout the UK, sponsored by *Sounds* magazine, the third local music weekly. The tour would run through June and July 1976. *Sounds* was the only magazine that hadn't abandoned rock music; their journalists included Jeff Barton, Dave Lewis and Phil Sutcliffe, who all loved AC/DC. This was a major departure from most other critics in London, including the important *NME* and *Melody Maker*, who for the most part hated the band. We got all the usual 'ocker'/'colonial'/'Bruce' crap from the critics, who seemed to think Australia was stuck in some beer-swilling time warp.

The tour coincided with the band's first front cover of a major music publication outside Australia. Not surprisingly, that magazine was *Sounds*. It featured a great piece written by Sutcliffe, who'd bravely spent a lot of time with the band on and off the road—and survived well enough to document it. The band had been very forthcoming about their Melbourne exploits, both in Lansdowne Road and at the Freeway Motel, which prompted his headline: THE DIRTIEST STORY EVER TOLD.

Things were really starting to heat up for the band. The great thing was that the audience they were building were genuine rock music fans, unlike the teen girls back in Oz wanting to tear their clothes from their backs, or the drunken yobs in beer barns throwing stuff at them. The *Sounds* tour reached Scotland, taking in Glasgow, Malcolm and Angus's birthplace, which made for an emotional homecoming. Backstage passes for the Youngs' extended family were always out of control back in Sydney—they seemed to come from everywhere—but in Glasgow they set new records. It felt like half the population of the city came backstage after the gig, all eager to see young Malcolm and Angus for the first time. I found out that George had also played in Glasgow while with The Easybeats, on a tour with The Rolling Stones.

There was a running joke among the Young clan that their father, William, had been lucky enough to be born with a musical dick. But it takes balls to uproot your family and move to the other side of the world in order to give them a better life. Now that Malcolm and Angus were back in Glasgow with AC/DC, the remaining Youngs could see that William's decision had been right. Australia had helped the boys become great musicians and provided them with a huge opportunity—even if 'our Angus' still dressed like a schoolboy, for reasons that seemed to elude the gathered Young clan.

After Scotland, the tour headed south to Liverpool, the home of The Beatles, the band that got most of us started in music. AC/DC played at the Liverpool Stadium, an old, dilapidated warhorse of a venue. It felt a lot like Festival Hall in Melbourne; it was once an old boxing venue, too.

But at this gig I caught a glimpse of things to come. The crowd, mostly teenage boys, let off more steam that I'd ever witnessed at an AC/DC show before, which is saying something. They went wild, trashing seats and genuinely threatening the architectural integrity of the rundown old joint.

What the fuck do they put in the water in this town? I asked myself, watching the carnage unfold. Maybe it just poured straight out of the Mersey, which we took in the next day from a ferry, making our way to the Isle of Man for another over-the-top show.

Our return to London was marked by a show at the famous Lyceum Theatre, just off the Strand. Excitement was running high; this was an important gig. But during set-up, just prior to soundcheck, our quiet and unassuming Aussie lighting guy, Herc, fell off a high ladder after getting a huge electricity jolt. Herc landed on the floor, breaking both his arms. The gig went ahead while Herc was rushed to hospital and pieced back together. The gig always went ahead.

I visited Herc a few times in hospital before making arrangements for his return to Australia. Years later I was told by a mutual friend that I was the only person to visit him, which hadn't impressed Herc at all. Upon reflection, this said a lot about the AC/DC mindset: if you couldn't do the job, you were out. Everyone was disposable. Dog eat dog.

After the *Sounds* tour, Richard booked a string of dates in Scandinavia in mid-July as part of an exchange, of sorts, with ABBA, who were to tour Australia. At the same time, there'd also been a trickle-down effect from the London shows; people were talking up the band's live reputation. A natural curiosity about anything from Australia, which had been the first country in the world to embrace the Scandis' beloved ABBA, also helped the band.

We sailed from Plymouth in the direction of Hamburg, after which we would drive through Germany and on to Sweden. Finances were very tight; we had no budget for sleeping cabins aboard the ship, so we all bedded down on bar chairs joined together, or whatever else we could find. After sufficient Carlsberg Elephant beers—with the exception of Angus, of course—we all tried to sleep. On arrival, customs decided to give us the once over, making an uncomfortable night with practically no sleep even more unbearable.

We finally cleared customs and made our way out to collect a hire car. There was just one problem: the car hire company insisted on a credit card, which weren't all that common then— they certainly weren't readily available to managers of up- and-coming rock bands. I had a brainwave and produced my Australian Ansett Airlines card, which to the German assistant at the counter looked official enough. We drove off in the latest Model 5 BMW, the crew in a van, headed for Scandinavia. The BMW eventually ended up in London, a mere shadow of its former glorious self.

We were living right on the edge, touring Europe with very little cash, no credit cards or any other convenience. To boost our non-existent budget, we'd stockpiled English ten-pence coins and swapped them for deutsche marks to pump into the German vending machines, loading up on snacks and cigarettes.

Angus was the voice of gloom, continually reminding me what a ridiculous undertaking this was. As amusing and likeable as he could sometimes be, there were also times when I could have throttled the little prick. Moan, moan, moan.

While I'm sure no band in their right mind would attempt to do it today, to me this adventure we were on was just the way it was. It really was a case of putting one foot in front of the other—and going for it, even if it meant playing gigs in Malmö and Växjö or Anderstorp. The only other option, as I reminded Angus, was sitting on our asses in London, waiting for some punk-obsessed radio station to program our record. For me, there was no choice. We had to push the *High Voltage* album and the 'Long Way' single, which were receiving hardly any airplay. It was up to us to get the band's music heard.

The gigs certainly made up for the discomfort and hassles along the way; it was a revelation to see the band play to a non-English-speaking audience for the first time. European audiences didn't seem to have a problem with language—they either didn't care about the lyrics or were just getting off on the music. Who knows, maybe they understood English. Something clicked.

We returned to London for our Marquee residency, which began on 26 July. Another band from Richard's agency, Eddie and the Hot Rods, currently held the Marquee attendance record, but by the second week of their residency, AC/DC had smashed it to pieces. I'd never seen so many people packed into a venue, even in the Aussie beer barns; the Marquee walls were like waterfalls of sweat. AC/DC absolutely nailed it—and word of mouth around London was running hot.

The audiences were genuine fans who knew their music and loved the band for all the right reasons. Some were even turning up in school uniform. The word also got out among musicians and celebrities, who decided to see what the fuss was all about. One Marquee regular was local loon Screaming Lord Sutch, who used to sing live while in a coffin, or dress as Jack the Ripper. You couldn't miss him. Deep Purple's Ritchie Blackmore turned up one night wanting to jam—and was subsequently knocked back. Not enough time had passed since that ugly Sunbury punch-up. Then again, AC/DC were usually too intense for that kind of thing. For them, every gig was a case of getting on stage and going flat out until the end, then coming off totally wasted.

Doug Clifford and Stu Cook, the rhythm section of Creedence Clearwater Revival, came along to the Marquee on another night. They were so impressed that they contacted Atlantic and put their case forward to produce an AC/DC album, which was flatly rejected by the band. They were more than satisfied with their current production team; after all, everyone at Alberts was family.

In terms of simple numbers, AC/DC was probably the most successful band to have played at the Marquee. They would certainly join the ranks of the famous bands to have started out there, although this fact seems to have escaped the venue's owners, who haven't mentioned them in a proposed doco about the Marquee. To me, it seemed like another example of the condescending British attitude towards us 'colonials', something that we learned to cop sweet back in 1976.

Still, we were making progress. True music fans were starting to really love AC/DC.

KICKING AGAINST THE PRICKS

Despite the great response from *Sounds*, recognition from *NME* and *Melody Maker* took some time. Both were still besotted with the whole punk thing, declaring on almost a weekly basis that some trumped-up act were the new saviours of rock'n'roll. It was all a bit hard to swallow.

Being an Australian wasn't exactly the ideal calling card in the UK in the mid-1970s, either. There were a lot of preconceptions that all Australians were crude and uncultured (no truth whatsoever in that belief, of course). The likes of Bazza McKenzie and Chips Rafferty hadn't made things any easier for Aussies trying their luck in the UK.

Even when we finally got some attention from the 'other'

music magazines, the headlines said it all: MORE CHUNDER FROM DOWN UNDER screamed *Melody Maker*. The *NME* responded with I WALLABY YOUR MAN. Both thought they were the funniest things since Derek and Clive.

The odd thing was that we were underplaying the band's Australian background and focusing more on the Scottish connection. Still, it was hard to shake off some narrow-minded preconceptions.

We had more luck when it came to equipment. The band had shipped over some very ordinary old Marshall gear. Now, with the word about AC/DC starting to spread via musos into the all-important music equipment shops, I decided it was time to give Jim Marshall a call. Jim was a pioneer, the man who built the iconic Marshall amps, an essential for any serious rock band. I was pleasantly surprised when Jim told me he was fully aware of the band, so much so that he decided to give us a sponsorship deal. He handed over two sets of Marshall 'stacks' and some bass gear for Mark Evans, as part of an ongoing arrangement. Phil Rudd soon got an endorsement from Sonor, the German percussion manufacturer.

All this served a couple of purposes: it showed that respect was building for the band, and it also saved us some serious dollars. AC/DC was starting to become a genuine force in the hard-to-crack London music world.

On 29 July 1976, the band appeared at the annual Reading Music Festival, a three-day-long, mud-caked outdoor event that typically drew upwards of 50,000 music fans. The band's late afternoon spot, just before the set of American guitar- and gun-nut, Ted Nugent, was their reward for having done so well at the Marquee.

Along the way, we dropped into Richard Griffiths' parents place, a stately home in upper-class Ascot, for a spot of croquet on the lawn and morning tea. It was a very civilised build-up to an afternoon spent—hopefully—blowing the heads off thousands of bedraggled music fans.

Upon arrival at the site, Phil Carson, who may have spent too much time hanging out with Led Zeppelin's Peter Grant, had the bright idea of clearing the stage of all personnel and hangers-on before AC/DC would appear. When I asked why, he assured me that this would give the band more backstage 'presence' and star quality. I should have been smarter; this smacked of Deep Purple's arrogance at Sunbury, on reflection. And look how that had ended up.

Phil was usually right about most things but this was a disaster. MC John Peel, an important BBC 1 DJ, got the shits with the band's posturing and the vibe just went downhill from there. Once on stage, despite a set list that included 'Livewire', 'High Voltage', 'Jailbreak' and 'Baby, Please Don't Go', the band seemed to choke for the first time, unable to connect with a crowd that yawned in the sunshine, barely noticing their set. What should have been a triumph and a pivotal moment turned into a very ordinary gig. First the Sunbury debacle, now Reading. It seemed that there was some kind of curse when it came to AC/DC and big outdoor festivals. If there was a lesson to take away from this flop, it was that we should never again listen to Carson's advice on matters of backstage etiquette.

Later on that evening, at the band's house in London, there was a lively post-mortem, which led to a brotherly punch-up between George, who was in town, Malcolm and Angus. It was possibly the beginning of the end for Mark Evans, too, who'd had a particularly bad gig. The Youngs certainly didn't hold back on letting him know about it. When Mark tried to intervene in the brawl, the Youngs turned on him. 'There's a lesson to be learned here,' Mark wrote in his terrific book *Dirty Deeds*, 'never try to break up a fight between brothers, especially when there's three of them.'

A couple of nights later Richard Griffiths and I invited George to join us for dinner at the Speakeasy. It all seemed very civilised, when out of nowhere George let loose.

'Come on, guys, when are you going to get serious about the band?' George roared at us. Richard and I exchanged a 'What the fuck is he talking about?' look.

'Okay,' I said to George, 'there's now been one crap gig, but everything was going to plan. Things are still looking great.'

George wasn't buying it and the night quickly fell apart.

Later I made an observation to Richard.

'Don't worry,' I said, 'it's the Mike Vaughan factor rearing its ugly head.'

Clearly, George hadn't shaken off his bad experience while with The Easybeats. I also had the feeling that his trip to London, the brothers' fistfight and George's negativity were an exercise in reminding us that Alberts was still pulling the strings back home. I shrugged it off, but Richard wasn't so sure.

'I think George is out to screw you,' he warned me.

Shortly after Reading, the band played a series of small gigs throughout Germany, including a gig for Wolfgang 'Bubi' Heilemann. Bubi was a very high-profile and powerful contributor to *Bravo* magazine, a guy who could make or break artists, a sort of German Molly Meldrum. Luckily, Bubi became a big fan and supporter of AC/DC and helped pave the way for the band in Europe.

Things were happening for me away from the music, too. The fourth of November 1976 was one of the best days of my and Julie's life, with the birth of our daughter, Billie, at London's Paddington Hospital. We named her after singer Billie Holiday, a musical hero of mine. Richard, by now a close friend, was there to help me through with cigars and loads of warm Pommie beer. My daughter would be a traveller virtually from the cradle. Our family life was in motion; we had no idea where we'd end up living. Everything was dictated by the band's journey—and we were enjoying the ride, loving life in England. Right now it felt like home.

By late November, the band, after a turbulent but successful beginning in the UK and Europe, was scheduled to return to Australia for a national tour, promoting the *Dirty Deeds* LP. My itinerary took me in a different direction, west from London to New York, for my first meeting with Atlantic head honcho Jerry Greenberg. I'd reconnect with the band in Australia.

I'd done my research on Jerry, who I learned was a totally passionate music guy. He'd become President of Atlantic Records in 1974 at the ripe old age of 32; he was the youngest president of any major label. In London, I'd been told how Jerry had to approve everything before things could really happen for AC/DC. So it was great to finally sit down with the man; it was a crucial meeting for me and the band.

Our meeting took place in his office at the Atlantic Records HQ in the imposing Rockefeller Plaza complex (more recently, the site of TV show *30 Rock*). In terms of significance, this was right up there with my first meeting with Ted Albert in Sydney. But instead of Ted's walnut-panelled walls and colonial trimmings, Jerry's office was crammed with rock'n'roll paraphernalia—a classic 1950s jukebox, containing all the great Atlantic Records recordings through the years, sat in one corner. The green shag-pile carpet was so thick and lush I got an electric shock every time I touched something metallic.

I liked Jerry a lot and could quickly see why everyone was in awe of him. He was an impressive guy. But while Jerry was very gracious, I sensed that he didn't really get the band, at least not yet. AC/DC, for the time being, was 'Carson's folly', an act Jerry was stuck with, that Carson had signed without his blessing. I was hoping to get a commitment from Jerry to get the band to the States pronto, but no major breakthrough or commitments were agreed upon. I couldn't help but think that Jerry was out to punish Carson in some way for signing the band without his okay.

Also in the meeting was Jim Delahunt, Atlantic's head of A&R. He seemed more interested in discussing Skyhooks, of all bands, whom he seemed to love. They'd been having problems with their US label, a condition known to insiders as 'Mercury poisoning'. I got the sense that Delahunt would rather have been working with Skyhooks than AC/DC. Had I reported this little bit of information back to the band there would have blood on the streets.

The band hated the idea of going back to tour Australia; they told me that it felt like they were going backwards. They'd made some inroads in the UK, why couldn't they continue with that? Though it was never said out loud, maybe they feared that once they were back in Oz, they'd never leave again. They also felt that their fanbase in Australia was wrong, there were too many young girls; they'd well and truly moved on from their five minutes as 'pop stars', *Countdown* favourites.

But the high overheads that came with being London-based and touring Europe and the UK made the trip home unavoidable. They needed to make some money. Although Atlantic in the UK was behind the band and selling records, the American parent company was doing neither.

The band's reluctant return to Oz in December 1976—named the 'Giant Dose of Rock'n'roll' tour—had barely begun when I got a bombshell call from Phil Carson.

'Atlantic America want to drop the band,' he told me from London. They'd heard the *Dirty Deeds* album and just didn't think it would work in America. There was a 'drop notice' on the band; as far as Atlantic America was concerned, they were history. Toast.

He explained that Jerry Greenberg just didn't see their potential, nor was he able to mount the necessary internal support for the band. I'd sensed this during my first meeting with him and Delahunt in New York.

This was a disastrous piece of news.

'I'll do what I can to get them to change their minds,' Carson promised before hanging up.

He had a lot to lose, too. After all, we made the deal with Carson while Jerry was on leave. If anyone was in the firing line, it was Carson.

Carson reached out to Nesuhi Ertegun, the suave, sophisticated Turkish-born co-owner of the company, and pointed out some facts. The *High Voltage* album, which had been recorded for a mere $25,000, had been selling okay: some 12,000 copies in England, another 10,000 in Germany. The numbers weren't awe-inspiring, but their investment had been recouped.

Carson finally managed to convince Ertegun that they should hang onto the band, but it came at a price. The agreed album advance for their next record was reduced from $35,000 to $30,000; somehow this saved the deal, and probably the band. But we'd still have to fight to survive.

The band, Harry and George and Alberts were all shocked, but accepted that we just had to swallow the lesser advance and keep moving. At least we still had a label. Still, Atlantic's near dumping of the band hurt a lot and kept everyone on edge.

Ray Evans and my old partner and good friend Michael Gudinski promoted the 'Giant Dose of Rock'n'roll' tour, which kicked off in Perth on 2 December. It was a 20-date, coast-to-coast run, with big shows at the Hordern Pavilion in Sydney, the Myer Music Bowl in Melbourne and Festival Hall in Brisbane.

Before leaving the UK I'd heard a song on BBC 1 called 'I'm Stranded' by Australian punk band The Saints, who were also starting to get some attention from the London music press. I'd called Chris Gilbey at Alberts in Sydney.

'You should check out The Saints,' I told him. 'Maybe Alberts would be interested in them.'

When I got to Australia, I organised for The Saints to open for AC/DC at their Surfers Paradise gig in mid-December. Personally, I didn't really care for them live; there was a lot of pseudo punk posturing going on, which annoyed me. I reported back to Chris, who, nonetheless, flew to Brisbane and signed them up on the spot at Brisbane Airport—not to Alberts, but to himself. He was now The Saints' manager and promptly quit Alberts—who didn't appreciate him, anyway—and off they went to London to follow up on the hype. Ted Albert's response was to promote Fifa, who now controlled the day-to-day running of the label. He hired me as consultant on the worldwide licensing arrangements for the label, duties I performed while travelling with AC/DC.

With Gilbey's departure, Alberts' viability as an independent record label diminished. The chemistry that Chris had helped build between the production team and marketing went into decline. The only things Alberts had going on was AC/DC, which I was driving, and Rose Tattoo.

The Australian tour, which the band was now calling a 'Giant Dose of Grief', ground on towards Christmas. Angus was the chief complainer; he'd grumble about anything and everything, and he continued to give me hell about the band 'going backwards'. He really didn't want to be on the road in Australia.

'Yes, Angus,' I'd reassure him. 'One step backwards, two steps forward.'

It wasn't as if I wanted to be in Australia right then, either, but we had no choice: we needed money. My recent telephone conversation with Phil Carson didn't help any, either. A 'fighting fund' was more crucial than ever, if we were going to continue on our shared journey of world domination.

There also seemed to be a whiff of resentment and jealousy in the air from a new contingent of Oz punk bands towards AC/DC. They believed that the band belonged to some kind of old order and had somehow sold out along the way. What a load of bullshit.

We'd already weathered this shitstorm in Britain and we weren't about to let a few delusional tin-pot Aussie punks bother us. AC/DC was the real thing; they were more punk than punk. Their credibility was based on their playing and songwriting skills, as well as their street smarts and amazing work ethic. There was none of the pretensions and bullshit that seemed present in these upstart punk bands. To me, this was just another case of tall poppy syndrome, a negative mindset originally imported from England that had been taken to new lows in Australia. An absolute crock.

The 'Dose' tour was further marred by controversy surrounding the song 'Dirty Deeds', in which Bon read out the fictitious phone number, 36–24–36. It turned out to be the real number of a wealthy Sydney widow, who didn't appreciate all the calls enquiring about 'dirty deeds done dirt cheap'. Added to that, record sales had slipped, and not all the gigs were selling out. Angus, meanwhile, was getting into trouble for his latest on-stage stunt: mooning the audience. Even one of their greatest allies, Sydney station 2SM—owned by the Catholic Church—declared they'd no longer play AC/DC's records, at least not until they decided if they were a strip act or a rock'n'roll band.

Still, by late December, we'd achieved our objective: the coffers were full again, even if the 'Giant Dose of Grief' tour had been one almighty pain in the arse. Everyone had had enough of the tall poppy syndrome. We were all ready to make our second escape from Oz, although there was one task left—to make a great new album.

THE ROADSHOW KEEPS ON ROLLING

It was apparent that to make further inroads internationally, the band needed to cut a tougher record. So before leaving Oz, along with their production team of good ol' 'George and 'arry', they disappeared into Alberts Sydney studios to record their fourth LP, sessions that ran between January and February 1977.

The album was named *Let There Be Rock*, and for good reason: this time the producers took more of a live approach, letting the band jam on the songs as if they were playing a gig. George and Harry simply captured it all on tape, which was a bit of a throwback to the old Billy Thorpe and the Aztecs/ *Hoax is Over* days. Everyone completely embraced the live and raw concept, so much so that while recording the blazing title track, smoke started billowing from Angus's amp, filling the studio. Angus looked up at his brother George, who mouthed 'Don't stop!' from the control room. By song's end, Angus's amp simply gave up and died.

The recording done and the Atlantic deal back on track, everyone was prepared for a return to the UK for more touring, but there was a final gig in Perth at the Entertainment Centre on 13 February 1977. The local promoter made a big mistake: he'd neglected to remove the seats. The fired-up crowd trampled all over them; the place ended up looking as though it had been hit by a bomb.

On the morning of their departure for London, Malcolm and Bon decided to hire a catamaran and do a few laps on Perth's beautiful Swan River. Their London flight was scheduled to depart mid-afternoon, but the local wind known as the Fremantle Doctor failed to blow. They were marooned, stuck out in the middle of the river somewhere.

Meanwhile, the crew, the rest of the band and I packed our gear and headed for the airport, where there was no sign of our intrepid sailors. Malcolm and Bon finally turned up at the airport with minutes to spare, still in their swimming trunks. They boarded the plane dripping wet and duly froze in the air-conditioned cabin, headed for a British winter. The perfect start to the next stage of the band's career.

Atlantic in the UK had been careful about the amount of hype they generated about the band. It can be a big mistake to go too early; with a group like AC/DC, the fans could be well and truly put off by a lot of big talk. People like to think they discovered the band, and the smell of hype can be deadly. But now, with a new album in the can, due for release in March, it was time to turn the marketing up a few notches, to really let rip.

Promotional coverage in the UK music press was the yardstick as to whether a record company was seriously behind an artist and their latest release. Anything less than full-page ads across the board in all magazines was considered unenthusiastic. Personally, I would have preferred no ads at all. One of my early influences was Canadian philosopher Marshall McLuhan and after reading his book, *The Medium is the Message*, I concluded that the way in which the message was relayed was actually far more important than the actual message itself. Small, seemingly apologetic ads for something as significant as an album release, in my opinion, said the label actually don't really believe in the band. Why bother?

The biggest statement of all was a double-page spread. As I reminded Atlantic, this was what they'd given Led Zeppelin. I believed AC/DC deserved the same coverage, in order to establish the perception within the industry that the band had now arrived. While I chipped way, Atlantic organised a 'Let There Be Rock' competition, bringing in a retail chain to encourage sales of their new single. The next day there was a report in the *Evening Standard* about a giant rock that Atlantic had dumped on King's Road. The hype had well and truly begun.

Richard Griffiths and I met with the prestigious UK tour promoter Fred Bannister, who ran a company named Tredoar. We believed Fred's involvement would improve the quality of the band's touring presentation. Fred was best known for staging the annual Knebworth Festival, a huge outdoor event, which the Stones had headlined in 1976.

Fred put a tour together that culminated with a gig at one of London's prestigious venues, the Rainbow Theatre, in early March 1977. I invited American talent agent Doug Thaler, who'd been showing some interest in representing the band in the US, along with Aerosmith's manager David Krebs, half of the powerful New York–based management company Leber and Krebs. He was in London on business. Both would figure prominently in the band's future.

The Bannister-staged tour achieved its purpose, upping the band's profile considerably. I was now in full 'take no prisoners' mode and knew, with some reluctance, that I needed to have a conversation with Richard Griffiths about his ongoing role as the band's agent.

I had no complaints about Richard's work; in fact, I thought he'd been great, very supportive of the band, who also respected and liked him. He and I were also good friends. But I knew it was time to part company. I just wasn't getting the band on the type of tours they needed to elevate them to the next level. It was always a case of 'dog eat dog' with AC/DC; if they didn't keep moving upwards they'd let you know about it. What we needed was an agent who could secure opening slots with big acts, particularly around Europe.

Richard and I met in a Mayfair bar, the type frequented by the upper-class type from the House of Lords, just up the road from the Shepherd Market red-light district where I was living and running the business. We ordered a couple of dry martinis and I spelled out the situation.

Richard, being an absolute gentleman, said that he understood my dilemma and accepted his termination with grace. Our friendship survived the sacking, and he soon moved on to very big things of his own.

The band signed to a new agent, John Jackson at the Cowbell Agency. John had a rep for making things happen in Europe, and soon enough had the band touring the continent with Black Sabbath. It kicked off in Paris on 5 April 1977 at the converted old city abattoir, a big barn of a venue. It was one of those gigs you hope to forget: everything that could go wrong did; the band sounded like crap; their equipment started conking out. After about 20 torturous minutes they trashed their gear and stormed off stage, expecting boos and jeers. Yet something strange happened: the audience went crazy. They loved it, probably thinking all the on-stage demolition was some kind of punk statement. Hardly. The band was pissed off.

As the tour progressed, Bon and Ozzy Osbourne connected with each other via footwear, of all things. Both singers shared an appreciation for brothel creepers while on stage. They became kindred spirits, bonded by shoes. But relations between the two bands—one on their way up, the other in a slow decline—weren't always good. Malcolm and Geezer Butler from Sabbath had an incident in a hotel where Malcolm thought Geezer had pulled a knife on him, which got a big ugly. It turned out to be a plastic flick knife, a strange thing for a grown man to be carrying around, admittedly. Eventually things got sorted out and the tour ended in reasonable spirits, even if the band took to heckling Geezer from sidestage during his interminable bass solo.

Meanwhile, there'd been more trouble with the cover art for the UK release of *Dirty Deeds*. Atlantic, with my blessing, had assigned the prestigious UK designers Hipgnosis to design the image. They'd worked on album artwork for Pink Floyd, T. Rex and Led Zeppelin, among others, and were the leaders in the field, highly regarded. Atlantic's Phil Carson would state that the idea for *Dirty Deeds* was from some earlier project that had been rejected; he claimed to have had it lying around and recycled it to save some money and time. I dispute this, because I had meetings with the designers as it was being created.

Hipgnosis came up with a menacing image, which had a *One Flew Over the Cuckoo's Nest* kind of feel, featuring a selection of shady, sinister characters with their eyes blacked out, lurking ominously outside a cheap motel. I loved it. It was clever and timeless, but it turned out to be a bit too tricky for the AC/DC market, who liked things a bit less layered. There was no big love from the band towards the cover, but neither did they reject it. Hipgnosis were highly rated; it's fair to say everyone trusted them.

In September 1977, the band undertook their biggest tour so far, a 23-date with Ritchie Blackmore's Rainbow, promoting the *Let There Be Rock* album in Europe. The tour kicked off in Belgium, then headed to Scandinavia, where the dates were promoted by Erik Johansson. Ritchie and his band loved to play tricks on this likeable promoter. On one occasion Erik returned to his hotel room to find it totally empty of any furniture; it was completely stripped bare. He headed downstairs and returned with the hotel manager, by which time the band had restored the room to normal. It was a real mindfucker, the kind of thing that's necessary to relieve tension when you're on the road.

The tour went very well for AC/DC; the German audiences worked themselves into hysterics. But Ritchie had enormous problems with this giant electronic rainbow, which ran the width of the stage. It was forever shorting power supplies. Then there was that stressful night in Hamburg, when a harem of his ex-wives turned up at the show and sat in the front row, looking on. Backstage, loads of schnapps helped ease the man's pain.

Back in London during May, Malcolm said we needed to have an urgent meeting. I thought it might have been about Bon, who, despite his undeniable on-stage charisma and brilliance with lyrics (which Bon called his 'toilet poetry')—and shiny new chompers, courtesy of the British health scheme—spent most of his time away from the stage getting into some kind of trouble. He was overdoing the pills and the booze and, most likely, harder drugs. Bon was still with Silver, which didn't make things any easier. There was also grumbling from some quarters that Bon's voice was 'inaccessible' for the mass market, which most of us laughed off. He was a great rock'n'roll singer.

But Bon wasn't the problem. He may have caused Malcolm and Angus serious frustration at times—which can happen when you're not sure your singer has survived yet another binge—but they respected his talent and the contribution he made to the band. As for me, I always found Bon to be professional and reliable, in his own unique way.

Instead Malcolm and Angus had a problem with their bass player Mark Evans. Mark and Angus had been arguing about trivial stuff for a while; there'd been some simmering musical 'issues' and there was also the train wreck at the Reading

Festival, where Mark had expressed his frustration towards the placid crowd, for which he'd been duly caned by the Youngs afterwards. During that lively post-mortem, Mark had also made the mistake of trying to physically stop the brothers from killing each other. A family punch-up, as it turned out, was not the place for 'outsiders' like Mark to intervene.

Then there was an evening in London when Angus was holding court, as usual, mouthing off about The Beatles during their 1964 Australian tour. Mark called Angus on this, after figuring out that he would have been all of nine at the time. Mark asked a lot of questions—'How did you get to the show, Angus?' 'How much did the tickets cost?' and so on, which pissed Angus off badly. (Not hard, admittedly.) This may have been the last straw.

'He has to go,' Malcolm told me. 'And, Browning, you have to tell him.'

Perhaps Malcolm didn't quite grasp how significant this was. The band was everything to Mark, who'd come from a working-class background not vastly different to the Youngs', in the housing commission ghetto of Prahran. Now I had to tell Mark that his world, as he knew it, was coming to an end.

I knew that Mark would be shattered. Malcolm has been quoted to the effect that I chose Mark for the band, that it was a 'management decision', which isn't true. The first time I met Mark he was already playing in the band. I certainly nodded my approval because I thought that he looked great with them, but that was it. I wouldn't be able to say the same about his replacement.

As Mark documented in his great book *Dirty Deeds*, the sit-down took place in the flat shared by Malcolm and Angus. The entire band was there, even Bon, who spent most of the brief meeting with his arms crossed, staring at the ceiling. I got Mark a cup of tea and then told him straight.

'The guys in the band want to get another bass player,' I told him. I wasn't savouring this job as executioner.

Mark knew he had no option but to reluctantly accept the decision, although it was clear this was the last thing in the world he wanted. 'If that's what the guys want, Michael,' he mumbled. Within days I drove him to the airport for a flight back to Melbourne and a new, post-AC/DC life. His problems with the Youngs and Alberts lingered for years, but we've remained friends.

I didn't feel good about the decision—Mark seemed perfectly acceptable to me—but my job now was to make sure they found a replacement, and fast. The band's first tour of America, scheduled for November and December 1977, was looming very large on the horizon.

Angus Young showing the Poms who's boss at London's Marquee in July 1975. AC/DC established a new house record, with hundreds of people squeezing into the tiny room.

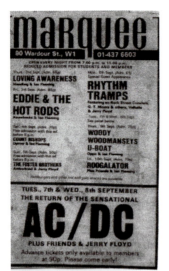

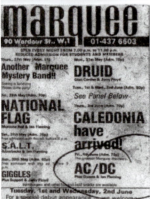

LEFT and BELOW: Various early UK listings for AC/DC, 1975, including the tour that never happened —with Paul Kossoff's Back Street Crawler.

BOTTOM: The band and I with The Beatles' press officer Derek Taylor (back row, middle), Atlantic's Dave Dee (back row, far left) and Phil Carson (front row, middle), who first signed the band. © Paul Canty

OPPOSITE TOP: A page from AC/DC's ATI accounts for August 1977, a time when they were still 'netting' as little as $250 per show. That would change soon enough.

OPPOSITE BOTTOM: Angus unleashes his 'snot cyclone' at London's Nashville club, April 1975 (bottom), while my first wife, Julie, and my sister Coral (centre) look on. Ralph the Roadie tries to keep up with Angus.

ARTIST'S STATEMENT

August 26, 1977

CONTRACT NUMBER	DESCRIPTION	DATE	ENGAGEMENT GROSS	DEPOSITS	COMMISSION	ADVANCES	EXPENSES	TOT.
	AC/DC							
17265	Armadillo World/Austin, Tex.	7/27/77	$ 350.00	$ -0-	$ 35.00			
17243	Mun. Aud./San Antonio, Tex.	7/28/77	1,000.00	500.00	100.00			
17241	Ritz Music Hall/Corpus Christi, Tex.	7/29/77	500.00	250.00	50.00			
17244	Aud./W. Palm Beach, Fla.	8/5/77	750.00	375.00	75.00			
17245	Col./Jacksonville, Fla.	8/6/77	6,761.78	1,750.00	676.18			
17287	Mississippi Nights/St. Louis, Mo.	8/9/77	400.00	400.00	40.00			
17282	Mem. Hall/Kansas City, Mo.	8/10/77	500.00	250.00	50.00			
17286	B'Ginnings/Schaumberg, Ill.	8/11/77	500.00	250.00	50.00			
17285	Agora/Columbus, O.	8/13-14/77	4,652.40	750.00	465.24			
17293	Stone Hearth/Madison, Wisc.	8/16/77	500.00	250.00	50.00			
17283	Riverside Thea./Milwaukee, Wisc.	8/17/77	500.00	250.00	50.00			
17284	Circle Thea./Indianapolis, Ind.	8/18/77	250.00	125.00	25.00			
17327	Hara Arena/Dayton, O.	8/19/77	750.00	250.00	75.00			
17343	Tomorrow Thea./Youngstown, O.	8/21/77	500.00	-0-	50.00			
17344	Agora/Cleveland, O.	8/22/77	500.00	-0-	50.00			
17340	Palladium/New York City, N.Y.	8/24/77	375.00	-0-	37.50			
	Purolator Sky Courier	6/21/77					$ 27.50	
	Copy Art	6/27/77					28.57	
	Copy Art	7/1/77					18.63	
	Harley I. Lewin, Esq.	7/1/77					500.00	
	Copy Art	7/25/77					13.99	
			$18,789.18	$5,400.00	$1,878.92		$588.69	
	Amount due AC/DC							$2,932.

18,789.18,
5900
12,389.18

TOP: The band receive the keys to the city of North Miami, August 1976, a PR exercise cooked up by Atlantic's Barry Bergman (back row, centre), whose cousin was the mayor.

ABOVE: Bon, whom one critic described as sounding like a 'weasel on heat', with yet another of his female admirers. There was a sensitive soul behind the leer. © News Ltd/Newspix

TOP LEFT: Angus and Bon prepare to take on the American winter and a new audience, 1977, travelling pretty rough in a rented station wagon.

TOP RIGHT: Coral and Billie in the UK office, Billie doing her bit to plug *Let There Be Rock*. My family life was intertwined with AC/DC's for the years we worked together.

ABOVE: AC/DC during their first US tour, 1977. Atlantic's Michael Klenfner (back row, with moustache), was a huge supporter in America, along with Perry Cooper (in glasses).

TOP: Back briefly in Sydney, I try my hand at 'tagging', while Bon, Malcolm and Alberts' Fifa Riccabono look on. Why I'm dressed up as a police officer escapes me. © Philip Morris

ABOVE: Coral (behind Angus), me (back row) and UK WEA staff with the band, celebrating the release of *Let There Be Rock*, July 1977. © Chris Horler

TOP: Bon and Angus backstage in Atlanta, Georgia, 1978. The 'Bon and Angus show' was an integral part of AC/DC's trailblazing early days. Great chemistry. © Rennie Ellis Photographic Archive

ABOVE: Bon with the groupies known as the 'Heathen Girls', 1978. Bon loved touring the US, where the groupies were many and generous—and the dreaded 'jack' was scarce.

© Rennie Ellis Photographic Archive

As soon as I met INXS's Michael Hutchence, I knew he was something special (above).
Just like Bon, however, he blazed too brightly and died way too young.
I signed Michael and INXS to my label Deluxe.

I Send A Message

(Andrew Farriss & Michael Hutchence)

INXS

on WEA records

DELUXE MUSIC PTY. LTD.

Sole Selling Agents
chappell music
99 FORBES ST. WOOLLOOMOOLOO, N.S.W
P.O. BOX KX250, KINGS CROSS, 2011

$2.75

I thought Heaven had what it took to break America, then realised the odyssey was more about me than the band (top). Lead singer 'Uncle Allan' Fryer with my daughter, Billie (above).

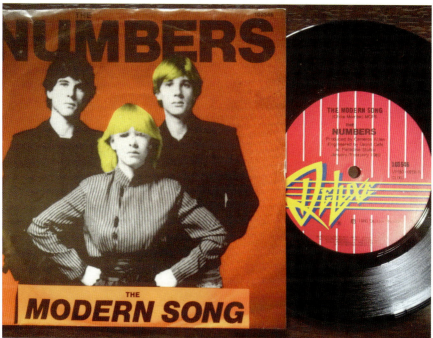

TOP: Warrior were an American hard rock outfit I signed to Richard Branson's Virgin label.
They were way ahead of their time but failed to connect.

ABOVE: Sydney three-piece The Numbers, another early signing to my label Deluxe.
They were the definitive cool, early 1980s inner-city band, loved by critics.

JON STEVENS   9.92   COLUMBIA

LEFT and OPPOSITE: Jon Stevens, whom I spotted on *Countdown* in the early 1980s when he was a solo star in New Zealand. Jon and I worked together after Noiseworks split.

BELOW: I managed and helped develop The Change, better known as Noiseworks, into one of the biggest Australian bands of the late 1980s and early '90s.

Noiseworks stopped the city when they played on the steps of Victoria's Parliament House in early 1989, not far from where my journey began in Melbourne's clubs many years earlier.

TOP: Jon Stevens (in cap), my lawyer Warren Cross (back row, far right) and various Sony staffers, including Chris Moss (back row, far left) and MD Denis Handlin (front row, second from left), signing Jon as a solo act.

ABOVE: With my family (from left to right)—Bert, Rosie, Elizabeth, Billie and James, to whom this book is dedicated. © Tim Wirth

Bon was right—it truly is a long way to the top if you want to rock'n'roll.
Photographed in Sydney, June 2014. © Paul Christie

TAKING ON AMERICA

For Mark's replacement, Malcolm and Angus were keen on recruiting Colin Pattenden, from Manfred Mann's Earth Band, who'd impressed them when they saw the band play back in Australia. This seemed to contradict something Malcolm told me early on: 'Good bass,' he said, 'should be felt and not heard.' Colin was too distinctive a player for that. He was also too old for the band, as shallow as that sounds. I strongly believed that the last thing AC/DC needed was someone from another era who might be written off by fans as some 'old fart'. Image has always been crucial in rock'n'roll; AC/DC was no different. Colin wasn't approached.

I called Barry Earl, an Aussie friend of mine who'd been

living in London for some time and knew a lot of people in the business. I offered him a ten quid 'spotter's fee' if he could find a good candidate for the job.

A couple of days later he called.

'There's this guy Cliff Williams,' he told me.

Cliff had previously played with the bands Home and Wishbone Ash and, crucially, knew a bit about AC/DC, having seen them a few times on TV.

I met with Cliff the next day. He certainly looked the part, even if he may have been a bit too good-looking for the job. He had a solid reputation as a player and seemed like a good guy, somebody who'd fit in and contribute to the band's overall appeal without overshadowing the 'Bon and Angus Show'. The next thing was to get him over the line with the group.

I'd given Cliff a heads-up about a couple of things: I told him to learn the song 'High Voltage' inside out, because that's what they'd jam in an audition. I also told him that the Youngs preferred their bassist to use a pick—and he had to hit those strings hard. With that stored away, off he went to the audition.

The next day Malcolm called me.

'He's perfect.'

I didn't let slip the advice I'd given Cliff, but everyone came out a winner—certainly Cliff. AC/DC had their new bass player who'd just nailed the gig. The drama with Mark was consigned to history, Barry Earl got his ten quid and everyone headed off to the land of opportunity, also known to some as the Highway to Hell.

◾

Atlantic Records America had released the *High Voltage* LP in late 1976, combining tracks from the Australian versions of *High Voltage* and the *TNT* albums. They repackaged it with a photo of Angus on the front cover and put it out to radio, without much of an effort or anything resembling a marketing campaign. *Rolling Stone* did review the album, but they hated it, slagging Bon ('truly annoying'), Angus (taking an easy shot at his schoolboy outfit) and the album itself, stating: 'Stupidity bothers me. Calculated stupidity offends me.' They'd come to eat those words.

Not surprisingly, little happened for the band or the record, with the exception of a few pockets of interest, one being in Jacksonville, Florida, where the local radio station programmed the whole album and kept it 'in rotation'. The other was in the college town of Columbus, Ohio, where they also received a massive amount of airplay—and some decent sales.

This was an encouraging sign, just what we needed to convince Jerry Greenberg and Atlantic's new A&R guy, John Kalodner, that the band had legs. Jim Delahunt, who'd considered AC/DC too meat and potatoes for his sophisticated taste, was gone.

Along with some not-so-gentle prodding from Phil Carson, it was enough to get Jerry and Kalodner on a plane to Hamburg to see AC/DC play for the first time, in April 1977. Phil Carson joined us. This was a huge opportunity, the chance we'd been hoping for. If it went well, it was a case of 'USA, here we come'— way beyond the tour we had lined up. But if it went the other way we might be in the market for a new label.

As it turned out, much to my and Phil Carson's relief, John Kalodner loved them; it seemed that unlike Delahunt, AC/DC was right up his alley. We needed an ally like Kalodner.

It was a win–win situation: Jerry was happy and Kalodner had just discovered the dirtiest rock'n'roll band on the planet. (He'd later sign the even-dirtier Guns N' Roses to Geffen Records.) Jerry thought it appropriate to celebrate (we didn't argue) and he treated us all to a lads' night out on the Reeperbahn in the red-light district, which ended with a live sex show at a spot close to the Star Club, where The Beatles had learned many of their early life lessons. In an extreme example of multi-tasking, the sex club's bouncer doubled as the male participant in the show.

Back in New York, Jerry appointed a new executive, Michael Klenfner, who he'd just poached from Arista Records. Michael was an imposing figure, a big man with an even bigger moustache, from Brighton Beach, Brooklyn. He'd joined Atlantic as Senior Vice-President. Michael had done time in virtually every aspect of the music business, starting at legendary venue the Fillmore

East as 'outside security man'. Over the years he and famous promoter Bill Graham became extremely close friends. When Michael was approached about the role of program director at WNEW-FM, Graham said he'd fire him if he *didn't* take the job. Scott Muni, another of Michael's mentors, did the poaching.

From there, Michael became Columbia Records' first album promo man, which brought him to the attention of label boss Clive Davis, who made him Vice-President of Arista Records. Michael was then brought into Atlantic to shake things up, something he was especially good at. AC/DC, the label's problematic band from Oz, was his first priority.

I met with Michael in New York for lunch, not long after our Hamburg breakthrough. We caught the lift downstairs and walked out into the street. Next door to Atlantic's HQ was the 21 Club, an exclusive haunt of the rich and famous. As we neared 21, I thought to myself, 'What a great way to start a working relationship.' But then he stopped just short of the club's entrance, at his favourite hot-dog stand. He ordered us two dogs with mustard and ketchup, as my dream of fine dining at the 21 Club swiftly dissolved. There are some people in the music industry who are renowned for doing great lunch but Klenfner clearly wasn't one of them. I was getting way ahead of myself.

However, Michael was extremely well connected. On another occasion we were meeting in his office at Atlantic when there was a commotion. Michael's best friend, comic and actor John Belushi, was in the building.

'I've just heard on the radio,' Belushi wailed, bursting into Michael's office. 'Elvis is dead!'

I was saddened by the news—Elvis had inspired me to a life in music—but equally impressed by the company Klenfner was keeping. Michael would play a huge role in Belushi's future as a Blues Brother.

Michael brought over a colleague from Arista, Perry Cooper, who was appointed Atlantic's Director of Artist Relations. I quickly learned Perry was really great at following up on detail, making sure all the right things happened. He was very good at schmoozing with the band and keeping everyone happy—if they needed tickets to baseball games and gigs whenever they were in New York, Perry was the go-to guy.

J. Albert & Son's publishing interests in the US were represented by the New York publishing house Edward B. Marks Music. It was an old family business, not unlike Alberts, which had been established in 1894. It became one of Tin Pan Alley's most successful publishers. Edward B. Marks Music held a wealth of old copyrights, representing a who's who of African-American and Latin composers, including the Billie Holiday catalogue.

In 1977, the company was headed by Joe Oshlander, a sweet and caring guy not too far out from retirement age. Joe had been with the company for years and had seen the lot—or at least he thought that was the case until AC/DC entered his world. Here they were, a company steeped in musical culture and history, about to be invaded by a bunch of scruffy rockers from Australia with a lyricist who referred to his work as 'toilet poetry'. It was quite the shift for E.B. Marks.

Joe had recently hired a new professional manager named Barry Bergman, a young Jewish stockbroker with a Groucho Marx accent. Barry had decided to get out of Wall Street and follow his music industry dreams. When Barry commenced work at E.B. Marks he discovered that despite their wonderful heritage, they hadn't signed new songwriters of any significance in a long time. The company was in a sort of suspended animation, trapped in the past.

In 1976, an opportunity arose to sign the publishing rights of an up-and-comer calling himself Meatloaf, along with his writing partner, Jim Steinman. Barry forced the issue and they made the deal. Despite a slow start, Meatloaf's debut album, *Bat Out of Hell*, became a massive worldwide hit. Barry was now out to get the AC/DC project up and running in the United States.

Publishers had become known as the bankers of the music industry; they'd generally pay an advance to a writer against future royalties, in order to secure rights, but often that was the last you'd hear from them for some time. Barry was determined to change this perception.

While I ate hot dogs in a summery New York, the band was in London breaking in their new bass player Cliff, who they found fitted neatly into the whole AC/DC psyche. They were preparing themselves for their next onslaught on the highway to hell. Julie, Billie and my sister Coral remained in London for the time being, while I threw myself into the deep end in Manhattan.

Barry, Joe and I met and took an instant shine to each other. Joe even helped out with some office space from which I could run the management company. When he discovered we were about to embark on a US tour without credit cards, he very generously gave us an Exxon Card. At least we could pay for our gas.

Barry, meanwhile, hit the phones, along with an early ally at Atlantic, Beth Rosengard. Together they called radio stations, drumming up some airplay for the band's US debut, 'High Voltage', on the fiercely sought-after FM stations and college radio.

So between Jerry Greenberg, John Kalodner (aka the Rabbi), Michael Klenfner (whom the band christened Tons of Fun), Perry 'The Worm' Cooper, 'Gentleman' Joe and Barry 'Bilko' Bergman, we had quite the team in place, all with suitable nicknames. Barry wasn't especially happy about being likened to the famous TV sergeant, but the name did fit.

So here I was, a 'tolerated Goy', as a Jewish friend of mine described me, surrounded by a posse of ambitious New York

Jews, out to do whatever was required to make things happen for the band. How could it fail? I had a lot of fun with the team, learning Yiddish and discovering the delights of their cuisine. The venerable Carnegie Deli on Seventh Avenue became part of my daily routine.

I appointed Doug Thaler as AC/DC's US agent. Doug, who'd seen the band in London, was with the heavyweight agency ATI. Doug was a former muso, who'd been in a band called The Black Sheep that had once played with The Easybeats. A great guy with a hot temper, Doug was as driven as the rest of the team, fiercely committed to the band. (He'd go on to co-manage Mötley Crüe.) ATI was the big rock agency of the day, a company that knew how to package rock tours and get them into small to medium-sized arenas. With our first US date set down for 27 July 1977 in Austin, Texas, this was exactly what we needed.

◼

AC/DC was all about momentum. While in Australia, our target had been to get to the UK and get a record deal. Once established there, we had our eyes on the bigger prize, America. We just kept rolling towards our next collective goal. It all now seemed very much within reach.

But America was different to the UK and parts of Europe, where word can spread quickly about a band through print media. America was going to be a long, hard slog; in some ways it was like having to make inroads into 50 Britains, one state at a time. You could be big in Florida and unheard of in New York, massive in Texas and nobodies in California. Most big cities had their own radio stations and media, their own favourite acts. We understood the challenge but were totally up for it.

Loaded up with the help of our new best friends, Ryder Truck Rentals, the crew left New York in late July 1977 headed for Texas. The band and I followed on an Austin-bound flight. There was no way I was going to miss witnessing the first run of AC/DC dates in America, first in Texas and then Florida, where the band already had solid radio support.

Excitement was running high in the band, at least as high as it could within a group as outwardly reserved as AC/DC. The bass player drama was now behind them, as was Silver—Bon escaped to America a free man. And boy was he in for one lively ride.

On arrival in Texas we hired a station wagon from Budget, another company about to do well from AC/DC. It was our ride for the entire six-week tour. We drove straight to Austin's Red Roof Inn, America's cheapest hotel chain and yet another soon-to-be regular AC/DC haunt. The place was no Hilton; it was right next to the freeway in the shabby end of town, although the swimming pool and hot Texan weather lifted our spirits.

I was given a token tour support budget from Atlantic, moderate to say the least. Straight away, I was the brunt of the band's 'tightarse' jibes, but I knew if I was going to be able to keep them on the road in America for some time, which I felt was essential, I had to be tight-fisted. There were no luxuries or rock star indulgences. US-based bands would rock up to their gigs in elaborate tour buses, whereas AC/DC would arrive in the station wagon, sometimes having to convince security that we were actually that evening's entertainment.

That first night in Austin, after settling in, we experienced our first taste of American hospitality. The Atlantic promo guy took us out for an authentic Texan-style Brontosaurus steak dinner. We'd heard that everything was bigger in Texas and here was the proof. They ate dinosaurs.

The next day it was down to business. AC/DC's first US gig was at the Armadillo World Headquarters, a big barn of a venue, sort of a Texan version of the Matthew Flinders Hotel in Victoria. There was a capacity crowd of about 1500, mostly young males, all of whom seemed to have slugged down a six-pack on the way to the gig and were now off their faces on pot. The venue, after all, was partly owned by Willie Nelson, country music great and marijuana advocate.

AC/DC was opening for the Canadian band Moxy. The place was hot and steamy and reeked of pot. I'd seen condensation running down walls at the Marquee gigs in London, but tonight there was what looked like a gushing waterfall of sweat coating the walls. When mixed with the smoke coming from the many joints circulating the room, it looked as though cloud cover was forming inside the venue. Phil Rudd was right in his element, as this was his kind of rowdy place, while the rest of the band looked like they were playing under the shower. When Angus did his usual once-round-the-venue routine perched on Bon's shoulders, he probably got stoned for the first time in his life, courtesy of second-hand dope smoke. Thanks, Willie.

The Texans lapped it up. After the gig in the dressing room, Angus removed the plastic pick-up cover on his SG Gibson guitar and emptied out what looked like half a pint of rank sweat. AC/DC's first American gig had the lot: pot, drunks, sweat, stink. If the rest of the tour was going to follow suit, we might just score a home run.

Next stop was the Fox Theatre in San Antonio, a city that claimed to be the 'Rock & Roll Capital of the World'. It was hard to argue with the claim; nowhere in the world had I seen locals so passionate about 'kickass rock'n'roll'. (Love those American terms.) The city lived and breathed rock and AC/DC delivered exactly what they wanted. It was a huge buzz to watch this going down; the band was really connecting.

When I was a kid, I was obsessed with the *Davy Crockett* TV show; a model of his hat was one of my prized possessions. So away from the music it didn't get any better for me than being in the place where the King of the Wild Frontier had made a name for himself. As for the band, they shrugged it off, showing little interest. The thing they lived for was getting up and playing.

Life on the road was about to get a little smoother. Atlantic Records were starting to receive some good feedback and helped us out with a little touring money. Even Angus had stopped whingeing. That was a blessing.

Corpus Christi was next, passing thru Lubbock, the home of Buddy Holly, along the way. The landscape was so flat and boring I couldn't help wonder what the guy did there other than make some amazing music. Probably nothing. I'm sure he wrote about a mountain somewhere nearby, where horny teens would go 'parking'. Maybe it was just in the man's vivid imagination.

And so on went the tour and the band, one foot in front of the other. But it wasn't a grind, it was a blast; the place felt very much like home. Texans seemed to love AC/DC, especially the vivacious, long-legged groupies, who'd pursue the band in their flashy Pontiac Trans Ams and Chevy Corvettes. This was a whole new concept for the band; the girls in Melbourne would get around on buses or trams, and hang about until the band got the shits (or the jack) and turfed them out. Not now. Once the Texan girls got what they came for, they'd simply jump in their sports cars and head off to our next destination.

Never before in his life had Bon been more in his element. He quickly flicked the band's station wagon for his admirers' sportier rides. There were no irate fathers to deal with, and the best-looking groupies on the planet were hanging on his every word—and attending to his every need. For Bon and the band it was the beginning of a long and mutual love affair with the Lone Star State, and its citizens. Especially the women.

We reluctantly left Texas, headed for Florida. The first date was at the West Palm Beach Auditorium, supporting arguably the world's most boring band (with a name to match), REO Speedwagon. Ironically, they were managed by a young Irving Azoff, one of the music biz's more interesting characters. He eventually made a big name for himself as the manager of the Eagles. I guess he had to start somewhere.

The Coliseum at Jacksonville was AC/DC's first American headlining gig; they played to a full house of 11,000 newly converted fans. We had some traction in Jacksonville thanks to Bill Bartlett, the Program Manager from WBQ FM, who'd programmed the entire *High Voltage* album, which he'd played even when it was an 'import' and not yet available Stateside. He was a real trailblazer for the band; I hoped Atlantic would pay attention and see if they could replicate this throughout the US.

When Bill first played 'It's a Long Way to the Top', he said the station's phones 'lit up'. AC/DC even outpolled Southern rock poster boys Lynyrd Skynyrd, a massive achievement. Interestingly, when an Atlantic rep first paid a call on Bill, the rep had two records to pitch: the American release of *High Voltage*, along with a release from a newly signed band named Fotomaker, under his arm. The latter was his priority; the order from Atlantic was to get Fotomaker 'added' to WBQ's playlist.

The rep was surprised to find that the station was housed in a one-room tin shed, on a lonely highway, miles from nowhere, its only distinguishing feature the big rooftop-mounted aerial. Bill thanked the rep for both records and promptly turned his attention to AC/DC. It's fair to say that Bill almost single-handedly saved the band in America. Without his support Atlantic would probably have dumped them. I'm not sure what happened to Fotomaker.

The Jacksonville gig was a triumph. Afterwards, there was a big backstage gathering of the local bands and music community, invited by the local promoter and well-known Jacksonville scoundrel Sidney Drashin. Doug had warned me about Sidney. 'When you do the reconciliation at the end of the night,' he joked, 'watch out for dog tags instead of ticket stubs.' When Drashin had promoted a Deep Purple/ZZ Top show at the Coliseum a few years earlier, he'd been forced to break into a local music store in the dead of night to find the right guitar for Ritchie Blackmore. Anything for the show.

Sidney had invited Jacksonville's favourite sons Lynyrd Skynyrd to the gig. They'd heard AC/DC a lot on WBQ FM and were keen to see them play and hang out at what was essentially Skynyrd HQ. A strong friendship formed that night backstage.

Just to bring us back to earth with a thud, the next night, 7 August, we played to barely 100 people in Fort Lauderdale, Florida. Everyone was gutted; it was a bleak reminder of how far we still had to climb. Next stop was Miami, for Atlantic's annual convention. We had a free night, and decided to go shark fishing in a chartered boat in waters very close to the Bermuda Triangle.

Angus's idea of a big night away from the stage was spent eating, smoking, watching TV serials and practising his guitar licks, ideally at the same time. Shark fishing wasn't his style. In fact, anything involving the great outdoors wasn't his style, so he passed. But for the rest of us, the fishing trip was an interesting experience; we'd haul in the sharks and while we looked on the guys who ran the boat would put them out of their misery. With a baseball bat.

We hadn't really thought this through. I mean, what do you do with a hefty catch of sharks? In the back of the guys' minds, they were hoping some of their new female friends might cook up something special, so we decided to store the sharks in the hotel's ice machine. This was fine until the management discovered our catch and all hell broke loose. They were never going to get the stench of those poor battered sharks out of their machine. Being on the road does make you do some crazy things. We should have eaten the damn things and not been so wasteful.

The next day we were given the keys to the city of North Miami at a civic reception held in the band's honour. It seemed pretty impressive but in fact it was a savvy little promotional effort cooked up by Barry Bergman, whose cousin happened to be Mayor Michael Colodny. Later that day, along with country act the Charlie Daniels Band—of 'The Devil Went Down to Georgia' fame—they performed at a charity event named Day for the Kids, to raise money for muscular dystrophy. It was held at the Hollywood Florida Sportatorium.

During this Miami visit we met up with a guy passing himself off as Randy Bachman, from the band Bachman-Turner Overdrive ('You Ain't Seen Nothing Yet'). This imposter took us all for a ride, literally and otherwise, in his limo to Disneyworld, via a music store where he conned all sorts of gear, pretending he had a sponsorship deal, which he then lavished on the band. His rental limos, we found out later, had been fraudulently acquired. The guy was obviously very disturbed, but he was a dead ringer for the real Randy. The only giveaway, on reflection, was that he smoked; I'd read somewhere that the real Randy hated cigarettes so much that he'd install fans on stage to blow the smoke back towards the audience. After we said our goodbyes, the limo company told us he'd absconded without paying them, confirming our suspicions. For a while there, though, he really had us going.

The Atlantic Records convention was staged in your typical low-ceilinged, Mafia-run joint called the 4 O'Clock Club. It came 'equipped' with the worst acoustics and the least band-friendly environment I'd seen for some time. It's always puzzled me why venues that trade on live talent put so little effort into creating a good vibe. The musos' comfort always seems to figure last. This was hardly the best way for the band to play a showcase for the very people whose job it was to build their career.

The band plugged in and commenced to play at their usual glass-shattering level, but not for long. Michael Klenfner was designated with the unenviable task of telling them to turn it down, a dangerous job at the best of times. They had no choice but to comply. The band got through the gig and endured the usual post-show schmoozing, with no-name execs crapping on about how 'You guys really killed it!', when only an hour before they had been demanding that the band turn it down so they could chat. Talk about having to sing for your supper. Just not too loudly.

When we reached St Louis, we had another dodgy gig at another dodgy Mafioso club, this one called the Mississippi Nights. The subject of volume came up again, but this time the band decided to not take any more crap. I'd had a gutful of venues like this, willing to book heavy rock bands and then complaining about the noise. The guys felt the same. We were forced to fight our way out of the club, quite literally, with a little help from Phil Carson, visiting from London, who turned out to be pretty handy in the aggro department.

This wasn't the last problem we had on what was a key tour. When we reached the Palladium in New York on 24 August, sharing a bill with The Dictators and the Michael Stanley Band, we were screwed over by the production crew, who denied us a soundcheck. *Who cared, right?*, they seemed to think—we were only the support band. But we were stuck; this was New York, a big music centre, so we were forced to play. The band grumbled about being shafted and then got on with the job. With Bon and Angus in blazing form, they blew the so-called headliners clear off the stage. It wasn't the first or the last time this would happen with AC/DC.

After the Palladium, Klenfner had organised a late-late gig in the Bowery, at CBGB, the ground zero of East Coast punk. This hole-in-the-wall venue had given rise to the Ramones and Patti Smith and Television. Typically, this would have been a no-go zone for AC/DC, who didn't relate to punk rock in any way, but this was the only chance for Ahmet Ertegun, Nesuhi Ertegun's brother and legendary chairman and founder of Atlantic, to eyeball the band. In its own way, having Ahmet see the band and get on board was as important as any gig on the 1977 summer tour.

AC/DC had honed their skills in venues like this; sweaty, cramped, dingey dives, and they more than held their own, connecting with an audience of NYC punks in a way that surprised the band. We all met Ahmet backstage, who was a very charming and charismatic man. I would come to learn that Jerry Greenberg used Ahmet as a sort of secret weapon in matters of artist relations. Musos loved him; they were in awe of his rich musical background and air of sophistication. He was very tight with stars like Robert Plant, Jimmy Page and Mick Jagger.

Ahmet was later overheard saying that AC/DC were a 'little derivative and scruffy', but he could see their potential. That was all we really needed to hear.

The next morning we flew west, for a three-night stand at Whisky A Go Go in LA, another famous American venue. During the tour, Klenfner had introduced Bon and Angus to Ken Schafer, the inventor of the wireless guitar and microphone. This was handy, because a feature of the Angus and Bon Show was disappearing into the audience, usually with Angus perched on Bon's shoulders. The crew would frantically follow in their wake, hoping they had enough guitar lead for the job, or that it didn't get tangled up in the usual melee in the audience. Ken flew to the LA gig, specifically to present Angus with a wireless transmitter and Bon with a wireless mic. A whole new world opened up for the pair; they were now officially free to roam.

Ken was a technical genius, no doubt about it. There'd been an annoying buzz in the Whisky's sound system for years. When someone mentioned the problem to Ken while he spoke with us, he excused himself and tracked it down to the cash register at the front of house. Problem solved.

An unlikely face backstage after the gig was Johnny Young, the host of Australian TV's *Young Talent Time*. Given how squeaky-clean and family-friendly that show was, you just wouldn't have expected to spot him at a rock show in sleazy LA. But Johnny was an old friend of Bon's from the days in Perth; he didn't seem too concerned. Johnny had just driven around America on vacation with his son.

'You have no idea how sore my arse is,' he told Bon.

Unfortunately, Bon had forgotten to flick off his wireless mic. Now a full house at the Whisky knew the unfortunate state of Johnny Young's arse.

Also among the usual backstage gathering of musos, groupies and label people was Iggy Pop, who dropped in with his entourage. Bon was particularly impressed. Another new fan in attendance was Gene Simmons from shock rockers KISS, a big AC/DC convert. He especially liked Angus and invited the two of us to a late night supper at Denny's Diner on Sunset. Gene was a great talker and kept us engaged for hours. He also proposed some shared dates on KISS's upcoming US tour.

Over supper, talk turned to Angus's wireless transmitter. Gene revealed that he was on the verge of discovering a frequency that, when transmitted through the PA at a show, would drive women to orgasm. It was a great story—who cared if he was simply blowing smoke.

For the most part, AC/DC's first US foray had been a huge success. The band had laid down foundations for the future, struck up new connections, won over Atlantic staffers, gained some airplay and broken some hearts. Hardly the kind of band to sit back and smell the roses, they now flew to London where within days they'd start their biggest tour of the UK. Talk about take no prisoners.

MY VERY OWN ROCK'N'ROLL DAMNATION

It was good to be back in London. It was still where I based my operations and where Julie and Billie lived. We'd rented a house in Belgravia Mews, owned by Lady Lucan, wife of Lord Lucan. The Mews was attached to the main house, the scene of the murder of their nanny a few years earlier that Lord Lucan had been accused of committing, before his sudden disappearance. The place had some strange history.

The AC/DC office was housed in a converted garage, which was originally the stable. Clearly I'd been away for a while—some months—because Billie didn't have a clue who I was when I got back from the States. Still, it felt like home, the food tasted real—and I could get a decent cup of tea. Julie was pregnant again, too, with our second child, James.

The band's upcoming UK tour was promoted by Midland Concert Promotions—MCP—a company headed by Maurice Jones, a jovial and well-heeled music man from Birmingham. It was Maurice's first major national tour as promoter, and another big run of dates for the band. Maurice liked to give me grief about not attending the few AC/DC gigs he'd already promoted in and around Birmingham, but I laughed it off—he was someone we all got to know and trust. He was a good friend of Robert Plant from Led Zeppelin and was forever telling me that AC/DC needed to get even heavier, 'a bit more Zeppelin-ish'. (In hindsight, maybe he was onto something, because the band did grow a bit heavier over time.)

Maurice invited us all over for dinner one night during the tour, hosting us at his sprawling period home in outer Birmingham. Angus took a stroll around Maurice's pride and joy, his sizeable and beautifully manicured garden, which he off-handedly referred to as a 'backyard'. Maurice was underwhelmed. Backyard, indeed.

Most of the shows were sold out, and the tour included two full houses at London's Hammersmith Odeon in late October 1977, a major venue and a big accomplishment for everyone involved. The scope of the event was somewhat lost on Bon, who only showed up about 15 minutes before the gig, looking a bit confused. With no regard whatsoever towards my 'no public transport' policy, Bon had made his own way to the gig on the Tube—and duly boarded the wrong train. I hired a photographer to shoot the Sold Out sign on the marquee; Bon turned up in the background of the shot, wandering around in search of backstage.

By now, with Christmas 1977 fast approaching, the band had established itself as a legitimate live attraction in Britain and Europe. It was time to knuckle down to the huge challenge of achieving the same level of success in the United States, the centre of the musical universe. As much as I loved London, and as much as I'd miss a good cup of tea, I would set up an office in New York, where Coral would work with me—and this time I was taking Julie and Billie. World domination awaited.

The hardships Bon had written about in 'It's a Long Way to the Top' were ringing very true: things were tight. A tropical island getaway would have been very welcome, but it wasn't going to happen any time soon. However, we were all down for the long haul; on that, the band and I were united.

From the band's very beginnings, the AC/DC logo was designed in handwritten graffiti style, with the lightning flash between the two sets of letters. It was now album art time for the upcoming *Let There Be Rock* album, and I met with designer Bob Defrin, who was the head of Atlantic's New York art department. Bob didn't love the existing logo. Influenced by the new album's (sort of) biblical title, he produced an early version of what would become the band's signature logo. With my okay, he then commissioned graphic designer Gerard Huerta to produce the finished piece.

Bob and I sat in his office, unaware of the significance of the moment. It's a rare day now that I don't see that logo, on a T-shirt, a cap, an album cover. It's everywhere, West, East, Free World, Third World—even cred-hungry supermodels get around nowadays in an AC/DC T-shirt. It's one of rock'n'roll's best-known icons and a huge merchandising money-spinner.

Bob became a key player in the development of the band's image, working on numerous album covers, including the notorious *If You Want Blood (You've Got It)* cover, which shows Bon hovering menacingly over an impaled Angus.

The band's second US tour commenced in mid-November 1977 in Poughkeepsie, New York State, supporting the Canadian prog rock band Rush, another not-quite-right match-up. Then they headed south on another of ATI's tour packages, this time with British metal act UFO and pub rock band The Motors. Those dates ran through to early December, when the band returned to New York.

Perry Cooper from Atlantic had an idea for a live album, to be recorded at the Atlantic studios—a promo for WQ10 in Philadelphia, attended by competition winners. The resulting album was pressed and packaged as an FM radio-only release, and has since become a collectible. (My one copy, perhaps the only one in Australia, was stolen from my house many years later. I caught the thief trying to sell it, after a tip-off from a record store. At least the bastard had good taste.)

The band's anywhere/everywhere approach continued, as they played Knoxville, Chicago, Milwaukee, Memphis and seemingly all points in between, sharing bills with Cheap Trick and the Blue Oyster Cult. They also opened for KISS, Gene Simmons staying true to his word. As far as I could see, no women in the crowd had spontaneous orgasms, although I'm sure Gene tried his best.

I kept tabs on things from my office in New York, joining the tour for key shows and special events. Okay, I'll admit that if they were playing in a place I was keen to visit, I'd check that gig out, too. But I found touring an extremely tedious affair; at least the band had a stage and an audience to look forward to at the end of the day, something creative and satisfying. I just had another hotel room and a long list of calls to return.

My creative desires were fulfilled in the office. But it did leave me wondering sometimes what other managers were out there, circling the guys. The band would also sometimes question what I was up to back in AC/DC HQ. It was a tricky situation—there was essential work to do in the office to keep the machine working, but I sometimes wished I could be in two places at the same time.

Even a band built for the road like AC/DC hit the occasional pothole. I'd learn that Phil Rudd suffered from occasional anxiety attacks. Phil, a motoring fanatic and a wizard behind the wheel, loved to drive, and in America that sometimes meant driving for as much as 1500 kilometres a day, through all kinds of extreme weather. This could take its toll on anyone. I do wonder, though, whether Phil's anxiety might have been brought on by the fair amount of pot he was smoking. Cheap Trick's drummer Bun E. Carlos chipped in to help during one gig, when Phil wasn't up to it. Bon was feeling a little strain, too, but that was mainly with the lyrics for the upcoming album sessions. Bon's rep as a rock'n'roll street poet was spreading; he had to come up with more stuff that was funny and irreverent and honest, his lyrical trademarks.

The last date of another bridges-building US tour was on 21 December at the Stanley Theatre in Pittsburgh. Then all of us, with the exception of Cliff, flew home to Sydney to commence recording work with Harry and George on *Powerage*, studio album number five. The AC/DC bandwagon just kept on rolling.

There was a problem, though. Cliff didn't have a working visa for Australia, and the Australian Musicians Union—then a ragged mob of crusty and embittered musos—were advising the immigration department against granting him a visa. The way the union saw it, Cliff was denying an Australian musician work. I'm sure only the recently departed Mark Evans saw it that way.

Cliff lingered in the US while I sorted this out. After much negotiating and persuasion—'No, Mr Williams is not taking the food out of someone's mouth' and all of that—his visa was finally granted. He reached Alberts in January 1978, just in time for the recording sessions.

■

The recording of the new album spread over January and February, a little longer than usual. But the stakes were now significantly higher. Harry, George and the band knew they needed to deliver a powerful musical statement—and, ideally, a hot radio track or two for the American market.

When the work was finally concluded, Cliff and I returned to London. Julie, Billie and our newborn son James, meanwhile, stayed in Australia, in a house I'd managed to buy a few years earlier, in North Sydney. I needed to set plans in motion for continued touring and the release of *Powerage*, which was scheduled for worldwide release in May. The rest of the band planned to follow in the next few weeks.

In London, during a night out with Cliff, we started talking about the new record.

'What do you think of it?' Cliff asked me.

Typically, I kept my opinion to myself, at least until I sat down with the entire band and talked things through. But a few weeks had passed and I'd had time to digest the new music. I felt that I could confide in Cliff.

'I have mixed feelings,' I admitted. 'Personally, I love it—it's got good songs and great grooves. Bon's vocals are bluesy and soulful. But,' I added, 'my gut's telling me that it doesn't have the right songs for radio in England and America.'

It was a strange thing: I genuinely felt that the record made the right kind of statement, that the band were growing bigger and bolder. Their fans would get it and love it—even Keith Richards, when he heard the record, said, 'You can hear it; it has the spirit.' And if anyone knew about rock'n'roll spirit, it was Keith. But at that time I was worried about radio's reaction to the record, and that, too, was critical. To me, the hits, the big songs, just weren't there.

Cliff was a bit shocked. It was his first record with the band and he loved playing on it. The other guys felt likewise, he told me. I'm not sure if Cliff ever relayed my opinion to the rest of the band, but my instinct proved to be correct. Soon after that discussion I got a call from Phil Carson at Atlantic.

'I'm just not sure there's anything here I can take to radio,' Phil told me. He insisted that the band get back with Harry and George and cut some hotter tracks.

Not surprisingly, the band and their producers were unhappy—they truly believed they'd given it their all and come up with their best album yet. Still, they knew they had no real choice but to do as Atlantic directed.

AC/DC was a band that responded well to a crisis. They returned to the studio and emerged with 'Rock 'n' Roll Damnation', which became the band's first British Top 40 hit in June. Atlantic's rejection had brought about a breakthrough.

Breaking the Top 40 meant that Atlantic was able to book the band onto *Top of the Pops*. This was a standard British label marketing strategy: get the single into the Top 40 by selling enough records via a concentrated effort during a given week. Then get them on this much-watched TV show, whose rule was to book only artists with a single in the Top 40. Hopefully, with a powerful performance the single would take on a life of its own and continue selling on its merits.

At least that was the plan.

There was a British musician union rule stating that for a song to be heard on *TOTPs*, it had to have been recorded in the UK, which wasn't the case with 'Damnation'. A record company rep—who will remain nameless—quickly arranged for the band to go into Island Recording Studios to re-record the track, with the musos' union guy supervising. The engineer was under strict instructions to switch back to the Australian recording at the end of the session, which he did without the union guy noticing. It was one big charade.

The union guy didn't have a clue and the band duly made their first appearance on *Top of the Pops*, miming to the original recording, on 8 June. This was no *Countdown*—Bon wore jeans and a red jumper, rather than dress in drag, and they weren't the best mimers in the world, but it did the trick.

After a brief stint in the UK it was back to the grind Stateside for the band's third and longest tour yet, a huge run that started in late June and continued until early October '78. They had dates with some big acts: Alice Cooper, Foreigner, Aerosmith, Journey, Rainbow and Cheap Trick, again, who were now opening for AC/DC.

Although the band was making great inroads into America, financially it was still very tough. The enormous costs of staying on the road outweighed any income we generated. We were still dependent on Atlantic paying for tour support; I was continually requesting more money from Jerry. My position towards the tour support was that it was commissionable; that is, it was paid to the band in lieu of record royalties that would be eventually deducted from accounting once sales kicked in.

Ted Albert, unfortunately, didn't quite see it this way. We had a disagreement on the issue and I was forced to stop taking the Atlantic commission. Ted failed to understand my argument, that I was building the band's brand for the future, which they'd own in perpetuity. He just didn't see it the same way as me.

My contract only had a couple more years to run; I had no real idea how I might fare with a renewal. With the loss of this income, it was becoming difficult for me to sustain an office and Coral's salary, plus run a family household.

At the same time, I needed to find a person I could work with, someone with whom I could bounce around ideas. I began to explore a possible co-management deal with Aerosmith's manager, David Krebs, who I'd got to know fairly well and liked. The management company that he ran with his partner Steve Leber was very successful, with a stable of A-list clients. We set up a meeting and to my surprise, also present was one of David's employees, accountant Peter Mensch. Peter was a smart young guy on the rise who'd got to know AC/DC quite well while on the road with Aerosmith. He was showing a lot of interest in my band.

As the discussions progressed I happened to mention that I'd been freelancing with Ted Albert in Sydney, consulting on the international careers of The Angels and Rose Tattoo. I proposed the idea of a co-deal for all the Alberts bands, even though I didn't have any management interest in Rose Tattoo or The Angels. I was simply just shooting the shit, fleshing out any possibilities. AC/DC had always been my main point of business.

Before I could blink, I had a fiery call from Malcolm.

'What's this I hear about you trying to sell us as part of an Alberts package?' he yelled. I explained that wasn't really the case, but it was a wake-up for me. Clearly, Mensch was not to be trusted.

Michael Klenfner, meanwhile, had been hammering away at his good friend and old boss Bill Graham, finally securing a slot for the band at 23 July's A Day on the Green event at San Francisco's Oakland Coliseum, along with Aerosmith, Foreigner, Van Halen and the Pat Travers Band. This was a highly prestigious gig, playing before a crowd of almost 60,000.

I'd heard a lot about promoter Bill Graham, an equally feared and revered music industry figure, not only in the California Bay Area but throughout the entire United States. He was the kind of guy who got things done, by whatever means necessary. I don't mind admitting that I was in awe of him, like all of the top-level people that I'd met so far. In 1973, he'd produced a show in rural New York featuring the Grateful Dead, the Allman Brothers and The Band, attended by more than 600,000 punters—and unlike Woodstock, everyone paid to get in. As proud as I was of my involvement with Sunbury, that festival just didn't rate with something of this scope. Bill also ran the legendary Fillmore East and West, two of the country's best rock'n'roll venues.

Bill was a great producer of amazing events, someone who had absolute respect for the performers—and he was fantastic to deal with, an amazing host. I'd never encountered such particular attention to backstage hospitality, regardless of whether you were the opening band or the headliner. Bill was one of a kind.

Yet there was some conflict at this gig. Bud Prager, the manager of Foreigner, and I went head to head backstage, with Klenfner acting as reluctant referee. Foreigner, like AC/DC, were signed to Atlantic, which didn't make things any easier for Klenfner. The problem was simple: Foreigner didn't want AC/DC to go on before them, as had been arranged. Because Foreigner was a hot band in the States at the time, with the hits 'Cold as Ice' and 'Hot Blooded', Prager had the final word. But it was enough of a problem for us to nearly come to blows.

A stage manager intervened, smiling, while we shouted at each other, sarcastically suggesting that we resolve the dispute the 'American way'. Disagreements of this nature, he told me, were generally resolved by the combatants placing their cocks on display, one to the other, sizing them up. Biggest dick wins.

'Well, not me, pal!' I let him know. 'That's not how we do things back home.' Bud, thankfully, was as horrified by the notion as I was.

I should add that our dispute was taking place in a crowded backstage hospitality tent, hardly the kind of place to just whip it out and slap it on the table. So Bud won by default. Klenfner was convinced, bizarrely, that Bud got away with this kind of stuff because he was blessed with a magnificently thick head of fabulous grey hair. I was follically challenged, brought on years before by the stress of working with Billy Thorpe and the Aztecs. Thanks to medical breakthroughs, I was at least vainly trying. But Bud, bless him, was the victor, at least on this day.

I knew the reality: AC/DC didn't care who went on stage and when. We were accustomed to dealing with the paranoia of so-called headliners. At A Day on the Green they did as they always did: they went on stage and gave 100 per cent, leaving it for the audience to decide who rocked the hardest. The huge crowd loved them.

The band had little time to chew over the backstage battle of the penises. They had yet another show to play, this time at the Paradise Club in Boston, where the photo for the *If You Want Blood* cover was taken after the gig. Then it was down to New York to play the Palladium with Ritchie Blackmore's Rainbow. Following AC/DC's performance, Ritchie decided not to play due to a buzz in the PA system. Once again, the problem was his bloody enormous, trouble-plagued rainbow lighting rig. Because they didn't require the three billion volts that Ritchie's rainbow sucked out of the system, AC/DC had a great gig.

The promoter, Ron Delsner, was forced to cough up a refund for all ticket holders, but AC/DC, once again, left a deep impression.

In LA, the band recorded a set for NBC's highly-rated *Midnight Special*, followed by more gigs with Cheap Trick, Thin Lizzy, KISS and Aerosmith, as the tour criss-crossed the country. Clearly, the band's first A Day on the Green performance resonated with Bill Graham, now a fan of the band, who booked them for their second appearance at the Coliseum, on 2 September. This time it was Ted Nugent headlining—and I kept my fists in my pockets, and I was not challenged to unzip and compare dick sizes with anyone. Thank Christ for that.

Since leaving Australia in 1976, AC/DC had performed over 1000 gigs, a staggering workload, and had established a worldwide reputation as an awesome live band. This had all been achieved by constant touring and hard work—major radio airplay remained elusive. This lack of airplay was seen as a big problem, but I think it was actually the making of the band. Okay, they agreed, if we can't get our songs heard on radio, let's play them live and loud and often, and win fans that way. They'd taken the ultimate grassroots path to making a name for themselves.

But as another hot US tour wound down in early October, Atlantic America was beginning to make some very loud noises about the band's troubles with radio. A question was raised about their ongoing production relationship with Harry and George—Atlantic thought that might be the problem. For Michael Klenfner, this tricky subject, loaded with all kinds of personal and professional complications, became his number-one priority.

HIGHWAY TO HELL

Up to now, AC/DC albums had been recorded according to the true spirit of the band. George and Harry, with the backing of Alberts, had made sure of that. But fuelled by Michael Klenfner, the feeling coming out of Atlantic Records was that a change of producers was necessary. The (hell's) bells were tolling for Harry and George, and very loudly.

Accordingly, Michael Klenfner flew to Sydney in late 1978 for discussions with Alberts, George, Harry, the band and myself. It wasn't going to be an easy conversation.

The band still genuinely believed that George and Harry were essential members of the team, and that they'd produced their music with a strong sense of integrity, without any kind of compromise. They'd never sold out. If Harry and George were to be sacked, which was Atlantic's view, the fallout could be devastating, especially for Malcolm and Angus. The professional and personal were deeply intertwined in the world of AC/DC.

Michael Klenfner's master plan was for the band to record with Eddie Kramer, a well-known studio veteran who'd worked with Traffic, Small Faces, the Stones, Jimi Hendrix and, more recently, Led Zeppelin and Peter Frampton. Kramer was a heavy hitter, well established; his name would give the band some clout. Kramer was Klenfner's one and only choice, and he pushed hard for him. The unspoken message was this: if AC/DC wanted to keep recording for Atlantic Records, we didn't have an option.

Soon after, Kramer flew to Sydney where we all met. It was obviously a difficult situation for Eddie to navigate: on one hand, he needed to sell himself as someone who could take AC/DC to the next level, but he also needed to be sensitive to the band's relationship with Harry and George and Alberts. Fortunately, Eddie was a reasonable man and we all got on well. And he did have an impeccable track record.

Understandably, we were all feeling a bit strange and apprehensive about this, although few things were said out loud. George and Harry, to their absolute credit, put the band's future first. As for the guys, while obviously disapproving of what was going down, they knew that they had to keep moving. Ted Albert, tellingly, kept his distance. He'd been through a similar situation in the 1960s when, as producer of The Easybeats, he'd been discarded by United Artists for Shel Talmy, who'd crafted huge hits for The Kinks and The Who. It was déjà vu all over again for Ted. I don't recall having a single conversation with Ted about this; he was MIA. Then again, we weren't exactly seeing eye to eye on a few other matters, especially after our disagreement about the Atlantic money.

The one thing we reluctantly accepted was that this was Atlantic's decision. The band, of course, would have preferred me to tell Atlantic to back off, and then get back to work with George and Harry. But my gut had been telling me for some time, probably back to the *Powerage* LP, that Atlantic was right in believing we needed to change producers. If not Eddie Kramer, then someone who understood the nuances of the FM radio–dominated American market, which had a distinctive sound and feel.

This was the toughest challenge I'd had to confront in my time managing the band, but the deal was done. What I'd also done, quite unintentionally, was sow the seeds of my own eventual breakup with AC/DC.

◼

The band flew to Miami in early 1979 to commence pre-production with Eddie. Meanwhile, I flew back to my office in New York. I was in the midst of an apartment change and was kindly offered the use of a friend's vacant place, only to discover it was now crawling with cockroaches. I happened to mention this to Cedric Kushner, an upstate New York promoter I'd met through Doug Thaler. Cedric very kindly invited me to stay with him, in his penthouse apartment overlooking Central Park, no less, on West 58th Street. Some place.

Also staying there was music publisher Clive Calder, a South African, like Cedric, who was establishing his Zomba publishing company, along with his partner Ralph Simon. He also managed record producers, including Robert 'Mutt' Lange, a Zambian-born Brit who'd worked on records by The Boomtown Rats, The Motors and City Boy. Lange was travelling with Clive and—as fate would have it—also staying at Cedric's crowded house.

The apartment on West 58th was a great place for me to be; the conversation was always stimulating and informative, and I learned a lot about the business of music publishing and recording deals. We would spend hours listening to songs that Mutt had been working on and discussing music in general. All this interaction would prove to be incredibly handy.

We'd occasionally shift down a block, to the corner of Sixth Avenue and 57th, to Wolf's, another of New York's legendary delis, where the conversation would continue in earnest over one of their famous pastrami Reuben sandwiches. Mutt was very quietly spoken and likeable, a gentle man with a down-to-earth disposition. I could sense his greatness and his capacity to draw the best out of an artist.

Although AC/DC was now committed to making this album with Eddie Kramer, I gently put the feelers out to Clive and Mutt; maybe Mutt would like to work with the band. Clive, a very switched-on guy, recognised the band's potential, but I'm not sure Mutt had a strong opinion about AC/DC one way or the other. At this stage he simply saw them as another band having a crack at making it in America. I was about to change this perception.

Two weeks into the Miami trip, I received a desperate phone call from Malcolm.

'Get us the fuck out of this situation, Browning,' he pleaded with me. 'It just isn't working.'

The band were used to receiving more input on song arrangement and playing than Eddie was giving them. George would have them play potential song ideas on the studio piano. If they didn't sound like a good tune on the piano, George figured, then all the guitars and production techniques in the world weren't going to change anything. Eddie Kramer was basically a very hot engineer who could pull good sounds, but didn't offer the band anything else.

Malcolm told me that instead of helping them develop their own songs, Eddie was trying to persuade them to cover 'Gimme Some Lovin'', the old Spencer Davis Group hit, although Eddie has since denied this. To Malcolm and the band, their fears about 'selling out' had suddenly become very real.

Eddie, when pressed, blamed the band's problems on lack of preparation and Bon's drinking. Maybe that did play a part.

Regardless, something had to be done and quickly. This was costing the band money and losing everyone momentum.

Malcolm's last words to me were desperate. 'Find someone else. I don't give a fuck who it is, just get us the fuck out of here.'

I said I'd do what I could, put the phone down—and looked over at Mutt.

'You've got to make this record,' I said to him, point blank. 'This isn't some dime-a-dozen heavy rock band, these guys are special.'

By now, Clive had a rule of thumb for Mutt—he'd only have him produce artists whose records had sold more than 500,000 copies in the United States. AC/DC, despite their live success, hadn't reached that level. But Mutt had a connection with Atlantic, through his work with City Boy—although I kept his role with The Boomtown Rats quiet, knowing full well that the AC/DC guys would hate it. More importantly Mutt had been working on some unreleased songs with his ex-wife, Stevie, who was in a band named Night. When he played me those songs, I knew it straight away. He could definitely make AC/DC sound as great as they should.

When I called Malcolm back, he asked me, 'Mutt who? Never 'eard of 'im.'

I persevered and really got to work on Clive, using the Barry Bergman technique of hammering away until he couldn't take it anymore and agreed to Mutt producing the album. Malcolm was still unsure, but I told him, in true rock'n'roll managerial style: 'Trust me, it's going to be fine.'

Of course, I had no real idea, but all they needed right now was another producer. Still, I had this instinct that Mutt was the right choice.

While the band was okay with the change, I now had to convince Michael Klenfner, who'd championed Eddie Kramer in the first place.

I called Klenfner, who didn't agree with my decision. We met up later that night with Clive. Michael, who was never afraid to speak his mind, said a few things that Clive thought were insulting to Mutt. The next morning, Clive pretty well crucified Klenfner in a telephone conversation with Jerry Greenberg. It was all getting very heated.

While Clive Calder was still very much a music man on the rise, there was a feeling in the industry that he was destined for greatness, so his opinion was valued—Michael, unfortunately, had picked a fight with the wrong guy. Atlantic sacked him the next day. I felt the loss strongly; I knew that Michael had played a huge role in AC/DC's success to date. His wife, Carol, later said that Michael's 'oversize personality' gained him some enemies within the company, and I'm sure that was true. But Michael had been a huge help to me and the band—he'd simply gone too far with Clive and paid the price. He'd have future success, though, and we remained friends despite this big disagreement.

For the record, I'd like to set things straight: no one person was more crucial to the band's US success than Michael Klenfner.

Atlantic sprang into action and quickly arranged for the band to fly to London to commence recording with Mutt at Roundhouse Studios in London's Chalk Farm.

Bon had a memorable first discussion with Mutt. He'd just read a review that described his voice as 'a weasel on heat'. That was new.

'Is that something you can work with?' Bon asked, flashing a grin.

Despite their early scepticism, the band locked in with Mutt. But he was very different from any producer they'd experienced before. Mutt was a perfectionist, someone who worked very slowly. He insisted that Angus record his guitar parts while sitting next to him in the control room. Mutt sometimes even told him what to play, which took a bit of getting used to on Angus's part. Mutt also managed to extract great, weasel-free vocals from Bon, while his lyrics were up to their usual high standard.

As I'd hoped, it all came together; they made a great album, which they named *Highway to Hell*. It was also the beginning of a long and incredibly fruitful relationship with Mutt.

Mutt has made a point of never doing interviews during his career, but he did once let it slip that he too had been sceptical about the situation at first. But I'd told him this band was special, and he agreed after working with them on *Highway to Hell*.

Back in New York, I decided to bring Cedric Kushner into the management company, having shelved the idea of a co-management deal with David Krebs. I'd been dragging my wife and kids around the world for years with very little income and I needed a reasonable injection of capital, to set up a decent living space for my family of four and continue running my management company.

Cedric, having been a successful promoter, was able to provide the funds that I needed to make this happen, and Coral and I shifted into his 57th Street offices, putting things in place for *Highway to Hell*. It felt very much like the right decision to go with Cedric, even though it would prove to be a deadly mistake on my part.

In April 1979, the band flew in from London and we sat down and listened to the new record together. Not only did it blow us away, but we knew we had the one song—the title track—that would provide the missing link between the band and radio. 'Highway to Hell', the song and the album, was going to break the band wide open.

During this sit-down, the subject of album art was raised. I'd only just heard the album in its entirety, so it was a case of shooting the breeze on the subject of art. In the past, the band didn't pay that much attention to the topic—although they'd readily let me know when something sucked—and had left it up to me to deal with the various designers. However, I was being pressed for a concept, and what popped into my head was the art direction for *Cheap Thrills*, the Big Brother and the Holding Company LP, which turned the cover into a sort of cartoonish board game. What I had in mind was a rock'n'roll version of snakes and ladders, played out on the 'Highway to Hell'. As spontaneous ideas go, I didn't think that it was too bad. Thoughts of related pinball machines and video games also sprang to mind. AC/DC merchandising.

Out of nowhere, Angus turned on me.

'What a fucked idea, Browning,' he spat.

Angus was never easy to please, but this seemed over the top. I was starting to get the sense that something was amiss.

While the band was in New York we met with Atlantic's art director, Bob Defrin, who'd developed the AC/DC logo, and arranged a photo session for the album cover. It was going to be a band shot, with Angus wearing some horns and a bit of a snarl. Considering their meat and potatoes approach to art, it was probably the way to go, as much as I liked the board game concept.

That in place, and with a few days rehearsal at SIR studios in New York under their belt, the band hit the road. Their first date on the tour was in early May and the roadshow would roll on for three months. This was it, the big time.

I flew into Nashville on 22 May 1979; the band was headlining a show at the Tennessee Theater. It was a typically strong show, but as soon as they came off stage, an almighty argument erupted, with me on the receiving end of various insults courtesy of Malcolm and Angus, with the odd sharp comment from Bon and Phil. It was right then I knew I was screwed. My radar had been correct; something had been brewing, probably stemming from the time Peter Mensch had a post-meeting word in Malcolm's ear. Now I knew how Mark Evans must have felt.

As I'd discover, there were a number of issues irritating the band. These included the sacking of Michael Klenfner and my bringing Cedric Kushner into the fold, someone they didn't care for. Perhaps I should have taken my chances with the cockroaches, I thought—but then I'd never have met Mutt.

Once he was aware of my dilemma, Cedric, in a last-minute attempt to retrieve something for himself from a band that he'd only met twice, went directly to the guys, who fed him some bullshit about how much they hated and resented me, and how this whole drama was of my creation. They couldn't bring themselves to tell Cedric that he was one of the reasons for the breakdown in the relationship.

Sure, we'd been through some tough and unpleasant times: just recently, the firing of Harry and George, the switch of producers from Eddie to Mutt, and the fallout with Klenfner. Getting on the wrong side of Ted Albert was a big problem, too. I was on the AC/DC shitlist, no doubt about it. But I felt I deserved some credit for where I'd taken the band, and in such a relatively short time. I'd preserved their relationship with Atlantic in America when it seemed as good as over, and I had connected them with Mutt Lange, a relationship that would prove crucial for the group and their career. The band didn't want to consider any of this. They just wanted me gone.

There was another issue. While still with AC/DC, I'd received a call from the Van Zant family, who wanted me to fly down to Florida to discuss possible management for Johnny Van Zant's band. Johnny was the younger brother of the late Ronnie Van Zant, of Lynyrd Skynyrd, who'd died in a plane crash with bandmates Steve Gaines and Cassie Gaines, and assistant road manager Dean Kilpatrick in October 1977, not long after befriending AC/DC. Cedric was my partner, and it was logical that we should consider taking on other bands, building our roster. Cedric came along to the meeting, but while the family wanted me to manage Johnny and the band, they didn't relate to Cedric and the deal didn't happen. But AC/DC had issues with this, regardless of how it played out. In hindsight, I can understand why they didn't want to share their manager.

There was one thing I hadn't shared with the band. While they were recording in London with Mutt, I'd returned to Australia briefly, only to be detained for six weeks. I was having visa problems with the US Consul, dating back to my old drug bust in the Doug Parkinson days. I had a strict policy—no drugs backstage or anywhere near the band—and here I was with my own drug-related drama. I never shared this with the band because it would have made me appear hypocritical.

Bon was in the same boat. His long-ago bust caused him all sorts of grief, including the cancellation of a Japanese tour, after the equipment had already been shipped; a strong following had been building in Japan during the *Powerage* era. I had my own drug-related problems with the Japanese immigration officials.

Angus hated anything to do with drugs. He'd seen at close range the damage inflicted on and by Stevie Wright, whose talent had been destroyed by hard drugs. In hindsight, I made a big mistake in not taking the band into my confidence; perhaps this was another contributing factor to my removal, to be replaced by Leber and Krebs.

Some time later, David Krebs said that Ian Jeffrey, the band's tour manager, had been a thorn in his side, which led to his sacking and Ian's elevation to band manager. Jeffrey had allegedly reported to the band about me, telling them I'd squandered thousands of dollars in air tickets. This just wasn't the case. What I'd done was purchase round-the-world air tickets, which would enable the band to stop at any destination, as long as they were heading in one direction. It wasn't entirely practical, and we did have a lot of unused tickets, but the saving was substantial.

Ian, I'll admit, was a very good tour manager and also a great soundman; he'd become a valued part of the team. But he had zero entrepreneurial skills; this, combined with his penchant for stroking the band's ego, caused an almost fatal blow to their career further down the line. Full-page ads in *Billboard* magazine exclaiming that you are now the manager of AC/DC doesn't make you a manager. He was soon fired; then they appointed someone I suspect was an Albert plant, Crispin Dye, who was even worse. Thankfully, they realised they needed experienced management and hired a team that included Stewart Young, who'd managed Emerson, Lake & Palmer, and Steve Barnett, a true music madman and great wheeler and dealer, whom I'd once considered setting up shop with in Australia.

■

Management is a bit like a marriage when things start to break down. The smallest issues get blown out of all proportion. I remember hearing how Rod Stewart left his long-standing manager Billy Gaff because he didn't like the wallpaper in a hotel room. I'm sure the wallpaper wasn't the real issue, but that's how things can blow up in a relationship as close and complex as client and manager. I could absolutely relate to this story.

Bands who become successful normally have a short window of opportunity to make money and set themselves up for life, which makes them all the more ruthless in their business dealings. This I understand. But as it turned out for AC/DC, this just wasn't the case; they'd actually get bigger and bigger over time. I'd set in place so many things that would help them out for years beyond my involvement.

Rock'n'roll is a unique business. As a manager, if you seriously commit to the band on the basis of a commission remuneration arrangement, which I did, and nothing happens, then you get nothing for your belief and commitment. If a band breaks out big, it's not unreasonable to assume that you, too, should make a killing. But money wasn't my major motivation; my goal was to make things happen for AC/DC on a global level.

Being a manager is probably the next best thing to being in the band, particularly when you're seeing first-hand the impact of your decisions—and especially when you and the band have a great rapport. My education for the AC/DC gig came from the street. There was no college course that could teach me intuition and ambition, the two things all rock'n'roll managers need. I was a pioneer, taking AC/DC out of Australia at the time I did. There was no one I could ask for advice and guidance; no one had done this before. Nobody understood how things worked internationally.

My mentors were people like Norman Vincent Peale and Marshall McLuhan, who spoke about how 'the medium is the message'. I'd learned a lot about marketing from McLuhan. My father had told me that I should try to achieve something every day, which was a sound bit of advice. I'd also studied the methods and careers of Andrew Loog Oldham, who got the Stones rolling, and Led Zep's notorious manager, Peter Grant.

I'd also been inspired by something I'd once read in the book, *Zen in the Art of Archery*. It was a very Zen concept that was driving me, and therefore, by association, the band, at the time. Put simply, the Archer was able to split the arrow that was already in the bullseye with a second arrow, because in his mind, he had already done it. He was now working in reverse with the second arrow. So I imagined that AC/DC had already made it to the top, and everything we were doing was actually working in reverse. This Zen concept was driving me and constantly reinforcing my belief in the success of this journey that we were on. It was not something that I shared with the band, though; they would have called me a fucking madman.

Another key influence was the Ayn Rand book *The Fountainhead*, a bible for all aspiring architects of the 1960s. Her subject is someone who refuses to compromise his artistic integrity, a universal concept. They may not have even realised it, but the Young brothers had an ironclad grasp of this principle. Not once during my involvement with the band and beyond had they deviated an inch from their artistic and musical beliefs. That's huge.

The other key thing I learned from this fallout was a bit less philosophical: it would have helped to have an 'exit clause' in my management agreement. I didn't; my financial saving grace was the two years I had left to run on my contract, which meant our respective lawyers got to work negotiating a reasonable settlement—or something that appeared reasonable. A well-drafted exit clause would have allowed me to go about AC/DC business safe in the knowledge that if something fell apart and the band suddenly turned on me, as happened, then at least I would have been financially covered.

There is one thing I know for sure. If a band reaches the top, it's due to their greatness. If they fail, it's because their manager is an idiot.

LONG WAY—ENDINGS AND BEGINNINGS

My last encounter with AC/DC was a very solemn bus ride from the Tennessee Theater to the hotel. I didn't realise that I'd never talk to them again—but from now on, lawyers would relay everything the band felt I should know. We'd lived in each other's pockets for five years and most of the time I felt we were brothers in arms, out to conquer the world. This isolation was also a painful experience for Coral and my family, who'd followed me on this globetrotting odyssey. Suddenly I was persona non grata, and that hurt a lot. There were a couple of exceptions, including Alberts' long-standing New York lawyer, John Clark, and Barry Bergman from E.B. Marks; both knew what I'd helped accomplish and kept in touch. But the rest were nowhere to be seen. That hurt a lot.

Particularly disappointing was something that occurred soon after. I was back in Australia and I'd left a message for Ted Albert, whom I would have liked to speak with, but he didn't return my call. Of the entire team, Ted was the person I respected the most, and he was about to get a whole lot richer due, in part, to my hard work. I thought it was an ungracious and thoughtless way to treat me, someone who'd done his best to advance the development of his business interests. I expected it from Malcolm and Angus—that was just the way it was with them and their clannish style of dealing with anyone on the outer. Once out, that's it: you were as good as dead to them. But for some reason I hadn't expected it from Ted. Even Mark Evans was acknowledged for his great work when the band finally came back to Australia for their triumphant 1981 tour. Mark was invited to the Sydney gig and presented with richly deserved gold albums by Ted.

If it hadn't been for the thoughtfulness of both Phil Carson and Jerry Greenberg, who were both decent enough to remember me when *Highway to Hell* went gold, I would have very little on my wall marking my work with the band.

Despite my disappointment with Ted, my experience in dealing with him convinced me that he was a man of his word. I was shocked to read an interview with Shel Talmy in Jesse Fink's recent book *The Youngs*, in which he said the royalties he was owed for The Easybeats' hit 'Friday on My Mind' were never paid. Shel also made some highly disparaging remarks about Ted's integrity, which I found hard to believe and somewhat offensive.

Ted, who passed away in 1990, was a hard-nosed businessman, to be sure. But he was always honourable. I'd be inclined to believe that it was a misinterpretation, a contractual stuff-up of some kind. Ted did once ask me to make some enquiries into the revenue that Alberts were owed for their publishing interest on 'Friday on My Mind' and other songs, but that was more to do with revenue from cover versions, which he considered a bit low.

I've always wondered what went down on an international level, contractually speaking, during that whole Easybeats period. Both Ted and George were very cagey and tight-lipped about it, always very quick to blame management for their failure to capitalise on the success of 'Friday on My Mind'.

In Jane Albert's book *House of Hits*, she made a reference to me setting up some kind of New York branch office for Alberts, which had 'been unsuccessful'. Well, that was news to me. I think I would have known had this been the case; I'd have been given a budget and a business plan. Ted did, however, hire me to handle some licensing arrangements for Alberts artists internationally, including John Paul Young's 'Love Is in the Air', which I'd overseen for US and UK release, along with numerous other activities. But the Alberts' New York office just didn't happen.

Some time after my dismissal I received a call from Mark Evans, who admitted he still felt shell-shocked about being fired from the band. On his return to Australia from London after his sacking, Mark was asked by Alberts to sign off from any future rights. An Alberts employee turned up to one of Mark's Sydney gigs with his new band, holding a cheque and a release document. Without the benefit of any legal advice, Mark duly signed.

I met with Mark and he showed me the document, which I gave the once-over. I made a point of staying out of the politics and didn't pass an opinion on whether it was fair. I simply suggested that Mark meet with my lawyer Warren Cross, to discuss the release, which he did. This resulted in a much larger settlement for Mark, which, when combined with legal costs, clearly didn't thrill Alberts. I'd heard a rumour that Ted issued a directive that the name Warren Cross not be uttered in his building.

I believed then and still believe now that my advice was correct; that Mark should have sought legal counsel. It was the right thing to do. But for what I considered a perfectly reasonable suggestion to someone feeling very alienated, it made any chance of a friendly get-together between the band and myself even more remote. I was now—and remain—well and truly on the Alberts and Young brothers' shitlist.

It's hugely disappointing; there's nothing that would give me more pleasure after all these years than to see them and have a laugh. I always liked them, especially Malcolm, who I dealt with the most, and was without doubt the creative and driving force behind this great band. With the 2014 revelation of Malcolm's debilitating illness, my unfinished business with the band may up end staying that way.

In 1979, no longer managing a band on the brink of greatness, I had to get on with my life. The first thing I wanted to reclaim was my health. I'd smoked two packs of cigarettes a day while managing the band—I'd usually reach for a stress-relieving ciggie as soon as Angus opened his mouth. So my wellbeing was high on my to-do list—and besides, the cost of cigarettes in the vending machine in the foyer of my new apartment had risen to a dollar. Damned if I was going to pay that much.

Coral, meanwhile, remained good friends with Bon, keeping an eye on him when she could, being there when he needed a friend to confide in. So it was with the heaviest of hearts that I learned about his untimely death on 19 February 1980. Coral had been so conscious about looking out for Bon, but he was a grown man, in charge of his own destiny.

Sadly, Bon's large and diverse circle of friends was excluded from attending his funeral. Only immediate family and AC/DC members—including their new managers, who barely knew Bon—were asked to attend. Coral and I weren't invited to the funeral or informed about any chance to pay our last respects to an amazing guy. This was not the right time for band politics.

Bon was a fellow traveller, and our respective journeys intersected many times, dating back to the Valentines/Battle of the Sounds days. We shared esoteric and eclectic influences, the type of things Malcolm and Angus loathed.

Just before his death, Bon had been confiding to his friends that he was feeling isolated and lonely, and was also growing tired of continual touring. He wanted to put down some roots; he needed somewhere to call home. Sadly, it never happened. Bon was one of a kind; he always joked about 'dying young and leaving a good-looking corpse', an aside that proved to be eerily prophetic. Although he was portrayed by the media as a party boy, and he did play on his wild side, this was mainly AC/DC propaganda. The Bon his close friends and I knew was much more than that. He was a sweetheart and one of the best street poets the rock'n'roll world has ever known.

So, where to next? I'd achieved my ambition: to become the first Australian manager to break a band internationally. Glenn Wheatley, the former bassist from the Masters Apprentices, had recently broken the Little River Band, whom he managed, in America. Perhaps he could argue that he was the first, but it's not something we've ever discussed. And at the end of the day, who cares? We both did our best for our artists.

With AC/DC now attached to the New York firm of Leber and Krebs (with Peter Mensch also involved in the action), I remained living in New York with my family, working with the lawyers on a settlement and licking my wounds. Coral found a temporary job in Manhattan with her new Australian friend— and future TV star—Kerri-Anne Kennerley.

I began walking a lot, through Central Park and around the streets of New York, trying to regain some fitness—and clear my head. On one of my daily walks I noticed a chrome sign attached to the back of a Cadillac; it read Deluxe. For some reason, I suddenly flashed on a conversation I'd had with Clive Calder, when I was living in Cedric's apartment. He'd looked on as I had another stressful phone conversation with Malcolm.

'Michael,' Clive told me when I hung up the phone. 'Get into the music publishing business. Copyrights don't call you up in the middle of the night and tell you the truck's broken down.'

When the lawyers finally reached what I then thought to be a satisfactory settlement, I decided that I was going back to Australia to live in Sydney, to start a record and publishing company, which I'd call Deluxe. It was time to go home.

DELUXE, INXS AND A VOLCANO NAMED MURPHY

With the drama of the last few months well and truly behind me, a sense of wellbeing finally returned. We moved back into our North Sydney house, and it felt great, as it always had when I returned to Sydney. I was now officially a non-smoker, and that felt great, too. I was raring to get back into something.

I soon discovered there was a terrific buzz in Sydney, with rehearsal studios and garages full of potentially great bands. There seemed to be a pub with live music on just about every inner-city street corner, with bands playing nightly to full houses. And there were still huge beer barns operating to capacity throughout the suburbs. It was the golden age of what we now call Oz rock.

A new management company named Dirty Pool had emerged, operated by John Woodruff, an old friend and manager of The Angels, along with Rod Willis, who managed Cold Chisel, and Ray Hearn. The stranglehold that my old partner Michael Gudinski had on the live music business, dating back to the days of Consolidated Rock, and later on Premier Artists and the Harbour Agency, was being challenged for the first time.

Dirty Pool was doing things differently, providing a very artist-friendly style of service. They introduced performance 'door deals'—in which the acts performing would get a slice of money paid at the door—and negotiated fairer recording deals for their artists. I got the strong sense that the local live music industry had entered a new and more sophisticated era.

I was still thinking about my Deluxe concept. I'd made the conscious decision not to sign any heavy rock bands, acts that would be dependent on hefty financial tour support, who'd take time to develop. I'd just lived through that scenario with AC/DC. Instead, I was looking for bands with more of a pop sensitivity, who I could break quickly through radio and TV and would be less dependent on gaining a reputation through playing live. This was, of course, the antithesis of everything I'd done so far, and I found that really exciting. A new and different challenge.

Globally, the new wave movement was in full flight and I started to hear about some interesting prospects in Australia. Okay, this wasn't my area of expertise—I'd been schooled in Billy Thorpe and AC/DC, loud, credible rock'n'roll acts—but I felt that this was the best move for me, at least for the moment. Besides, what heavy rock band was I going to find that could even compare to AC/DC?

I began the search for talent. I'd be in venues till all hours most nights. Sydney's Stagedoor Tavern, not far from Central railway station, was one of my haunts. This place was something else. The punters would be packed in like sardines; there was no chance for the bartenders to keep up with demand so all they served was canned beer. The turnaround at the bar alone must have been astronomical. The Stagedoor also had a novel way of tidying up from the night before. Instead of the old-fashioned method of brooms and vacuums and human sweat, they'd hire a team who'd arrive at 4 am and sweep the empty cans into a huge pile on the floor—and then hose the joint out.

Bands like The Angels, Rose Tattoo, Cold Chisel, The Church and Midnight Oil would pack the place to the rafters and beyond, night after night. Ironically, the Stagedoor, which must have broken every liquor licensing law ever drafted, was housed in the basement of the New South Wales police headquarters. Welcome to Sydney!

I had been really missing out on something living in America; the live scene was fantastic. The major Australian record companies, however, were still living in the past, blind to what was all around them. The worst offender, I observed, was RCA Records. They had what you might politely call an image problem, and almost zero local talent on their roster, although Elvis Presley and ABBA sales kept the cash coming in. There was a joke doing the rounds, about a kid who wanted a cowboy outfit for his birthday, so his dad bought him RCA Records. That summed them up.

But despite their major shortcomings, or perhaps because of them, I arranged a meeting with the head of the label, Morrie Smith, in 1979. I had the feeling he might be interested in a new label to distribute. I was right; Morrie welcomed the idea with open arms. He was a good music man, a true gentleman, someone who recognised the company's dire need for an injection of energy. And he backed me all the way with finance and support. Voila! Deluxe Records was born.

RCA would pay me advances to cover recording costs, and then they'd market and distribute the records. My job was to find the talent and provide direction and advice to both the artists and RCA. I kept my newly formed Deluxe Music Publishing company well away from the RCA deal, a decision based partly on Clive Calder's advice.

I set out to sign some artists, armed with my new super secretary-cum-personal assistant, Michelle Bennett. First I discovered a Melbourne band called Man and Machine, led by the enigmatic Eric Gradman. They were very inner-city cool, very Melbourne, art rock. Eric, who'd played in the Lou Reed–influenced Bleeding Hearts, was the vocalist and violin player. Regrettably, Eric's lawyers got in the way and the deal didn't happen. I'd had enough of lawyers to last me a lifetime.

I moved on and soon discovered The Dugites, named after a snake indigenous to Western Australia, the band's home. They were led by the tall and talented songwriter Peter Crosbie, who played keyboards, with Linda Nutter on vocals. They had an interesting twist on new wave, playing extremely well-crafted three-minute pop songs, with an early Phil Spector sensibility about them. I hired Bob Andrews, who'd been a member of Graham Parker & the Rumour, to produce their first album. Bob had been making a few waves in London, producing hits with Jona 'Stop the Cavalry' Lewie.

Bob flew over to Perth's Planet Studios and recorded their debut album, which spawned the hit 'In My Car', a sickly sweet but catchy little pop ditty that made the charts in June 1980. Deluxe's first hit.

Tim Murdoch, the managing director of WEA Records New Zealand, sent me his punk band called Toy Love (as in, the opposite of Real Hate), fronted by Chris Knox, one of New Zealand's most creative music minds. They recorded an album with Dragon's Todd Hunter at EMI's studio in Sydney. They were extremely vulgar and edgy, which I liked. Unfortunately, Australia just wasn't ready for them—they pulled good crowds when they played, but the audience was mainly homesick Kiwis. My younger sister and my brother-in-law were visiting me from Melbourne, and I took them to Sydney's Civic Hotel to see the band. They went home covered in spit, which we thought was funny, if disgusting. 'Gobbing' was a punk rocker's way of expressing their appreciation of a band; trouble was, you were bound to get hit if you were anywhere near the stage.

By now, quite a few players in the local music industry were starting to wonder what I was up to. Here I was, an ex-manager of a heavy rock band, dabbling in cutting-edge music. They seemed convinced that I'd been getting around town wearing a skinny black tie, masquerading as a new wave fan and then signing up all these new young bands. (I didn't own a skinny tie, by the way.) Frankly, I was enjoying the energy of the whole scene. It wasn't what I was used to but I was having fun—and I was about to land a band that would make them all turn a nasty shade of green.

Michael Chugg had been the first to tip me off to AC/DC and it was Chuggie again who told me to look into a band named the Farriss Brothers. I was also given the heads-up regarding a Sydney three-piece called The Numbers. I discovered that both bands were represented by Chris Murphy, a brash young Sydney player. Murphy ran an agency that he and his family had inherited from their recently deceased father. The company was named MMA—Mark Murphy & Associates.

While I'd been off on my AC/DC odyssey, Chris had been making a name for himself as an agent with the Sydney-based company Premier Solo. He'd struck up a deal with my old mates

Michael Gudinski and Frank Stivala, who ran Premier Artists in Melbourne, to represent a few of their artists in Sydney. Then he picked up some developing Sydney bands, including Cold Chisel and Midnight Oil, and set up MMA. In doing so he became a thorn in Gudinski's side, a man who to this day remains very protective of his market share. Chris had a way of making enemies; he lost Cold Chisel to the new agency Dirty Pool and then he lost Midnight Oil to a Melbourne agency called Nucleus. Now Chris was going out on his own, following in the footsteps of his late father, but the cartel was applying the screws. Chris needed to develop some viable clients for MMA—and fast.

I called Chris and introduced myself, and he invited me and my family to lunch the following weekend at his property in the country. Over lunch he played demos of two bands from his roster that he was particularly excited about. First up he played The Numbers, a powerful pop trio with a young (and as I'd find out) good-looking blond guy called Chris Morrow on guitar, and his equally attractive and charismatic younger sister Annalise on bass and lead vocals. Simon Vidale played the drums. Their sound, as far as I could make out, was a hybrid of The Jam and Blondie with some Who aspirations. I'd need to see them live, but they seemed like real contenders.

Chris then played me a tape of the Farriss Brothers, the other act Chuggie had mentioned. My immediate reaction was that despite some moments of musical brilliance, and exceptional vocals, they lacked a clear direction. What kind of band were they? But the more I listened the more obvious their nascent brilliance became to me. I also had a very strong feeling and appreciation for family-based bands, having seen how it worked with AC/DC and also watched from a distance the natural vocal blending of the Bee Gees. There is just something quite intuitive between brothers—and this band had three of them.

Chris may have had a habit of pissing people off, but we got on really well. He had a hefty ego but I liked his energy and enthusiasm—and he liked my knowledge and experience. I could give him some valuable insights into the machinations of the international music industry.

A few days later Chris took me to see the Farriss Brothers play at an old disused cinema in suburban Maroubra, and their lack of clear direction was on full display: it was almost like watching a cabaret show band. Everyone in the band felt the need to demonstrate all their multi-instrumental skills; it was too much. Okay, this would need to be sorted out, but their qualities still shone through. I could sense they had something special. Their singer, a kid named Michael Hutchence, was especially interesting. He was very young but he had a Jagger/Jim Morrison–like presence. He wore the usual adolescent acne scars, but when he flashed his vulnerable, irresistible smile, I could just tell he was destined to become a big star.

A few days later Chris and I watched The Numbers play at the Civic Hotel. They too were great; ever since the Jimi Hendrix Experience I've loved trios. Annalise had a striking, unusual voice and she was great on stage—in fact the whole group sparkled. Signing both these bands was now my number-one priority.

There was, however, one problem. I learned that Chris had already been considering setting up his own label for the two bands. We talked it through one big night—over dinner, lots of booze and a bonding fishing trip, at four in the morning, in a rented 'tinny' on Sydney Harbour—and agreed to join forces as Deluxe. We'd sign both bands to recording/publishing and management deals.

I'd handle the record company and publishing side of things, which suited me fine. Chris would manage the two bands, although he lacked hands-on experience as a manager. But he certainly had the passion. Chris was from the same school of life as me, full of ambition and raring to put his street-fighting skills into action.

After a lot of discussion, the Farriss Brothers agreed to change their name to INXS. It looked and felt right. The band agreed it was time to move beyond the 'apprenticeship' stage of their careers, their years as the Farriss Brothers. What better way to do that than change their name?

INXS's musical direction was still a big matter for all of us to address. Chris had just made a trip to London, where ska music was all the rage via such bands as The Specials and The Beat. In his excitement, Chris returned home and threw ska into the mix, just to make things even more confusing. Given my background in heavy blues-based rock, and spotting Michael's potential as a genuine rock star, I tried to push them into trying out a dirtier, harder-edged guitar sound. I thought their use of keyboards—all the rage in the early 1980s—was dominating everything else, making them sound a bit clinical and trendy. In short, I wanted them to become a rock'n'roll band.

Michael just had so much promise. It's unusual, almost impossible, to find someone who has the whole package: a great voice, poetic sensibilities, smart and sexy as hell. A lot of it had to do with his upbringing; he'd attended Hollywood High School. And he'd had an unusual, exotic childhood in Hong Kong. Michael had an affinity with art and decadence, the kind of worldliness that came with the life of an international rock star.

The Farriss brothers, Tim, Jon and Andrew, were a handsome lot, all good players. But most importantly, they had a talented songwriter in Andrew Farriss. Along with Michael's poetic lyrics, INXS was formidable.

To produce their first album we hired Duncan McGuire, an old friend of mine from Doug Parkinson's band In Focus. Money was tight—I think we had ten grand in the budget—which ruled out a bigger name producer from overseas. So we agreed to take a more organic, homegrown approach. As the band was still evolving creatively, we figured Duncan was the right guy to encourage this process naturally, rather than have someone force their own agenda on the band.

Their self-titled album came out in October 1980, just a few months after AC/DC's monumental comeback, *Back in Black*, which was fast-tracking its way to a peak of number four on the US Billboard chart. Considering the stage of INXS's evolution, while the album wasn't a world-beater it worked just fine as a starting point, spawning a few hits along the way, including 'Just Keep Walking' and 'Simple Simon'.

On the back of this, Chris was now frantically booking them into every bar, club and pub in Australia, and they developed a loyal following. I'd not seen such a hard-working band since AC/DC, or a manager with the same drive as Chris (who reminded me of a younger version of me, frankly). INXS would drive the 500-kilometre round trip from Sydney to Newcastle simply to put up posters for the gig the following night. Then they'd put in another 500 kilometres to play the gig. Like the best bands, they showed an enormous commitment to achieving their goals.

INXS were never the darlings of Australia's rock critics; they were considered too mainstream, simply not cool enough. From my perspective, the 'cool' tag was a kiss of death. Interestingly, the critics championed The Numbers, who were considered very cool. Strange. INXS shrugged it off and set to work making their legend through hard work, perseverance and sheer talent.

THE ARSEHOLE NO ONE ELSE WANTS TO BE

Ever since my days running clubs in Melbourne, I'd been a big fan of The Loved Ones; they were a great band. Their singer, Gerry Humphreys, was one of a kind, a great frontman in the tradition of Van Morrison and Mick Jagger. By 1980, The Loved Ones were long gone, another outstanding Australian band that didn't quite make it. I'd last seen Gerry in London in the early 1970s when I was there with Billy Thorpe. He told me he was working for the gas company in Tooting. Considering his enormous talent, this almost made me cry.

I played the band's 1966 hit 'The Loved One' to the guys in INXS, who loved it straight away. It had the same gritty, blues-based qualities and feel that I'd been pushing for—I was convinced that INXS could record a great version of it. They agreed and it became the band's first major hit, breaking the national Top 20 wide open in April 1981. They were on their way.

The Numbers had built a strong local following with their residency at the Civic Hotel, and had also made some commercial impact. They had their first national hit with 'The Modern Song' in April 1980, followed by 'Five Letter Word' a few months later. No longer a Sydney sensation, they started to tour the country. Meanwhile, The Dugites' self-titled album, released in mid-1980, had gone gold. They, too, were touring everywhere. RCA hadn't had a local artist in the charts for years—they were over the moon. Deluxe Records had made a perfect start.

I travelled to New York, with the intention of talking up INXS, with a little help from my lawyer John Frankenheimer. Phil Carson, my colleague from the AC/DC days, had set up his own label and I met with him, among others. I also met with the legendary music man Clive Davis, who'd helped launch the careers of Janis Joplin and Aretha Franklin, and was playing his part in the rise of Aussie band Air Supply. Clive passed on INXS, but was incredibly respectful and pleasant during our meeting. It confirmed something I'd learned over the years: the more important the executive, the more gracious they tend to be. It was the lower-down-the-line A&R guys that would give you attitude and never return your calls.

My trip, though, was a letdown. I was confident I had something special to offer with INXS. 'The Loved One' had been a big hit in Australia and was a song that American execs hadn't heard before—to them it was totally new. But no one expressed any interest in the band or the song. It was simply too early for the guys; they hadn't yet evolved to the point where newcomers would sense their potential.

While Deluxe had got off to a great start, Chris Murphy and I—and by association, INXS—were growing apart. I invited Richard Griffiths, AC/DC's first London agent and my friend, to join me in the running of Deluxe. One of his first roles was to work on this troubled relationship. But despite Richard's undeniable charm, things were shifting.

Chris had fallen well and truly under the INXS spell and wanted to focus all of his time and energy on their management, which suited the band just fine. I'd been the strongest advocate of this single-minded approach; it was a strategy that I had sworn by in the past. So I wasn't about to argue with him; I'd be a hypocrite. However, we had shared commitments to the other bands on the label, which needed to be addressed. We duly decided to go our own ways: I held onto Deluxe's recordings and publishing rights, and Chris retained the management rights. His focus from then on was managing INXS and making them stars.

INXS recorded their second album at EMI studios with Richard Clapton, a successful artist himself, during the winter of 1981.

The band was really starting to hit their stride, and the album, called *Underneath the Colours* and released in November, was a giant leap forward. It spawned three hits: 'Stay Young', 'Underneath the Colours' and 'Night of Rebellion'. Another gold record for Deluxe.

By now, though, Chris and I were starting to disagree a lot. His expectations were higher than an indie label with the limited resources of Deluxe could provide. It was beginning to fuel bad feeling that none of us—Chris, the band or myself—needed. INXS required a big label with a big budget. I knew I was screwed. Chris began to explore other options, including an exit.

The situation between us deteriorated to the point where our lawyers—I was represented by my good friend Warren Cross—were required to come in, sit down and work out a settlement. Deluxe retained INXS's publishing rights and received an override percentage payment on their future albums that would otherwise have been released during the remainder of their contract. Considering that they were now free to sign to a cashed-up multinational, and had a manager whose dreams were as big as the band's, I was now onto a very good thing.

INXS signed with WEA Records who, despite their enormous international resources and power, hadn't had much success discovering and developing local artists from scratch—with the exception of Cold Chisel. This was hardly an isolated case, to be fair; CBS had signed Men at Work and Mi-Sex, both of whom were enjoying success, but the majority of successful homegrown bands were coming out of Mushroom Records in Melbourne, as well as Regular Records and my own Deluxe in Sydney. Still, WEA had the resources that a band like INXS needed and deserved. I was okay with this; it was a win–win situation for everyone.

Out of this conflict grew a perception that Chris and I were raging, mortal enemies, likely to tear each other apart at a moment's notice. It just wasn't (and still isn't) true. While we've had our moments of unrest, we've been okay for many, many years. Chris was doing what he felt to be in the best interest of his band, just as I would have done back in the AC/DC era. You fight for your band. And I was happy with my override deal. Any nasty stuff was sorted out by our lawyers.

And, as history proved, Chris did the right thing by INXS, who became the biggest Australian band since AC/DC. He did an incredible job, although in typical Murphy fashion he pissed off a few people. Okay, he pissed off a lot of people. But he was on a mission and with his relentless support INXS became superstars.

Chris would never admit it, but I know that during the early stage of our relationship, I influenced his take on the management business, particularly the concept of thinking globally. I also influenced him in the art of embracing his role as the 'arsehole no one else wants to be', the person making all the hard decisions. Managers didn't have to be loved; that was the artists' job. Chris would set new standards for this concept.

■

At this point, I was starting to miss being involved with a heavy rock band. I'd promised myself that I would never go through the whole AC/DC scenario again, but deep down I knew that this was where I'd be the most effective. I was also missing the management side of the business. Record and publishing company business left me cold. Clive's advice had been wise, my health had improved, but I'd come to the conclusion that I needed the satisfaction I could only get via a management relationship with an artist.

Lobby Loyde had told me about an Adelaide band, now Sydney based, named Fat Lip—a name I hated—and I looked into them. I met their singer, a guy named Allan Fryer, who went to great lengths telling me that he'd been on the shortlist to replace Bon in AC/DC. Oh, really?

George Young, so he claimed, had considered him to be a good candidate for the gig and recorded his vocal on a few AC/DC tracks. I had no idea if this actually happened, or if it was, as I suspected, just a figment of Fryer's imagination. Not that Fryer couldn't sing well; he was good, but he was just a bit too close vocally to Bon and there would have been inevitable comparisons. He struck me as difficult to deal with, too; I could have imagined Malcolm and Angus ending up on a homicide charge if he'd somehow joined the band.

Despite a voice in my head telling me to forget it and walk away, my heart was saying go for it and I decided to sign Fat Lip. The first order of business was a name change: they became Heaven. I don't recall why, exactly; maybe it was like the Deluxe name, I must have seen it somewhere in some other context. Anything had to be better than Fat Lip.

Interest in hard rock in Australia in the early 1980s had almost completely faded away. AC/DC was based overseas, for one thing, and the country was caught up in the whole new wave movement, along with the last gasp of punk rock. Signing Heaven (to Deluxe and a management deal) was going totally against this trend, but I had a plan: I was confident there'd always be a healthy demand for good rock'n'roll bands in the United States. That was undeniable. AC/DC had never let trends get in their way, so why should I start to worry about such things now? And I knew the American marketplace.

The band also needed a new logo. I quickly arranged to have one designed; the brief was that we needed something with the feel of the Hells Angels logo. What the graphic artist delivered bore a striking resemblance to the bikers' world-famous motif. Too close. The band had barely re-emerged as Heaven when a pair of burly Hells Angels popped into my office for a friendly chat, pointing out certain design similarities. We agreed on a solution to the problem: as a penalty for our crime of plagiarism, we'd play a show at their clubhouse.

'You come too,' I was told. It didn't really feel like a request.

A few weeks later we found ourselves at their headquarters in a southwestern Sydney suburb. The club members could sense we were a little out of our comfort zone, and did their best to make us feel welcome. They were extremely hospitable, especially with their various substances. Lines of coke were placed under our noses—served up on the blade of a razor-sharp knife. We couldn't really refuse everything that was being offered. No one was interested in finding out what would happen if we politely said, 'No, thanks all the same.'

At one point I looked out of the heavily barred windows and observed, sitting just outside the compound, a busload of police in riot gear, patiently waiting for things to get out of hand. Interesting. It wasn't long before the Heaven guys were so fucked up they couldn't do what they were there for: to play and entertain our new Hells Angels buddies. They tried to play one song but collapsed in a screaming heap. To make matters worse, Allan Fryer recognised a young lady that he'd been with a few weeks earlier.

'Shit,' he whispered to me, pointing out that his female acquaintance was the girlfriend of one of our hosts. We began to case the joint for rooftop exits.

Fortunately, finally, the Angels took pity on us, saw how messed up we were and figured we'd paid our dues, so they escorted us home, eyeballing the cops warily as we left the compound. I couldn't get out of bed for two days. And the band got a new logo.

Heaven recorded their debut album at EMI studios in early 1982 with local producer John Bee, just as AC/DC's latest, *For Those About to Rock We Salute You*, became my former band's first US number-one LP. The Heaven record was called *Twilight of Mischief*; we shot a video for their first single, 'Fantasy', which copped a less than enthusiastic local response. There were line-up changes: their rhythm guitarist John Hayes was replaced by Mick Cocks from Rose Tattoo, joining Bradford Kelly on lead guitar, bassist Laurie Marlow and drummer Joe Turtur, with Fryer still out front. They were a hard rockin' band who I genuinely thought had the right stuff.

I wanted to provide them with a look that I could sell to the American record companies, fully aware how important image was in the world's biggest music market. I commissioned Norma Moriceau, the costume designer from *Mad Max 2*; she came up with a look similar to the apocalyptic feel of the film, a look that carried over into the album cover and video shoot for Heaven's next single, 'In the Beginning'. Overall, I felt we had a great package that I could sell to the Americans.

Things were changing in the local music scene. Thanks to the success of my label Deluxe and other indies like Regular and Mushroom, the major labels were now out there trying to sign all the new Sydney bands. Until recently we'd had the field all to ourselves; now I'd go and see a new band play and find the place jammed with numerous A&R guys, offering all sorts of stupid deals to every band that moved. This was the clincher for me: I decided it was time to go back to the States for a while, have another bash at breaking an Australian rock band overseas. This time it would be Heaven.

So once again we packed up the household and headed out on another attempt at cracking the international market. I was still driven, especially now that AC/DC were megastars. I just couldn't get the desire for world domination out of my system. I didn't quite realise something at the time: this was all about my ambitions. I don't believe the band really understood, or could have imagined, the possibilities. They just came along for the ride.

At least this time I was sufficiently cashed up to buy a comfortable house, just off Laurel Canyon, not far from Frank Zappa's old place. Laurel Canyon was great, the go-to location for Californian rock legends. My kids ended up attending a local primary school called Wonderland, where they studied alongside the offspring of legends. It was a stimulating environment.

I struck up a deal for Heaven with Michael Klenfner's new CBS-backed label, which he'd named Brighton Records, after his

Brooklyn hometown. I relocated the band to Los Angeles and with the advance I received from Brighton, paid everyone a weekly wage and put them on the road, just as I'd done with AC/DC.

Bill Elson at ATI booked the band's dates. Bill was the only guy in the music industry I'd met who virtually lived in a three-piece suit, regardless of whether he was in his office, backstage at a gig, or in 40-degree heat in the Californian desert at a rock festival. Bill booked what he described as a 'torture tour' for Heaven, similar to what ATI had booked for AC/DC a few years earlier. These were three-act bills, with Heaven down the bottom, usually staged in the middle of nowhere at far-flung places, often in the worst possible weather. Blizzards, storms, you name it.

I caught up with the band in Chicago mid-winter; we were scheduled to travel north. Visibility was zero; while one person drove, the others reluctantly stuck their heads out the window, navigating and yelling directions. It was genuinely scary. But Bill, whom I'd got to know pretty well from the AC/DC days, was great at packaging tours. He kept Heaven on the road, playing higher-profile supports for Judas Priest, Iron Maiden and Mötley Crüe, as well as their own headlining gigs.

Klenfner didn't love the band quite as much as he'd loved AC/DC, but he still did what he could, managing to get the 'In the Beginning' video into high rotation on the newly launched MTV. Practically every FM rock radio station in the country programmed the record, as well. I don't think an unknown Aussie band had ever been given such an amazing start. But for some reason the public just didn't connect; despite all the touring, airplay and TV exposure, they sold very few records. They clearly needed to make a better record and with the support of Brighton Records and Klenfner, we were in a position to make this happen.

I put up the band and their three-man crew (Rocky, Pat and Dave) in a nice family-style house in North Hollywood. The place had a swimming pool and cabana, and the house soon became the Valley's domestic equivalent of Sunset Boulevard's Rainbow Bar and Grill, Hollywood's famous hangout for rock stars. Heaven were the perfect hosts. I, meanwhile, footed the bills and pacified disgruntled landlords and neighbours, something I'd become very accustomed to in the days with AC/DC at their Lansdowne Road house. But instead of St Kilda strippers and hookers, I was now dealing with drug-fucked Hollywood groupies, real creatures of the night.

When they weren't in the mood to host, the band frequented the real Rainbow. They'd party with Mötley Crüe, Iron Maiden and whoever else was in town.

Iron Maiden's manager Rod Smallwood—affectionately known as 'Small Wallet', although I found him to be very generous—lived in an old mansion on the hill above the Rainbow, with a pathway connecting club and house. The place, which had once belonged to Jimmy Cagney, became Rod's own rock'n'roll version of the Playboy Mansion. For some reason, apart from his well-stocked bar and a bed, Rod didn't have a stick of furniture in this magnificent property. Maybe he didn't need any, because everything happened around the swimming pool. Rod's other band, hair metal act Wasp, shot a video poolside, with my daughter Billie making a cameo, reciting the pledge of allegiance.

Heaven loved the lifestyle, of course. What young, red-blooded rock guys wouldn't? But there was a key point of difference between them and the bands they were hanging out with: while the others loved to party, they also worked on their songwriting and playing skills, as well as everything else a band needed to do in order to be prepared for when a bit of luck came along.

I had some huge arguments with the band about this. I could sense that they were squandering a great opportunity. Mick just had to go; he was a great guy and made a good musical contribution, but he was also a terrible team player. There were occasions when he simply wouldn't get out of bed to catch the departing tour bus.

I pink-slipped him and hired Mark Evans. On paper this seemed a bit strange—Mark had played bass in AC/DC, after all—but he'd originally been a guitarist, and a very good one. Mark joined us in America and tried his hardest to instill some kind of work ethic, which he'd gained by osmosis during those early AC/DC days.

But Mark ended up clashing with Fryer. Allan could be a loveable guy; he'd dress up as a clown and entertain the kids at my daughter's birthday parties—she referred to him as

'Uncle Allan'. But he was also a very talented rogue, a bit of a trait among lead singers, as I've observed over the years. His nickname was 'Fast Eddie'.

I've been frustrated by musicians to the point of contemplating violence in the past, I'll admit that. But Fryer was the only guy I ever punched out. He could be really annoying, but I'd resisted the temptation to clock him until one day, during a band meeting, he pissed me off so badly that for reasons I no longer recall I swung a punch and connected with his jaw. The rest of the band was stunned. Allan sulked for a while and I felt like shit. We made up and, oddly enough, it didn't seem to make the slightest bit of difference; for some reason, I still liked the prick.

The band had a history of internal clashes. While in Oregon, supporting the band Steppenwolf, an almighty brawl broke out between the Heaven guys in the shared backstage dressing room, prior to Steppenwolf's arrival. The biggest casualty was the headliner's 'rider', which was splashed against the dressing room's walls, dripping onto the carpet. Steppenwolf only found this out after they'd thrown themselves into a set-closing, roof-raising version of 'Born to Be Wild'. They were not happy.

They recorded their second album in 1984 at Hollywood's Cherokee studios, working with a young and highly recommended producer named George Tutko. The album cover shoot took place in a park under the famous Hollywood sign, with two trained (and chained) black panthers as props. The concept was for Allan to lead the panthers, but he somehow managed to step on one of their tails. Luckily, the trainers had wire leads attached to the panther's collars; otherwise it would have been a case of goodnight Uncle Allan.

Their new album, titled *Where Angels Fear to Tread*, was well recorded, but just didn't have the songs they needed. It was the era of hair metal in LA, with bands like Poison and Mötley Crüe and Ratt on the rise, and Heaven would have fitted in perfectly— with the right songs. But there were none on this album.

The band continued to party hard and the inevitable internal problems started to arise. To be fair to the band, I'm blaming their lifestyle, but the partying was most likely a smokescreen for their lack of natural songwriting skills. We all learn lessons in life along the way; this proved to be an expensive one for all of us. It doesn't matter how smokin' the band is, if they don't have the songs, forget it, you're wasting your time. There was another problem, too: the image that I'd created for them in Australia had become diluted to the point that they no longer had a visual point of difference. Another big no-no in the world of heavy rock.

I decided to pull the plug in 1985 and sold my contract to Leber and Krebs Management, the same company that had taken over AC/DC after my sacking. Heaven didn't last long; they disbanded soon after and returned to Australia. All except for Fast Eddie, that is, who stayed in America and now resides in Texas, where he performs the occasional Heaven reformation gig.

A FEW FINAL SHOTS

Around this time I was seeing more of my old sparring partner Billy Thorpe; both our families were living in Los Angeles and we'd spend a lot of time together. Billy had a home studio set up in his Encino residence and I'd listen to tracks that he had been working on and chat about the possibility of working on different projects.

I ran one particular idea past him, based on the concept of The Highwaymen, the coming together of established solo artists who'd form a group for the occasional album and tour. It had worked a treat for Johnny Cash, Kris Kristofferson, Waylon Jennings and Willie Nelson. Surely there were some expat Aussies we could get together, give it a shot?

Billy got excited about the idea, so we called Max Merritt and Brian Cadd, who were both based in the US. They each had great musical and vocal chops, and Cadd could contribute his awesome songwriting talents. And we called Renée Geyer, also in LA, whom I'd known when she began as a professional singer; she was someone I greatly admired for her uncompromising approach to her art. Renée was the real deal—still is. Takes no shit from anyone.

Shortly after, we all met at Billy's local Mexican restaurant and over some tacos and margaritas we agreed to give it a go. After a few more margaritas, the subject of a band name was raised. The usual useless ideas were thrown around, then Renée looked at us with a grin on her face and said, without missing a beat: 'Let's call it Three Pricks and a Cunt.'

More margaritas were ordered. We loved it.

Billy, being the control freak prick that he was, started to dominate the concept and the other two pricks and Renée soon lost interest. The idea, which I felt could have been great, ended up the subject of a few dinner party laughs.

I didn't give up on Billy, though, and would hammer away at him with ideas. On more than one occasion I tried to talk him into moving to Nashville and becoming a country singer.

'There are no age barriers in country,' I explained, 'You don't have to worry about pop radio liking you.'

I also knew that this was a style of music Billy picked up in his early days as Little Rock Allen—it was in the guy's DNA.

Billy would kick his heels in, telling me that I was full of shit. He was, after all, an expert on everything, as much as I loved the guy.

My sister Coral had now been back working for me since my return to America. She'd discovered a band from San Diego called Warrior, led by a brilliant young guitar player, Joseph Al Kaddam (aka Joe Floyd); they also had an amazing vocalist with a huge set of lungs named Perry McCarty. Coral dragged me down to a rehearsal studio in Burbank to see the band, and I was blown away. Clearly, they'd been working very hard on perfecting what was a very original sound and concept. Most heavy rock bands were writing songs about partying hard, or were off on some Satanic trip; these guys had songs about saving the planet. A green rock band—Warrior were way ahead of their time.

We arranged for the band to record demos, in the hope of stirring up some record company interest, and the results were stunning. We then set up a showcase gig at West Hollywood's Troubadour Club, a career-making venue for everyone from Elton John to James Taylor. To promote the date we sent the demo to KMET, the big rock station in LA—to our delight they put the track 'Fighting for the Earth' straight into high rotation.

Before long we had record companies calling, wanting to get on the guest list. The gig was a huge success. Everyone was in. Capitol Records wanted the band; so did Ten Records from the UK, a subsidiary of Virgin Records now headed by my old

AC/DC and Deluxe buddy Richard Griffiths. They flipped over the band and definitely wanted to sign them, but first wanted label boss Richard Branson to meet the band.

On Richard Griffiths' behalf, Coral arranged for a limo to collect Branson from LAX. We called KMET and explained that Richard Branson would be in transit in a limo at a certain time—could they please play the track? We'd ensured the limo driver had KMET on, nice and loud. Everything was in place. By the time Richard met us at the designated restaurant he couldn't flash that Virgin chequebook around quickly enough.

Before the deal was signed, though, he insisted on flying us to London for a round of golf and dinner at his home in Oxford. How could we say no? Having now experienced the 'Richard Branson Show', we were all hooked on doing the deal. He was our guy.

Richard wanted the band to make the definitive heavy rock album—with no expenses spared. Thinking they had Virgin wrapped around their fingers, the band insisted on total creative control, meaning they'd be in charge of production, working with a studio crew of their choice who'd pull the sounds they were after.

This is generally a recipe for disaster; I really should have known better and put them in their place. Creative control is a wonderful concept and sounds really impressive, but it rarely exists, especially for a new band. Some compromises are always necessary. But they were highly talented, intelligent guys, who were very convincing, so I went along with them. The deal came together, but the recording process went on forever and the resulting album was way over-produced.

By the time it came out on Virgin Ten Records in Europe and MCA Records in the US—in 1985—the whole heavy metal thing was in temporary decline. The annual Abraham Radio Convention, a gathering of radio programmers from all over America, had just announced its demise, dismissing the form as 'Nazi rock'. Talk about the kiss of death. In the music industry timing is everything, and Warrior's time had been and gone. Another important lesson. The band hung in and played some dates in the US and the UK, but not much came out of it and they eventually decided to disband.

With the combined disappointments of Heaven and Warrior—and watching on from the sidelines as AC/DC's relentless rise continued—things were not going to plan for me. I wasn't used to failure and I wasn't taking it very well. My marriage to Julie was breaking down; it had been in decline for much of the period of my involvement with these two bands. I decided it was time to go home. I took Billie and James with me, while Julie stayed on in LA for a while. If we were to break up—which we eventually did—I didn't want it to happen away from our real home, Australia.

Career-wise, I had a fairly good idea what was waiting for me back in Sydney: a vibrant music scene, for one thing. I'd been having discussions with a long-time friend and a great vocalist, a guy named Jon Stevens. Maybe I had another shot left.

■

While living in LA I'd made the occasional trip back to Sydney, and would catch up with Stevens and Sydney guitarist Stuart Fraser, whom I'd introduced to each other. Stuart was a highly respected guitar player from a group called Blackfeather, whom I'd known and admired for many years. To my delight Jon and Stuart had been writing songs with the intention of forming a band.

I'd first noticed Jon on the TV show *Countdown* in 1980, where he was performing the single 'Montego Bay', his second number one in his native New Zealand. The other chart-topper was called 'Jezebel', which had knocked Michael Jackson's 'Don't Stop Till You Get Enough' from the number-one position. Jon was a huge star in New Zealand, but no one in Australia had heard of him. Not yet.

There was something special about Jon. First of all, he looked good—I later discovered that he was a combination of the best of his beloved Māori and Scottish parents—and I also thought that he had a great voice. But what really got my attention was evident in that first *Countdown* appearance; he was a complete unknown but the girls in the studio audience were going crazy for him. Looks, a great voice, sex appeal—it was Michael Hutchence all over again.

Jon had been signed to a deal with Air Supply's LA-based manager Lance Reynolds, who, after observing his sudden rise to fame in New Zealand, flew him over and began grooming him for the American market. But their relationship hit a snag when Reynolds made an unauthorised business commitment that Jon didn't care for. Jon cut himself loose and eventually settled in Sydney, like so many of his fellow Kiwis in the early 1980s.

During one of my Sydney visits, Kevin Stanton and Murray Burns approached me about managing their band Mi-Sex, who had parted company with their long-standing manager Bob Yates. Mi-Sex were a New Zealand–born band who'd had huge Australian success with their 1979 number-one 'Computer Games' and a few lesser hits in the early 1980s.

'I'm interested in working with you,' I said during our meet, 'but not as Mi-Sex.'

I spelled out my plan—I wanted to put together a band that I envisaged would be more suited to the American market (did I never learn?), with this vocalist I'd seen on *Countdown*, Jon Stevens. I meant no disrespect for Steve Gilpin, Mi-Sex's singer; I just had this different direction in mind.

I got in touch with Jon, who seemed keen, and we all met. Things seemed promising, but Kevin and Murray felt pangs of disloyalty towards Steve and decided against the idea. But by now I had really got to like Jon—and I was absolutely convinced of his potential. Before returning to LA, I'd introduced Jon to Stuart Fraser.

They eventually joined forces with Steve Balbi, a talented bass player and songwriter who had been writing with keyboardist Justin Stanley with the intention of also forming a band. With the addition of an old friend of Jon's, drummer Kevin Nicol, the line-up was complete in 1985. They called themselves The Change. There were now no less than four songwriters in the one group, something Heaven would have killed for.

With me still in Los Angeles, but checking in occasionally with Jon, they hooked up with the Australian-based, American-born session guitar player, Louie Sheldon, who'd previously played with Seals & Crofts and The Monkees. Louie had a big reputation and was highly respected both abroad and in Australia, especially in muso circles. The band engaged Louie to produce their demos in his home studio. Louie craved a bigger, more permanent role with the band, and by the time I'd settled back in Sydney with the kids, he'd offered his services as manager.

But I'd been having long distance telephone conversations with Jon about *me* becoming their manager, subject to hearing their final demos. I was now back in Sydney and itching to sign them up.

This created a dilemma for the band; Louie had been doing good work with them and had connected with the guys. Eventually I won, but not without Louie getting pissed off. He began to threaten the group with legal action, alleging that they had a verbal agreement. Eventually a settlement was reached, something I was becoming way too familiar with, and we all got on with it.

CBS Records in Sydney had just imported a new A&R man from London, Dave Novak, a serious young music chap out to make his mark in Australia. Dave heard the Change demos, and desperately wanted to make them his first signing. The deal was eventually done in late 1985. They signed what was a pretty standard 1980s contract, giving CBS worldwide rights, but they did offer a better than average royalty rate. CBS would cover all (recoupable) recording costs, as well as marketing costs. The band was happy; they'd found a home with some truly passionate music people who loved and believed in them.

Their publishing, meanwhile, was grabbed by my old cohort from the AC/DC days, Chris Gilbey. He'd discovered that the management business with The Saints in the UK was not his idea of a good time and had returned to Oz to run MCA's publishing business.

I decided to hire an assistant and was introduced to a young woman who'd previously worked for Rose Tattoo's Angry Anderson. Her name was Jane Norton. Angry had nicknamed her 'Snorting Norton', after the character on *The Jackie Gleason Show*. Hardly flattering, come to think of it. But she was tough—I called her my Iron Lady.

Jane was the world's most efficient secretary/assistant, without a doubt. She was particularly dynamite when it came to collecting money; grown men would quiver and cough up the cash when they saw her coming.

It was Christmas 1985 and I was about to meet the Australian head of CBS Records, Denis Handlin, for the first time. It was the night of the CBS staff fancy dress Christmas party. I'd heard a lot of stories about Denis, but I was unaware of what he looked like. I suddenly found myself discussing my new band's future with a bloke dressed as Davy Crockett. It had to be a good omen.

Denis had worked his way up through the ranks of CBS, starting in the Brisbane storeroom, and I'd never met anyone more passionate about breaking new artists. We got on very well and he made a commitment that night to do everything in his power to break The Change wide open. In true Davy Crockett tradition he'd always be as good as his word.

But he hit a bump almost immediately. We discovered a UK band was already using the name The Change, so we had to change ours. Everyone threw ideas into the proverbial hat. Mine happened to be DreamWorks—way before the movie company, I should point out—and the band sort of liked it, but they suggested one small change and Noiseworks was born. They held down a Thursday night residency at the St Leonards Hotel, and had built a solid following. Musos, too, would turn up in droves to check out this new band, always a good sign. A vibe was growing.

CBS hired producer Mark Opitz, who'd started out as tape operator for Vanda and Young at Alberts studios, working on some early AC/DC recordings, to produce Noiseworks' debut.

Mark had become a highly sought-after producer with a good ear; he made great-sounding records. He and the band settled in at Rhinoceros Studios in Sydney.

On release in late 1986, their debut single, 'No Lies', became an instant favourite with the Australian media. Radio loved it, too, adding the song straight away. Noiseworks were making all the right kind of noises.

The band headed out on the road as part of a high-profile package tour with Johnny Diesel and the Injectors and a now-solo Jimmy Barnes. The crowds were enormous. By tour's end, 'No Lies' was a genuine hit, a great start for the band. Their next single, 'Take Me Back', a heavy-hearted song Jon had written about the death of a friend, was an even bigger hit, reaching the national Top 5 in April 1987. Their self-titled debut album dropped in June and it was a smash, selling more than 200,000 copies and debuting at number two.

Noiseworks had fast-tracked their way to becoming a headlining band. MTV filmed a special in-concert performance at Selina's, a huge beachside beer barn in Coogee, a venue typically reserved for such established acts as Midnight Oil and Cold Chisel. Five hit singles were eventually lifted from their barnstorming debut. Even AC/DC and INXS—currently riding high in the US charts with 'What You Need' and 'Need You Tonight'—hadn't accomplished that.

Handlin and CBS put their money where their sales were and hired British producer Chris Kimsey, who'd worked on the Stones' *Undercover* and *Steel Wheels* albums, to produce Noiseworks' follow-up. Kimsey had also worked with Peter Frampton, engineering his massive *Frampton Comes Alive!* album; he would later engineer INXS's *Full Moon, Dirty Hearts* LP. A real player. CBS had given the band and me an enormous recording budget—more on that later—and work commenced in 1988, again at Rhinoceros Studios.

The catering costs alone for this album were more than a big album budget today. It was the 1980s, of course, the greed is good era, and there was money to be found everywhere— and then stupidly squandered, of course. Each night during the recording sessions, a fully catered banquet was laid on, with the finest food and wine provided. The band and recording team would wear long-sleeved T-shirts with a bow tie and lounge suit painted on them: formal dress, 1980s style.

While I was concerned by the spiralling costs, I did enjoy the occasional dinner with the band, which was followed by a mock cricket match on the ping-pong table, an empty vodka bottle substituting for a regulation cricket bat and an olive as the ball. It was like living in some Duran Duran video, with a few distinctly Aussie touches.

Everyone in the band took on a new name. Jon became Rangy Olsen, Steve was Vernon Weller, Stuart was Chet Fauquier, Justin became Stan Gruburg, Kevin was simply called Humphrey, Chris

Kimsey was renamed Cappy and I became Baz—for the second time in my managerial career I only needed the one name. Still, it felt a bit more inclusive and friendlier than Browning, which was how the AC/DC mob addressed me.

You'd think the new music would suffer with all this madness going on, but that wasn't the case; the only thing that really suffered was the budget, which was pushing towards a staggering $250,000. The *Touch* album, released in time for Christmas 1988, included the hits 'Simple Man' and 'Love Somebody', as well as 'Reach Out', which would become an Aussie classic.

Immediately prior to the album's release, Jon arrived at the annual CBS Christmas bash sporting a totally new look—a number-one, an Army-style crew cut. Hardly the style of a young rock'n'roll star. I was relieved that the album cover shot had already been taken.

Denis Handlin didn't look as friendly as at previous Christmas parties. He didn't say a word to me—he just burned a hole in me with his glare. On Christmas Day, just as I was sitting down for lunch with my kids, the phone rang. It was Denis—and he was going ballistic. He didn't give a fuck what day it was.

'What is with that haircut?' he roared at me. 'What is Jon thinking?'

Jon had a great, sexy image and the album's marketing was about to be rolled out, with the band's lead singer looking like a cross between a marine and a convict. Despite agreeing with

Denis, I defended Jon's free will—that was my job, after all—and we had an argument of monumental proportions. What did he want me to do—buy the guy a wig?

To launch the album, CBS Melbourne, in conjunction with Triple M FM and an anti-youth drinking campaign program, closed off the top end of Spring Street, not far from the old Sebastian's site, and erected a stage on the steps of Victoria's Parliament House. I was having my share of Melbourne and AC/DC flashbacks as everything was set up; a massive crowd assembled—just up the road from where my beloved Hard Rock had now been replaced by another bland corporate high-rise.

The band's dressing room was set up in a suite at the nearby Windsor Hotel, an exclusive old-world joint typically patronised by wealthy folks from the land. A rock'n'roll band in their pomp wasn't a common sighting at the Windsor. The launch was an unqualified success; estimates had the crowd at around 100,000, the kind of amazing numbers Thorpey and the Aztecs pulled at the Myer Music Bowl way back in the day.

The afterparty kicked on in the band's suite. The guys were joined by their many friends, including Baby Animals, a hard rock band fronted by one of the country's original rock chicks, Suze DeMarchi, and their manager John 'Woody' Woodruff. Nick Barker, a good mate and a budding rock star in true 'fucked-up Keith Richards style', was also in the house. Room service plied everyone with ridiculous amounts of liquor and when that dried up, the bar fridges were emptied. Everyone was wasted, just the perfect way to celebrate a gig sponsored by an anti-drinking campaign.

Keeping with the debauched rocker theme, Steve and Justin picked up a television set with the intention of hurling it out the fourth-floor window. I exchanged a worried look with a fellow manager (a well-known and respected man, who shall remain nameless), and we both turned white. No one had bothered to check the street below for pedestrians, nor had anyone noticed that the electrical cord was wrapped around Steve's leg. He was ready to go out the window with the TV set. My fellow manager and I suggested that Steve leave a job like this to professionals, and we duly removed the cord from Steve's leg and heaved the set out the window. Everyone watched it smash to smithereens on the pavement below.

We agreed now was the perfect time to get the hell out of Melbourne and prepared to make a hasty exit to Tullamarine for our flight back to Sydney. We didn't get far; on the way out of the hotel car park, the police pulled us over.

'Know anything about that TV set?' they asked, pointing to the wreckage on the footpath.

'Of course not, officer,' we lied.

They let us go, but the newspapers were all over it, of course, as we continued to deny any knowledge.

'You might want to talk to Nick Barker,' I suggested. Always the manager, I thought it might be good for his image.

As far as I understood, CBS must have paid the bill and shut down all the police enquiries. I was in a meeting a few days later with Denis in Sydney—and nothing was mentioned. It was as if it never happened.

The *Touch* album was another huge hit, selling around 150,000 copies. Damian Trotter, the band's staunchest supporter at CBS, arranged a video shoot for 'Reach Out', complete with helicopters and horses on a rocky outcrop just outside of Kiama, a township on the New South Wales South Coast. All this was organised with the assistance of the first mobile phone I'd ever seen. The thing looked like a motorcycle battery with a conventional phone stuck at the end of it. Of course, not everything went to plan—the volume of the music scared the horses, who bolted into the nearby sleepy township, freaking out the locals. Just another day on Planet Rock'n'Roll.

Sadly, Stephen Priest, the producer of 'Reach Out' and some other videos for the band—along with clips for Duran Duran and David Bowie—died from AIDS soon afterwards. A true believer to the very end, he asked to be buried in a Noiseworks T-shirt.

Some interest in Noiseworks had grown internationally, as my thoughts once again turned to breaking a band globally. They'd toured Europe and the US, and countries like Sweden and Italy seemed to get the band. Europe was shaping up well.

CBS Records presented the band to the international community at the annual Midem industry get-together in Cannes in 1989. Immediately prior to Midem, I joined a contingent of Australian music publishers on an invited visit to Moscow, courtesy of the government. The USSR was going through its Perestroika period—things were beginning to open up to the West. (In 1991, Mikhail Gorbachev threw open the Tushino airfield to the Monsters of Rock festival, which AC/DC headlined. They drew a crowd of around one million fans.)

We held discussions with the authorities about bringing Noiseworks to Moscow, to play—of all places—the Hard Rock Cafe. Apparently I hadn't been the only person in the world to fancy the name. But not long after these discussions, the Berlin Wall came down and the Soviet Union was split up. Everything changed; Noiseworks gigs were hardly the first order of business and the plans were cancelled.

The US, meanwhile, was a hopeless situation. CBS America's commitment was minimal, to say the least. Their art department had for some ridiculous reason decided to photoshop the band's photo on the album's cover and there wasn't a single wrinkle left on their faces. They all looked ridiculously young—and vaguely Asian. There was very little airplay, no promotion and Noiseworks was dismissed as just another band that slipped between the cracks.

■

There was no bottomless budget for the band's third album, which would eventually be released in mid-1991, and titled—

not on a whim—*Love Versus Money*. The band produced the album mainly because the label weren't committed to spending big bucks on another imported producer. The songs were mostly recorded at Damian Gerard Studios in Ultimo, basically a demo studio.

The first version of the album was rejected by CBS. I wasn't about to argue with them; the record wasn't sounding right to me, overloaded as it was with bombastic string arrangements.

The lack of interest from the US had given CBS doubts about the band's writing, so Jon and Stuart were despatched to Los Angeles on a songwriting mission, where they were hooked up with a number of 'pro' songwriters, the corporate thinking being, 'If it worked for Tina Arena, surely it'll work for Noiseworks.' This was a big mistake; it polarised a band that had been one big happy rock'n'roll family until now. The band split into distinct camps: Jon and Stuart in one, Steve and Justin in another, who'd felt alienated when Jon and Stuart agreed to go to LA—not that there'd been much choice. Kevin was stuck somewhere in the middle, wondering why all this was happening to his best mates.

CBS was holding out for a more 'American-styled' album; they wanted stronger songs than they'd heard in the Damian Gerard recordings. While Jon and Stuart were in LA, a disgruntled Steve and Justin came in to see me. They entered my office, cynically dressed up in business suits and ties, figuring they would come to talk business.

'We want some money,' they told me, 'to go into the studio and record some more demos.'

The songs rejected by CBS, written by Justin and Steve, had been very Beatlesque. I told them they could have the time in the studio for the demos, on one condition.

'I want to hear sex, drugs, fast cars and rock'n'roll.'

A week later they returned with a demo of 'Hot Chilli Woman'. They later told me they were taking the piss, that it was written as a pot shot at me, but CBS loved it. I did, too. It was a hugely commercial rock song, very Noiseworks. CBS quickly arranged for Randy Jackson, a red-hot bass player for Bruce Springsteen's E Street Band, and a CBS house producer, to fly to Sydney and produce the track. Randy did a great job, coming up with a very strong-sounding record; he even wrote the 'middle eight' (for which I don't think he was ever paid). The band still thought it was a cop-out; they hated the song. It raced into the Top 10 in June 1991 and became their biggest selling single. I wish they'd hated a few more of their songs.

Suddenly CBS found money for the band. Marketing manager Chris 'Mossy' Moss, a maniac in the Billy Thorpe tradition, was never afraid of spending big bucks if he felt 'the vibe'. Mossy splashed out on a launch for the new album, staged at Sydney's Hordern Pavilion. The big concrete bunker was transformed into a casino for the night, with roulette tables, printed Noiseworks money—you name it.

The band didn't just play; there was a huge production, with pyrotechnics and the rest of it. It was the most expensive album launch in the history of the Australian music business, the bill topping $100,000. Yet even with Mossy's incredible hype, and despite a number-one chart debut, sales of the album didn't match its predecessors. The band's unrecouped recording costs were now huge. Noiseworks were on a downward spiral.

NOISEWORKS' BLOWOUT, JON STEVENS' RESURRECTION AND MY SWANSONG

While all this professional drama was going on, my private life was on the improve after my divorce. Things had changed a bit since the Billy Thorpe days, when I'd had a clear run with some gorgeous women. Now I was managing the best-looking band in the land—some of whom were single—and the pickings were slim. And I was getting on a bit. I'd been flirting with Mossy's secretary Elizabeth for some time, in an era when executives still had secretaries. Elizabeth was beautiful and also very gracious; she always made sure I received the proper attention. Bells started ringing for me; I really liked this woman. *Really* liked her. Hoping that Mossy didn't object, I asked Elizabeth to dinner at one of Sydney's fancier restaurants. Something clicked, because we were married six months later, in a glorious ceremony held in a marquee in the home of Elizabeth's family. This time, as well as family and friends, we invited many of my musical cohorts, including the Gudinskis, the Chuggs, the Woodruffs and the Gilbeys. My best man (and best friend) was Warren Cross—Noiseworks supplied the music. It was all pulled together by Tony Assness, a creative wizard, who now runs live events. During my speech I used my uncle Milton's line about looking at the mother and seeing how the daughter will turn out, but I said it with pride. We now have two children, Bert—named after my father—and Rosie, so named because of her beautiful strawberry-blonde hair (and nothing whatsoever to do with AC/DC's 'Whole Lotta Rosie', thankfully).

But Noiseworks, meanwhile, was falling apart. The animosity between the two rival factions was taking its toll. There were also problems about substance abuse. Justin came to see me one day and announced that he was leaving.

From day one, Noiseworks had a pact: one out, all out. If anybody left the band, they'd call it quits. They didn't want to hang around in slow decline, like so many other Australian bands. There was also a business consideration: all the red ink on their CBS balance sheet meant that without a big international breakthrough, they'd never see any royalties. Why bother?

Noiseworks version 1.0 played their last gig at Selina's

in March 1992, a very emotional experience for everyone, me included. They were such great guys, the best people I'd worked with. There was never any grumbling à la Angus, none of Thorpey's tantrums or Fast Eddie's slippery ways. It was just as sad an occasion for the people at CBS, who'd been incredibly supportive and had got tight with the guys.

Management is in my blood. Ever since those early days in Melbourne I've loved the feeling of being part of the creative process, the buzz of contributing to something that starts from an embryonic idea and finally gets out there, to become internationally acclaimed. It's nothing less than exhilarating.

With Noiseworks' demise, and the benefit of hindsight, I should have quit the business, gone out on a relatively high note. The band may have fallen apart—at least the original band—but they'd become the biggest act in Australia for a few years, and their music still blares out of radios today. But this business is also a sickness; it's hard to get it out of your system.

I kept thinking, 'One more big one, it's just around the corner'—it was incredibly addictive. It's also the way I identified myself—I was a manager through and through—and the role in which I connected with my colleagues and friends in the music industry. But it's a young person's business; when I lost the desire to get out and see new bands, to network, I should have known it was time to move onto something else.

Jon Stevens re-signed to CBS as a solo act, which was how he'd started out when I first saw him on *Countdown*. Before Jon recorded his first solo record, I got a call from Harry M. Miller, one of Australia's leading theatrical impresarios and a lively, colourful character, who'd worked with some amazing musicians.

'How would Jon feel,' he asked me, 'about playing Judas in *Jesus Christ Superstar*?'

I didn't think too long and hard before arranging a meeting. Harry later said that as soon as Jon walked into the room, he knew he had his Judas. But I was Jon's manager, and I had a few demands.

'Jon would like a bottle of Grange Hermitage on his rider— every night,' I told Harry. Jon wasn't drinking at the time, but Harry didn't need to know that. I thought that requesting a nightcap of Australia's most expensive plonk was merely part of the negotiation dance.

Harry didn't say anything. He simply stood up, went into his office kitchen and re-emerged with a teabag, which he slammed down on the table in front of us.

'Grange! This is all he'll be getting!' he roared, pointing at the teabag. 'After all, you're dealing with the guy who flew The Rolling Stones to Australia in economy.'

Jon did, however, get his Grange. And the gig.

The 1992 arena production of *Superstar*, directed by theatre giant Richard Wherrett, was a huge hit. The cast included Australia's biggest names, everyone from John Farnham to Kate Ceberano, Angry Anderson and John Waters. But Jon Stevens stole the show, night after night, tapping into a whole new, older, more upscale audience. The cast recording was a smash, shifting around 300,000 copies and eventually winning an ARIA in 1993 for highest selling Australian album.

After *Superstar*, Jon began planning his first solo album for CBS, which had morphed into Sony Music due to a huge international takeover. Jon and I went on another of the label's 'song-seeking' missions to LA, checking in with songwriters and publishers. We also went to Miami for a lunch meeting at Joe's Stone Crab House, a favourite hangout for the early Miami Mafia and J. Edgar Hoover. There we met with Tom Dowd, a legendary old-school producer with AC/DC's label Atlantic Records. He'd worked with Eric Clapton and Cream and Rod Stewart, as well as R&B legends Aretha Franklin and Ray Charles. Tom had recently returned to the spotlight via his work with southern rockers The Black Crowes.

Tom didn't end up working with Jon, but that didn't make his stories of the early days at Atlantic any less engrossing. With a bit of prodding he even let slip a few stories about the Manhattan Project; while in the military he'd been part of the team who had developed the nuclear bomb. You don't often get to hang out with such true legends. We enjoyed every moment of it.

Jon ended up producing his own LP. The alarm bells should have gone off; I'd been down this slippery slope before with Noiseworks and Warrior. But if those alarm bells did ring, I just didn't hear them. And it wasn't as though we'd been given many choices by the label. Fortunately, unlike the Noiseworks days, this time the budget was modest.

As a producer, Jon had trouble making the distinction between being a solo artist and the lead singer of a band. An independent producer would have been better equipped to get the 'band sound' idea out of Jon's system. The resulting album, *Are U Satisfied?*, which came out in October 1993, sounded more like a Noiseworks record than a Jon Stevens solo album. His newfound audience from *Superstar* just didn't connect. The album flopped and Jon and I went our separate ways.

Everybody from Noiseworks went off in different directions. Jon first went to LA—he even worked with Slash from Guns N' Roses for a while, with Geffen Records dreaming of some kind of band reformation, though nothing ever came of it. Sony then dropped him from their roster and he returned to Oz, where he spent a well-documented but relatively unrewarding time as Michael Hutchence's replacement in INXS, from 2000 to 2003. Not even someone as gifted as Jon could quite step into those rock star shoes.

But Jon deserves success. At the time of writing he's back in musical theatre with yet another *JC Superstar* production, as well as touring the world with his new band, The Dead

Daisies. Jon's definitely one of the best people I've worked with, a wonderful person and a great talent. He's also a highly principled guy, who'd rather walk away from something he doesn't feel is right. He has a bit of the old Thorpey habit of sometimes getting in his own way. Yet I still believe he can conquer the world.

Steve and Justin, meanwhile, formed a band called the Electric Hippies in 1993 and finally got to record their Beatlesque songs. Among them was something called 'Greedy People', which was directed at Jon and myself. At first I was pissed off. But my old mate Chris Gilbey pointed out that I should be flattered, and besides, it was a hit.

Justin went off to Los Angeles with his wife, Nikka Costa, daughter of the legendary Don Costa, Frank Sinatra's arranger, and became a successful record producer. Steve stayed in Australia and pursued a career as a solo act and record producer. Stuart shifted to Melbourne and became a gun guitarist-for-hire; he also joined John Farnham's band.

As for Kevin, he's the one member who felt the loss of his beloved band the most. He'd been so committed to the group—and then he suddenly lost his dream. He's now the driving force that may one day see a Noiseworks reunion in the studio.

My Iron Lady Jane, meanwhile, went off to live in London.

A few years ago I was driving along listening to the radio, when a song that totally blew me away came on.

'This has to be new Noiseworks,' I said to myself, thrilled that they'd finally managed to nail a track that had the potential to break them in America.

At the same time, I was wondering how this could have come together without me hearing about it. Then they back-announced the track.

'You've just been listening to new music from the Kings of Leon.'

As for me, like I said, I should have given it up, but I just couldn't make myself do it. I was a management junkie, totally addicted. I fought on for a few more years with all kinds of band projects, none of which amounted to much, despite some amazing talent. The problem was simple: my heart was no longer in it. I'd lost the love and passion that had been my driving force for so many years, through all those dog-eat-dog years with AC/DC—and beyond. AC/DC had managed to keep on rolling, recovering from Bon's death and, over the course of the next 30-odd years, becoming perhaps the biggest band on the planet. But I'd lost the drive that kept Angus and Malcolm and the other guys going.

In 2007 I finally decided to retire from the music business. Considering the ruthless nature of the industry, I was lucky to have come out the other side feeling fresh enough to pursue other interests. To the relief of politicians like Joe Hockey, actual retirement has no attraction for me; I plan to work till

I drop. But the sheer number of my fallen colleagues has been very sobering.

From an early age, under the watchful eye of the Knight family, I fell in love with the world of antiques, design and unique *objets d'art*. My wife Elizabeth and I run a company named Rust, a nod to Neil Young's *Rust Never Sleeps*. We deal in imported rustic furniture and *objets d'art*, mostly from Europe.

The amazing thing about it is its simplicity: I can purchase something for X and sell it shortly afterwards for Y. This simple economic concept had eluded me for most of my life. I'd been signing up bands and investing money in them and hoping to make it back one day, praying that the stars would line up, that someone in the band wouldn't spontaneously combust, take too many drugs, get pregnant, die, lose their mojo—the list of uncertainties was endless. Doesn't happen in the world of Rust.

But would I have done it any other way? Absolutely not. That ever-present uncertainty was one of rock'n'roll's greatest mysteries and one of its strongest appeals for me. Who'd have thought the world would have gone mad for a grown man in a school uniform, dripping sweat and snot and god knows what else while he played amazing guitar solos? I knew it, but I'm not sure many others did.

Rock'n'roll has changed since I first got involved; no doubt about that. It's now a lifestyle option more than an attitude, a cool catchphrase rather than a deeply held belief. Accountants, lawyers, politicians, kids—they all talk about 'rock'n'roll' and flash the devil horns sign. To me, rock's glory days are long gone. But maybe a whole new version of the beast is just around the corner. Fuck, who knows?

There are two things I can say for sure, after all my years at the coalface of the business, both of them sourced from the good book as written by Bon Scott. It absolutely is a long way to the top if you want to rock'n'roll. And Bon was right about one other thing. When it comes to the business of music, it truly is 'dog eat dog'.

EPILOGUE

My life in the music industry was both a rewarding and a harrowing experience. I happened to get through the adventure in one piece, financially okay and in reasonably good health. However, a lot of the people I have mentioned throughout these pages didn't make it to the end of the story. I would like to express my respect for them here.

The first casualty was my best mate Larry Shepard, then Paul Kossoff, one of the world's finest rock guitar players, whom I didn't get to meet, sadly, but the circumstances of his death proved to be significant for the future of AC/DC.

Then came the highly respected journalist Claudia Wright, who hijacked me on her radio show the morning after the

Hard Rock opening. RIP Claudia.

Terry Cleary from *Go-Set* magazine was a rascal who made me laugh.

Then there was Bon Scott, that loveable Peter Pan, a real one of a kind, who lived his life to the fullest. He told me that he had always planned on being the best-looking corpse going. Tragically, he got what he wished for, but in doing so broke the world's heart. He had been such an important part of my life.

From Rose Tattoo: Digger, the world's best swing drummer, Mick Cocks and the uber-cool Peter Wells. Obviously a dangerous gig.

When Ted Albert passed away he left a huge gap in the music industry. He was a class act, a man I respected. He was a major player in the development of AC/DC and another huge influence in my life.

Wayne and Rodney de Gruchy were the closest I came to having brothers. I miss them both dearly.

Then there was Billy Thorpe, AM, another one of my special friends, as close as family. His memorial service at the Sydney Entertainment Centre in 2007, conducted by Michael Chugg, said it all. It was totally over the top, just the way Billy lived his amazing life. His power was finally unplugged from a higher source. We all miss him.

We also miss the wonderful Michael Hutchence, another one of life's gems, an amazing talent who also pushed the boundaries and, tragically, paid for it. The world mourned his loss.

Michael Klenfner was a giant of a man, who had a huge influence on the rise of AC/DC in the United States. RIP Wayne 'Swampy' Jarvis—whose middle name says it all—and Norm Sweeney. They were both true road warriors.

Gerry Humphreys, Malcolm McGee and Mick Hadley were all great frontmen who should have been internationally famous. And, of course, guitar slinger Lobby Loyde, the wise one, who helped shape the sound of Oz rock.

The enigmatic Wendy Saddington. The great drummer Stewie Speer. The Wild One, the great pioneer of the Australian music industry, Mr Johnny O'Keefe. Stephen Priest, the video miracle maker. The loveable Shirley Strachan. Bob Bertles. Trevor Young, a Coloured Ball. The dear Rona Newton-John. Perry Cooper, Bruno Lawrence, Claude Papesch, Duncan McGuire, Steve Gilpin, Peter Grant, Keith Moon and that other madman Beat poet Adrian Rawlins.

RIP Dr Norman Vincent Peale, my earliest influence and my uncle Milton, another wise man. My wonderful early mentor Owen Knight. Vince Lovegrove, Bon's old cohort from The Valentines, Darryl Cotton, Laurie Allen, Kelly from Heaven.

Our beautiful receptionist at Deluxe, Georgina, who tragically passed away from an undiagnosed allergy after celebrating the upcoming Christmas holidays with Michelle and myself. God bless her.

RIP Bill Graham, another giant of a man. Likewise Tom Dowd, a pioneer of recording, engineering and historical scientific pursuits. Mickie Most, one of the pop world's most treasured and successful record producers. And John Belushi, Michael Klenfner's best mate and Blues Brother, as well as Foreigner's manager and mentor Bud Prager. The Beatles' publicist Derek Taylor, who was in the thick of things in London during the most exciting period of music history. Wally Meyerowitz from ATI, the only person to have ever paid AC/DC not to play, during a Florida festival that was running over time. Ahmet Ertegun, the co-founder of Atlantic Records, sadly died as a result of a fall at a Rolling Stones concert. He was always a class act and the nod of approval AC/DC received from Ahmet and his brother Nesuhi meant a lot. Ahmet, along with Phil Carson, saved the band from being dropped. Nesuhi sadly has also passed away.

Pat Pickett, Bon's best mate, the human matchstick. Hunter S. Thompson, one of Billy Thorpe's heroes. Phil Key from New Zealand's great La De Das. Jim Keays. Lynyrd Skynyrd's Ronnie Van Zant, Steve Gaines, Cassie Gaines and Dean Kilpatrick, who all perished in that tragic 1977 plane crash.

During the completion of this book, another of our national treasures, Doc Neeson, met his maker. I first met Doc when I booked the Angels to support AC/DC during their first Australian tour. Angus loved Doc and spent hours urging him to follow his creative instincts, which he certainly did. RIP Doc.

Last but definitely not least: my mum Nin and my dad Bert. And my in-laws Digby, Shirley and Dean.

RIP to each and every one of you. Everyone mentioned had a huge impact on my pursuits and my life. If, out of ignorance, I've missed someone, my apologies.

There are a number of remarkable and inspiring success stories featuring some of the players in these pages. They include Richard Griffiths, who first booked AC/DC gigs in London and who worked with me at Deluxe. Richard became a high-flying American record company executive and he now runs a management company whose client list features One Direction. From the world's biggest rock band to the world's biggest boy band. Who'd have thought?

Clive Calder, as part of his companies Zomba and Jive records, went on to sign Billy Ocean, Britney Spears, Backstreet Boys, *NSYNC and many more. He sold his companies to BMG for $2.4 billion, making him one very wealthy music man, with no more need for that red-eye flight from London to New York that he would always insist on taking.

And, of course, AC/DC: this book wouldn't exist without them. Conversely, nor would they have existed as we know them today, had it not been for some of the players in this book. Their success has been enormous, to say the least. Not only have they become one of the world's bestselling recording acts—*Back in Black* sits at 50 million copies and rising—they're also one of the planet's top-grossing live acts. Their most recent world tour grossed a staggering $226 million—$2 million a night. They have amassed millions of fans throughout the world, and power to them. They deserve all their success.

That wise old sage Lobby Loyde once lectured me on the meaning of being rich—and it had nothing to do with money. I sincerely hope the AC/DC guys are rich in more than material wealth. My thoughts go out to Malcolm Young, whose days of roving the planet with his beloved band may be in jeopardy. Malcolm wrote the lion's share of every AC/DC song, carried the burden of just about every decision ever made for the band and now deserves a well-earned rest. Get well, Malcolm.

INXS, as well as Chris Murphy, achieved great things, sold millions of records around the world and did Australia proud.

Michael Gudinski became the biggest player in the history of the Australian music industry, with his touring company, agency and of course his earliest passion, Mushroom Records.

Another early mentor of mine was Anthony Knight, who received an OAM for his service to heritage and the arts in Victoria. Chris Gilbey also received an OAM for his services to the music industry, as well as his charity work—he's one of the founders of the great annual fundraiser known as the Golden Stave.

John Woodruff bravely put his arse on the line when he signed Savage Garden. The entire industry thought he was a goner but he pulled it off and helped make them superstars. And he made a killing. Well done, Woody.

Huge in Oz, Peter Garrett and Midnight Oil might have had more impact internationally had their manager Gary Morris agreed to participate in a who-has-the-biggest-dick competition with CBS President Al Teller; it was a bizarre way to resolve conflict, one I'd rejected when I clashed with Bud Prager at that Bill Graham gig. Peter entered Federal politics, only to be scapegoated by Prime Minister Kevin Rudd.

Richard Branson, whom I first met with Billy Thorpe in 1973, progressed from owning The Manor, a studio in Oxford, and a single record shop, to creating Virgin, a global music empire, an airline, a finance company and god knows what else. He also became an international adventurer and hero. My best Richard moment? He was the chauffeur, driving his Roller convertible, at the wedding of Richard Griffiths and his wife Olivia. Well done, Sir Richard.

Michael Chugg became a monumental figure in the Australian music industry and a major international promoter. But tellingly, he became the most dependable and effective fundraiser for the many fallen heroes of the Australian music industry. In an industry where superannuation and health insurance are usually out of reach for many of its participants, Chuggy always rises to the occasion. He deserves recognition for this and although I'm a Republican, I reluctantly admit that Sir Chuggie sounds very good.

My sister Coral, who spent many years of her life supporting my pursuits, has fulfilled her dream of becoming one of the best garden designers to the stars, based in Los Angeles.

'Mutt' Lange became the world's most successful record producer, taking such artists as Def Leppard, Shania Twain—and AC/DC—to unimaginable heights.

Mark Evans dusted himself off, picked himself up and got on with the task of forging a career for himself post-AC/DC. He ended up writing a great bestseller about his life with the band. It's a shame that politics got in the way of him being inducted into the American Rock'n'roll Hall of Fame with the band. Mark deserved it. Come to think of it, I wouldn't have minded being invited to the event either.

Randy Jackson, who produced 'Hot Chilli Woman' for Noiseworks, became an international star as a judge on *American Idol*. But he'd always been a star, especially when he was the hottest bass player on the planet with Bruce Springsteen's E Street Band.

Roger Davies became one of the world's top artist managers, representing P!nk, Joe Cocker, Olivia Newton-John and Tina Turner. He originally made a name for himself with that 'tea-towel rock band'—cheers, Angus—known as Sherbet.

Damian Trotter and Denis Handlin have become the two giants of the Australian recording and music-publishing industry. Denis was almost a goner back in the mid-1990s when some disgruntled Sony employees attempted a *coup d'état*. Denis was forced to lay low for a few months but came back with a vengeance and now controls the entire Southeast Asian operation for Sony.

I also need to make a confession to all those pillars of society from Melbourne, otherwise known as Collingwood Football Club supporters. I switched allegiance to the Sydney Swans soon after they arrived in town. I just had to: my elder son James was ready to disown me. Collingwood President Eddie McGuire once said: 'If you were once a Collingwood supporter, you never were.' The dog-eat-dog nature of the music industry may have wounded me, but this was an almost fatal blow. Sorry, Eddie, but it was family.

Then there's my own family. James has become a major player in the international touring business and also carries on the tradition of representing New Zealand bands via his involvement with the very talented and funky Fat Freddy's Drop. My wife Elizabeth runs our very successful family business Rust. My elder daughter Billie is involved in the film industry. My younger son Bert is becoming a builder and my younger daughter Rosie is on the way to becoming a fashion magazine art director. I'm incredibly proud of them all.

It gave me enormous pleasure recently to present my old friend Doug Parkinson with a lifetime achievement award from the Australian club industry. Richly deserved. And the list just goes on. Everyone in these pages has a story worth telling.

ACKNOWLEDGEMENTS

Writing this book has been an enjoyable experience, made all the more enjoyable by the great amount of support I received from my family. But I'll admit that I've also discovered writing can be fraught with procrastination and self-loathing. My family's support made all the difference.

Many thanks to Jeff Apter, who made sense of my ramblings in the manuscript—he even made me sound good. He now knows more about me than I know about myself. And yet I somehow know so little about him. A journalistic talent, I suspect.

David Koch and Amanda Pelman were two early manuscript readers whose enthusiasm and support was crucial. The support of Jane Palfreyman from my publisher Allen &

Unwin blew me away; all my feelings of inadequacy suddenly just melted away. Thank you so much, Jane; likewise Sarah Baker, who helped bring everything together smoothly and efficiently. And thanks also to Mark Evans for his early encouragement. Thanks to my sisters, Coral and Jan, for their valued encouragement. Philip Morris, Phillip Knight, Debby Cheeseman, Suzi Parkinson, David Porter, the Rennie Ellis Photographic Archive and Barry Bergman for help with the photos. Bernard Busch for reminding me of the magnificence of Mount Macedon. And thanks to an old mate, that warrior of the live music business, Paul (PC) Christie, who fancies himself as a bit of a David Bailey, for taking my portrait. Given my vintage, it was always going to be a tough gig. The bastard tried to drown me once; he loaded me up with lead weights and took me deep-sea diving at Palm Beach in Sydney's Northern Beaches—and told me to jump off a rocky ledge into a swell. What doesn't kill you makes you stronger, apparently.

www.supportact.com.au / www.goldenstave.com.au

michael.dogeatdog@gmail.com

INDEX OF NAMES